MW00916276

THE SUBMARINE IN
WAR AND PEACE

Yours Sincerly

Simon Lake

THE SUBMARINE IN WAR AND PEACE

ITS DEVELOPMENTS AND ITS POSSIBILITIES

BY

SIMON LAKE, M.I.N.A.

*WITH 71 ILLUSTRATIONS
AND A CHART*

PHILADELPHIA AND LONDON
J. B. LIPPINCOTT COMPANY
1918

COPYRIGHT, 1918, BY J. B. LIPPINCOTT COMPANY

PRINTED BY J. B. LIPPINCOTT COMPANY
AT THE WASHINGTON SQUARE PRESS
PHILADELPHIA, U. S. A.

DEDICATED

TO

LEBBEUS B. MILLER

OF ELIZABETH, NEW JERSEY

An honest and patriotic man, who took up a poor young man, and who, through his thorough grasp of things mechanical, was among the first to see practical possibilities in the dreams of a young inventor. With his financial means he was able to assist materially in the development and perfection of an important weapon for the defence of his country, thus rendering a valuable service to the nation.

Without his assistance much of the development work described in this volume would have been impossible of accomplishment.

No greater tribute can be paid to him than to remark of him that he is one—and there are but few of whom this may be said—who has steadfastly refused to take advantage of conditions which offered him the opportunity to increase his personal fortune at the expense of other individuals or of the welfare of his country.

FOREWORD

Some twenty years ago the author began to collect data with the idea of publishing a book on the submarine at a future time. There was very little information concerning submarines available at that date, as the early experiments in this field of navigation were generally conducted in secrecy. There had been constructed, up to that time, no submarine vessel which was entirely successful, and for this reason inventors and designers were disinclined to reveal the features of the vessels upon which they were experimenting.

Since then there has been considerable dissemination of facts about the submarine; much of this knowledge has found its way into print, some in short historical sketches published by the author and other designers. However, most of the publications on this subject have come from the hands of professional writers and newspaper men, some of whom have not had the engineering knowledge to sift the practical from the impractical, and who have not had any actual first-hand acquaintance with the facts. They have not understood the mechanical details of the submarine and the principles governing its operation well enough to comprehend or to elucidate the various phases of the development of this type of vessel. The result has been that many inaccuracies have been published, both in respect to the history of the development of the submarine and in regard to the practical operation of such vessels.

There have been published one or two good works dealing with this subject in a very complete and intelligible manner, but intended for those engaged in engineering pursuits. One of the best of these was "The Evolution of the Submarine Boat, Mine and Torpedo, from the Sixteenth Century to the Present Time," by Commander Murray F. Sueter, of the Royal British Navy, published in 1907.

When this book first appeared the present writer felt that the subject had been so fully covered that there was no need for him to publish his own information. However, since the beginning of the world-war the prominent part played by the submarine has led to a demand for more knowledge about the workings of this weapon of mystery, and for information concerning its future possibilities.

The aim of this work, therefore, is to present to the reader in a simple, interesting way the facts relating to the submarine; its mechanical principles; the history of its development; its actual operation; the difficulty of combating it; and its industrial possibilities. These facts are presented, together with descriptions of the experience of the author and other inventors, in order to clarify in the reader's mind the difficulties, the trials and tribulations of both the submarine operator and the inventor. Furthermore, the narrative is not restricted to a discussion of the submarine question from a mechanical standpoint. The submarine to-day is a factor in the political and industrial life of the world. The submarine problem transcends a mere matter of mechanical detail, and a book upon this topic must, of necessity, deal with it in its broadest aspects.

SIMON LAKE

CONTENTS

THE SUBMARINE IN WAR AND PEACE

INTRODUCTION

Jules Verne, in 1898, cabled to a New York publication: "While my book, 'Twenty Thousand Leagues Under the Sea,' is entirely a work of the imagination, my conviction is that all I said in it will come to pass. A thousand-mile voyage in the Baltimore submarine boat (the *Argonaut*) is evidence of this. This conspicuous success of submarine navigation in the United States will push on under-water navigation all over the world. If such a successful test had come a few months earlier it might have played a great part in the war just closed (Spanish-American war). The next war may be largely a contest between submarine boats. Before the United States gains her full development she is likely to have mighty navies, not only on the bosom of the Atlantic and Pacific, but in the upper air and beneath the waters of the surface."

The fantasy of Verne is the fact of to-day.

Admiral Farragut, in 1864, entered Mobile Bay while saying: "Damn the torpedoes—four bells; Captain Drayton, go ahead; Jouett, full speed!"

An admiral, in 1917, damns the torpedoes and orders full speed ahead, but *not* toward those points guarded by submarine torpedo boats.

While the British Admiralty once held that the submarine "is the weapon of the weaker power and not our concern," to-day the British naval officers in the North Sea operations somewhat discredit the former official Admiralty stand that "we know all about submarines; they are weapons of the weaker power; they are very poor fighting machines and can be of no possible use to the mistress of the seas."

Even as late as 1904 the submarine was not considered by naval authorities as a weapon of much value. A British admiral expressed his views on the submarine at that time in these words: "In my opinion, the British Admiralty is doing the right thing in building submarines, as in habituating our men and officers to them we shall more clearly realize their weaknesses when used against us. Even the weapon they carry (the Whitehead torpedo) is, to all intents and purposes, of unknown value for sea fighting."

However, from the very outbreak of the war now being carried on in Europe, the submarine has made its presence felt as a most effective weapon. German submarines have translated into actuality the prophecies of Verne, and have altered the views not only of the English but of the world as to the efficacy of the submarine as a naval weapon.

THE PIGMY CONQUERER OF THE SEA.

THE PIGMY CONQUERER OF THE SEA.

A drawing made by the author in 1893 to illustrate the possibilities of his submarine boat, and called "The Pigmy Conquerer of the Sea."

On March 10, 1915, a former chief constructor in the French Navy, M. Lauboeuf, stated: "An English fleet blockades the German coast, but at such a distance that a German division was able to go out and bombard Scarborough. When the English tried a close blockade at the beginning of the war, the German submarines made them pay dearly by torpedoing the *Pathfinder*, *Cressy*, *Hogue*, and *Aboukir*. Similarly the French fleet in the Adriatic was compelled to blockade Austrian ports from a great distance, and the battleships *Jules Ferry*, *Waldeck Rousseau*, and *Jean Bart* had fortunate escapes from the Austrian fleet."

As I write, the submarines of Germany are holding the navies of the Allied Powers in check. The British fleet dares not invade German waters or attempt a close blockade of German ports. In spite of the mighty English navy, the German U-boats—the invisible destroyers— are venturing forth daily into the open Atlantic and are raising such havoc with merchant shipping that the world is terrified at the prospect. It is the German U-boat which to-day encourages the Central Powers to battle almost single-handedly against the rest of the world's great nations.

So it is in this surprising manner that the submarine torpedo boat has emerged from its swaddling clothes and has begun to speak for itself. Its progress and development have been retarded for many years by the lack of appreciation of its possibilities on the part of those who have had the planning of naval programs. These have been, for the most part, men of ripe years and experience, and perhaps because of these years of experience they have become ultra-conservative and have been inclined to scoff and doubt the capabilities of any new device until it has been tried out by the fire of actual experience. Notwithstanding the fact that the problem of submarine navigation has been successfully solved for the past fifteen years, it has been only within the past four years that any great naval authority has unqualifiedly endorsed submarines as being of paramount importance in naval affairs.

Admiral Sir Percy Scott, in a strong letter to the *London Times* shortly previous to the beginning of the present war, stated: "The introduction of the vessels that swim under water has, in my opinion, entirely done away with the utility of the ships that swim on top of the water."

He stated further: "If we go to war with a country that is within striking distance of submarines, I am of the opinion that the country will at once lock up their dreadnoughts in some safe harbor and we shall do the same. I do not think the importance of submarines has been fully recognized, neither do I think that it has been realized how completely their advent has revolutionized naval warfare. In my opinion, as the motor has driven the horse from the road, so the submarine has driven the battleship from the sea."

Sir Percy Scott, however, is an inventor, being the man who devised the "spot" method of gun firing, and has, therefore, the type of mind which is able to foresee and to grasp the value of new devices.

Sir A. Conan Doyle, another man of great vision and imagination, was so impressed with the potentialities of the submarine that he wrote a story which prophesied, with such accuracy as to make his tale almost uncanny, the events which are actually taking place to-day around the coast of England in the prosecution of Germany's submarine blockade.

In these pages, therefore, I may make claims for submarines which have not yet been publicly proved by actual performance, and such claims may impress many as being as visionary as the destructive capabilities of submarines appeared to be until Lieutenant Weddingen, of the German Navy, shocked the conservatives and put the submarine on the map as a naval weapon by sinking, single-handed, three cruisers within one hour of each other.

I shall be careful, however, not to make any claim for submarines which is not warranted by experiments actually made during my twenty-two years' continual study and experience in designing and building submarine boats and submarine appliances in the United States and abroad.

To men of imagination and of inventive faculties these claims will not appear preposterous. The achievements of the submarine, in the face of all the ridicule, scepticism, and opposition which surrounded its development, will, I hope, commend these advanced ideas of mine to the attention, if not the respect, of the more conservative.

CHAPTER I

WHAT THE MODERN SUBMARINE IS

What is a modern submarine boat? A modern submarine vessel is a complex mechanism capable of being navigated on the surface of the water just as is any boat, but with the added faculty of disappearing at will beneath the surface, and of being operated beneath the surface in any desired direction at any desired depth. Some submarines are able to wheel along the bottom itself, and are also provided with diving compartments from which members of the crew, encased in diving suits, may readily leave and re-enter the vessel during its submergence.

The principal use to which the submarine vessel has thus far been turned has been that of a naval weapon, for scouting and for firing explosive automobile torpedoes, either for defensive or offensive purposes. Its full capacity has by no means been realized up to the present time.

All submarines, regardless of their design, have certain essential features which will be described in the order of their importance.

The Hull.—This must be watertight and capable of withstanding a pressure corresponding to the depth at which the vessel is designed to operate. The hull in most submarines is circular in cross-section; the circular form is best adapted for withstanding pressure. In some cases this circular hull is surrounded by another hull or is fitted with other appendages which will both increase the stability and seaworthiness of the submarine and add to its speed.

Superstructure.—Most of the early military submarines built for the French, Spanish, United States, and English governments were circular in cross-section and of cigar-or spindle-shaped form in their longitudinal profile view. It is difficult, in vessels of this form, to secure sufficient stability to make them seaworthy. They are apt to roll like a barrel when light, due to a diminishing water plane, and when under way the water is forced up over their bows, making a large "bow wave" which absorbs power and causes such vessels to dive at times when least expected. In some instances this tendency to dive has caused loss of the vessel, and, in some cases, of the lives of the crew as well.

They are also very wet for surface navigation, as the seas break over their inclined sides like breakers on a beach. These difficulties led to the invention of the buoyant superstructure, first used on the *Argonaut*. This is a watertight structure built of light-weight plating— in some cases it has been built of wood—with valves which admit free water to the interior of the superstructure before submerging.

By the admission of the water, danger of collapse is prevented. By this expedient the pressure upon these light plates is equalized when the vessel is submerged. This combination of a circular pressure-resisting inner structure, surmounted by a non-pressure-resisting outer structure of ship-shaped form, is now common to all modern submarines of all navies of the world. This superstructure adds to the seaworthiness and habitability of submarine vessels and increases their speed, both in the light and submerged conditions, as it admits of better stream lines.

Stability.—The stability of a vessel refers to its ability to keep upright and on a level keel. It is desirable to have great stability in a submarine in order that it may not assume excessive angles when submerged. The measure of stability is expressed in inches of metacentric height. The metacentric height of a vessel when submerged is the distance between the centre of buoyancy—or submerged volume—of the vessel and the centre of all the weights of hull, machinery, stores, and equipment contained within the vessel. This distance between the centre of buoyancy and the centre of gravity must be determined very accurately in order to obtain conditions of ideal stability in a submarine.

The metacentric height of a vessel is a term used in naval architecture to express the stability of the ship. In surface ships the term may be used to express either the longitudinal or transverse stability of the vessel, and varies according to the load line and trim or heel of the ship. On the other hand, in submarine boats *when submerged* the metacentric height is constant and expresses the distance between the centre of gravity and the centre of buoyancy of the vessel, and is the same either in the transverse or longitudinal plane of the vessel. In other words, the centre of buoyancy of the vessel when submerged must be directly over the centre of gravity of the vessel to cause her to submerge on a level keel.

We then get the effect of a pendulum, the length of the pendulum arm being the distance between the two points, and the weight of the pendulum equalling the weight of the ship. Therefore, if a submarine has a submerged displacement of five hundred tons, with a metacentric height of twelve inches, her stability, or ability to remain upright, is equal to a pendulum of five hundred tons hung by an arm twelve inches long, and it would require the same force to incline the ship as it would to incline the pendulum. Therefore it is evident that the greater the metacentric height the more stable the ship, and the less likely she is to make eccentric dives to the bottom or "broach" to the surface.

Ballast Tanks.—All submarines are fitted with tanks which may be filled with water so that the vessel will submerge; these are called ballast tanks. When the vessel is navigating on the surface she has what is called "reserve of buoyancy," the same as any surface vessel. It is this reserve of buoyancy which causes the vessel to rise with the seas in rough weather. It means the volume of the watertight portion of the vessel above the water line. In surface cruising a vessel with great buoyancy will rise to the seas, while if the "reserve" is small the vessel is termed "loggy" and will not rise to the sea. In the latter case the seas will break over the vessel just as they break over a partially submerged rock in a storm. On such a vessel the men cannot go on deck in a storm; in a sea-going submarine a large reserve of buoyancy is therefore essential.

Now in a modern submarine, of five hundred tons submerged displacement, for instance, this reserve should be about one hundred and twenty-five tons, according to the best practice. This means that before the vessel could sink beneath the surface the ballast tanks must be filled with one hundred and twenty-five tons of water. On the surface these tanks are filled with air. The water is permitted to enter by the opening of valves for that purpose. These ballast tanks are located within the main hull and in the superstructure.

Propelling Machinery.—When on the surface the submarine may be propelled by steam, internal-combustion engines, or any other kind of motive power adapted to the propulsion of surface ships. For propulsion when submerged many types of engine have been tried: compressed air engines; steam engines drawing the steam from boilers in which water has been stored at high temperatures; carbonic acid gas engines, and the internal-combustion engines receiving their air supply from compressed-air tanks. Most modern submarines use internal-combustion engines for surface navigation and storage batteries delivering current to electric motors for submerged propulsion. The internal-combustion engine is best suited for surface work because it can be started or stopped instantly, which is a desirable feature in submarine work. It is not fitted for submerged operation because of its great noisiness, and also because its spent gases must be discharged from the boat, in which case these gases ascend to the surface in the form of bubbles and thus betray the presence and position of the submarine. The storage battery, on the contrary, permits the use of practically noiseless machinery and does not require any outboard discharge of gases, as the battery gives off no material quantity of gases when delivering its stored-up power.

I was the first to use successfully an internal-combustion engine in a submarine boat, the *Argonaut*. This first engine was a heavy-duty engine of rugged construction, and gave but little trouble. This type of engine, with but slight modifications, was installed in six other boats built subsequent to the *Argonaut*. They also worked satisfactorily for several years, and so long as I had knowledge of them they always gave satisfactory and reliable service.

The first gasolene (petrol) internal-combustion engines installed in the Holland boats were also of rugged construction, and I have been informed by various officers in our submarine service that they were reliable and gave but little trouble. It is known that, after twelve years' service, some of them are still doing good work. The boats in which these engines were installed were slow-speed boats, making only from eight to nine knots on the surface.

A natural desire on the part of the governments of various nations was to secure increased speed. They sent out requirements to submarine boat builders calling for increased speeds within certain limits of cost. The submarine boat builders said: "Certainly we can give you increased speed if the engine builders can give us engines of the necessary power to go into the available space, and within a certain weight, to thus enable us to get the power plant within a certain size vessel possessing the fine lines necessary to give the required speed." The engine builders said *they could do it.*

The first, as I remember, to break away from the slow-speed, heavy-duty type was a celebrated Italian firm. Then two large and well-known German firms followed; then a celebrated English firm, and certain American firms claimed that they could build reliable, compact, high-speed engines on very much less weight than we had been using. I remember one American firm which offered engines as low in weight as twenty pounds per horsepower. Fortunately, we had sense enough to refuse to accept an engine so light as that, but we, as well as all other submarine boat builders both in this country and abroad, did accept contracts which required engines very much less in weight than the old, slow, heavy-duty type first used, and there has been "wailing and gnashing of teeth" both by the submarine boat builders and by the engine-room forces in the world's submarine navies ever since.

The first light-weight engines built by the Italian firm "smashed up" in short order. The German engines followed suit, and the losses to this firm, or to the shipbuilders, must have been enormous, as a large number of engines were built by them before a set was tested out in actual service. The test of an engine in the shop, on a heavy foundation, open to inspection on all sides, and with expert mechanics in constant touch with the engine, does not mean that this same engine will prove satisfactory in the restricted space available in a submarine boat when run by other than expert engine-building mechanics. I was present at a shop test of one of the German engines referred to, and under shop conditions it appeared to work very well —so well, in fact, that I took an option for my firm to build from the same designs in America. When the engine was tried out, however, in one of the German submarines it rapidly deteriorated and pounded itself into junk in a few weeks. Cylinders and cylinder heads cracked, bed-plates were broken, and crank-shafts twisted or broken. It was evident that the design was too light all the way through.

There are some destructive actions in connection with large, high-speed, light-weight internal-combustion engines which practically all designing engineers have failed to grasp. Otherwise, engineers of all nationalities would not have failed to the extent they have; and I do not believe that there is a submarine engine in service to-day which has fully met the expectations of its designers and builders.

It is unfortunate for the engineering profession that government policy will not permit of a full disclosure of the defects of engines and other equipment in government-owned vessels. Were a frank disclosure made, other inventors and engineers would, in all probability, take up the problems and they might the sooner be solved.

All the earlier submarines were equipped with engines which used gasolene (petrol) as a fuel, but the gas from this fuel, when mixed with a proper proportion of air, is highly explosive. A number of serious explosions occurred in submarines due to this gas escaping from leaky tanks, pipings, or valves. Some of them were accompanied by loss of life. The most disastrous was that on board the Italian submarine *Foca*, in which it is reported that twenty-three men were killed. Therefore, several years ago, all governments demanded the installation of engines using a non-explosive fuel; and builders then turned to the "Diesel" engine as offering a solution of the problem.

As early as 1905 I had anticipated that such a demand would ultimately be made, so during that year I built, in Berlin, Germany, an experimental double-acting heavy-oil engine; but unfortunately the engineer in charge of the work was taken ill and eventually died. This engine was later completed and showed great flexibility in its control and in reversing. It, however, has never been put on a manufacturing basis.

In the meantime, others took up the work of developing the heavy oil Diesel engine for submarines. The first of the Diesel type engines to be installed in a submarine were built by a well-known French firm of engine builders. As we were then in the market for heavy-oil submarine engines, plans of these engines were submitted to me, but I found it impossible to install them in any boat we then had under construction, owing to their size and weight. I have been advised that engines of this design were installed in some of the French submarine boats. I have also been informed that the shock and vibrations produced by them were such as to cause the rivets in the boats to loosen, and this started the vessels to leaking so badly that it was found necessary to take them out. These engines differed only slightly from the vertical Diesel land engine.

The engine is the most important element in the submarine. Without this it is impossible to make long surface runs, and in the event of its disablement it is impossible to charge the storage batteries to enable the submarine to function submerged, which is, of course, what she is built for doing.

I think the demand for increased speed has come too rapidly. It is more important to have reliability than speed. The criticisms which have been made regarding United States submarines, if traced to their source, may be found to be justified so far as they apply to the engines, but the Navy Department cannot be held responsible, and neither can the designers of submarines. They have both searched the world's markets and secured the best that could be purchased. All naval departments were undoubtedly right when they decided to abandon the gasolene (petrol) engine and substitute therefor the heavy-oil engine. Eventually a successful heavy-oil engine will be produced.

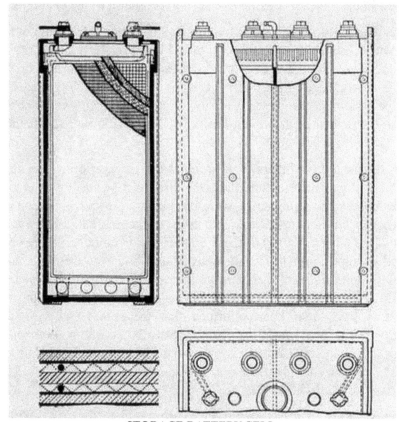

STORAGE BATTERY CELL

Gas suction arrangement.

Hard rubber tank.

A SUBMARINE CELL COMPLETELY ASSEMBLED READY FOR INSTALLATION

Storage batteries as used in modern submarines have been especially developed to meet the special needs of submarine-boat service. The requirements for this service are much more severe than those for any other service to which the storage battery has been applied. The batteries as first introduced in submarines were entirely too frail to stand up to their work, and the gases given off from them while being charged were the cause of much distress and danger to the crew, and have been in some cases responsible for the loss of both vessel and crew.

The Diesel engine, weighing practically five hundred pounds or more per horsepower, has functioned satisfactorily in land installations and has come into very general use, especially in Germany, but when the attempt was made to change this slow-speed engine of five hundred pounds per horsepower into high-speed engines of approximately fifty pounds per horsepower, all designers "fell down." It was but natural that naval authorities throughout the world should call for increased speed; they cannot be criticised for that, as it is a desirable thing, but experience has shown that they called for it too early in the game.

The expense of the development of a new type of motive power, such as the high-speed, heavy-oil-burning engine, for use in vessels whose prime purpose is to preserve the autonomy of the country, should be borne by the government rather than by individuals or private corporations. Millions of dollars have been expended in the development work of engines, but, although vast improvements are now in progress, the successful engine is not yet on the market.

Dr. Diesel has stated that he worked seven years before he succeeded in getting his first engine to make one complete revolution. Governments and the people must therefore content themselves to accept what they can get in a heavy-oil engine, imperfect though it may be, until such time as a satisfactory engine is evolved, built, and tested out under service conditions.

Storage Batteries.—It is impossible in a book of this character to go into much detail regarding the development of the storage battery. There have been two types in general use. They are both lead batteries, one known as the Planté type, in which metallic lead is used to form both the positive and negative plates. The other type employs what is commonly known as pasted plates, in which various compositions of materials are worked up into a paste and forced into metallic grids to form the positive and negative plates. The pasted type has greater capacity per pound of material used, but much shorter life.

In both of these batteries sulphuric acid solutions are used as the excitant between the elements. In charging, hydrogen gas is given off in the form of bubbles, the skin of the bubbles being composed of sulphuric acid solution. These bubbles, when taken in one's lungs, are very irritating, and if they collect in any quantity, or break up and allow the hydrogen gas to mix with the air, there is always danger of creating an explosive mixture within the hull of the vessel or in the battery tanks, which a spark would set off at any time.

The best method of installing batteries on a submarine boat is to have them isolated from the living quarters of the vessel in separate watertight compartments. The elements of the battery should be contained in non-metallic containers and sealed to prevent spilling of the electrolyte under excessive rolling or pitching of the vessel. Means should be provided to discharge the hydrogen gases from the boat as rapidly as formed. Special care should be taken to prevent leakages between the adjacent cells. Circulation of air to keep the cells dry is the best means of preventing this.

Mr. Edison has been working for a number of years on a storage battery suitable for submarine work, and it has recently been stated that he has finally solved the problem of producing a battery that will stand up longer than the lead type of battery, and that it has the further advantage in that it will not give off chlorine gas in case salt water should get into the cells. It should, however, be contained in a separate compartment, which should be ventilated during the charging period, as I understand the Edison battery gives off hydrogen gas the same as the lead batteries. Chlorine gas, as given off from the lead battery when salt water has got into it, has undoubtedly caused the loss of some lives. Mr. Edison claims that his battery, when immersed, will not give off poisonous gases of any kind.

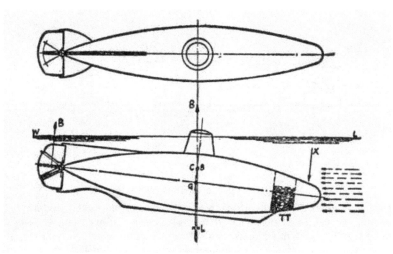

METHOD OF CONTROL IN DIVING TYPE BOATS

Horizontal rudder set down aft inclines the vessel down by the bow, in which condition, with only a small reserve of buoyancy, she will "dive." When she reaches the desired depth a lesser inclination of the diving rudder is supposed to reduce her angle of inclination sufficiently so that the pressure on the top of her hull will offset the tendency to rise due to her positive buoyancy. To be successful there must be no movable ballast, and variable stream line effect requires expert manipulation of the diving rudder.

Depth Control.—Practically all modern submarines use hydroplanes with a horizontal rudder for the control of depth when under way. Hydroplanes might be said to correspond to the side fins of a fish. They are substantially flat vanes that extend from either side of the vessel. They are set on shafts that may be partially rotated by mechanism in control of a man within the vessel. They readily control the depth of the vessel with a certain amount of either positive or negative buoyancy. For instance, submarines are usually submerged with a small amount of positive buoyancy. If a vessel has positive buoyancy she will float. We have seen that in a surface condition the five-hundred-ton submarine has about one hundred and twenty-five tons of positive buoyancy.

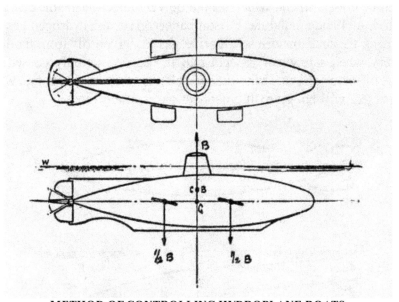

METHOD OF CONTROLLING HYDROPLANE BOATS

Showing a proper arrangement of hydroplanes and horizontal rudders. C B represents the centre of buoyancy of the vessel when submerged. G represents centre of gravity, which lies directly beneath centre of buoyancy. Now if hydroplanes are located at equal distances fore and aft their up or down pull is always balanced and does not cause the vessel to dive or broach, but holds her to a level keel. If stream line pull tends to upset this level keel, horizontal rudders may be used to correct it.

Now to prepare the vessel for a submerged run, we admit, say, one hundred and twenty-four tons of water; the positive buoyancy is then

24

reduced to one ton. Now if the forward edges of the hydroplanes are inclined downward (see diagram), and the vessel is given headway, the pressure of the water on top of the inclined hydroplanes, combined with the tendency for a vacuum to form under the planes, will overcome the one ton of positive buoyancy and will pull the vessel bodily under the water. When the desired depth is reached the operator sets the inclination of the hydroplanes so as to just balance the upward pull of the one ton of positive buoyancy, and the vessel proceeds at the desired depth. On modern boats the control of depth is most remarkable; it is very common for submarines to make continuous runs of several hours' duration without varying their depth more than a couple of feet. When the headway or motive force of the submarine is stopped, if she has reserved some positive buoyancy she will come to the surface. If she has negative buoyancy she will sink, but while under way with as much as a ton of positive or negative buoyancy the hydroplanes will absolutely control the depth of the vessel.

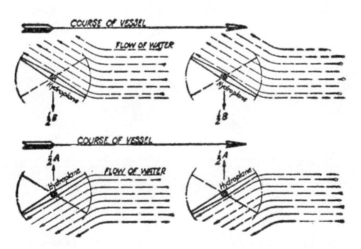

HOW HYDROPLANES CONTROL DEPTH OF SUBMERSION
The vessel being "under way" in the course of the arrow, the water contacting against the upper surface of the hydroplanes, as in the upper view, its course is thus diverted and adds weight to the upper surface of the planes. There is also a tendency to form a vacuum under the plane. Both these forces tend to overcome the positive buoyancy of the boat and force her under water and on a level keel if these forces are properly distributed fore and aft of the centre of buoyancy and gravity of the vessel.

Action of the Hydroplanes.—The diagrams are intended to demonstrate how it is that the Lake and other hydroplane boats can be so easily held at a predetermined depth and controlled vertically on an even keel.

The hydroplanes are symmetrically disposed on two sides of the vessel. They should be equal distance forward and aft of amidships. This symmetrical disposition, with equal forces acting on each hydroplane, compels the boat either to rise or sink on an even keel, depending upon which face of the hydroplanes is presented to the passing water during the boat's progress.

In the upper diagram the entering edges of the hydroplanes are inclined downward, and the force of the passing stream lines strikes upon the upper face of the blades. This exerts a downward force which causes the boat to sink, as indicated by the arrows marked "A, A." The opposite of this takes place when the forward ends of the hydroplanes are lifted. This brings the force of the stream lines against the under side of the hydroplanes, and the resultant is a lifting impulse in the direction of the line of least resistance, which is here indicated by the arrows marked "B, B." It is the lifting force so applied that makes it possible to raise hydroplane boats from the bottom even when having considerable negative buoyancy.

ON PICKET DUTY

This is a field of service to which the anchoring weights and the diving compartment of the Lake boats lend themselves conjointly with especial fitness. The illustration represents a submarine doing picket duty on an offshore station. A junction box is placed in a known locality with telephone or telegraph cables leading therefrom to the shore. The submarine, having taken her position on the surface, lowers her

26

anchoring weights, reduces her reserve buoyancy to the desired extent, and then draws herself down to the bottom by winding in again on the cables connecting with the anchoring weights. Having reached the bottom, the diving door is opened and a diver passes out and makes the necessary connections between that junction box and the instruments in the boat.

Holding Depth When Not Under Way.—If it is desired to bring the boat to rest while submerged, but when no motive force is being used, other methods must be used than that just described. One method is to have an anchor or anchors to hold the vessel at the desired depth. If it is desired to lie at rest off the entrance of the enemy's harbor to wait for her ships to come out, the submarine proceeds to her station submerged with a small amount of buoyancy,—which is the usual method of navigating submerged. When she arrives at the desired station the speed is reduced and an additional amount of water is gradually admitted to give her a small amount of negative buoyancy. At the same time her anchoring weights are paid out until they touch bottom. As soon as they do so water is forced out of the ballast tanks by compressed air until positive buoyancy is restored and the vessel stops sinking and remains at rest anchored between the surface and the bottom, like an anchored buoyant mine. By winding in on the anchor cables a submarine may then be hauled down nearer the bottom, and by paying out the cables she may rise nearer the surface. On picket duty off harbor entrances she remains sufficiently near the surface to project her telescoping periscope occasionally above the crest of the waves to keep watch and see that an enemy ship does not enter or clear. In this condition there is no necessity to have any machinery running on board the submarine, therefore she can remain for weeks at a time on station without exhausting her fuel supply. It is only necessary for her to renew the air supply now and then, which can be done at night. Another method for holding a vessel at rest is by taking in and forcing out alternately small quantities of water so as to keep her in equilibrium between positive and negative buoyancy. Another method is to use vertical propellers operating in wells extended from the sides, and by running these it is possible to exert an upward or downward pressure and so hold her at a depth. Neither of these methods is as satisfactory, however, as the anchor weights, because the vessel will not hold a definite position on station, but will drift off with the current. They also make a drain on the storage battery and require constant attention on the part of the members of the crew. By the anchor weights scheme the vessel may stay on station as long as the food and fuel supply holds out.

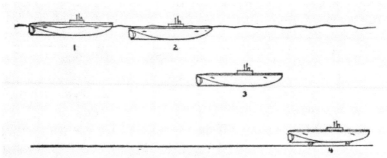

SHOWING VARIOUS CONDITIONS IN WHICH A SUBMARINE OF THE LEVEL KEEL TYPE FITTED WITH BOTTOM WHEELS, MAY NAVIGATE

1, running light on surface; 2, awash, ready for submergence; 3, submerged, depth controlled by hydroplanes; 4, running on bottom.

The above facts set forth simply the outstanding mechanical principles upon which the operation of the submarine is based. The submarine of to-day, however, has many auxiliaries, to describe which in detail would require several volumes of technical description.

I will briefly enumerate a few of the more important of these devices and describe their function as applied to the war submarine.

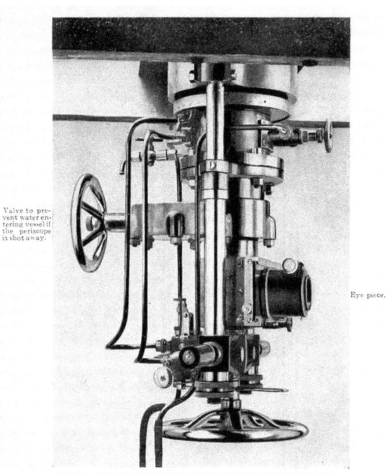

Valve to prevent water entering vessel if the periscope is shot away.

Eye piece.

THE LOWER PORTION OF GALILEO PERISCOPE

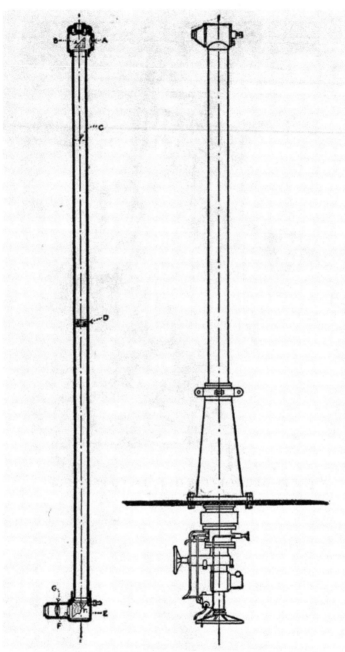

THE PERISCOPE IS THE EYE OF THE SUBMARINE.
(See description.)

The Periscope.—The periscope is the eye of the submarine. In its
simpler form it consists of a stiff metallic tube, from fifteen to twenty

30

feet in length and about four inches in diameter. Referring to Figure 1, on page 23, it is made up of an object glass, *A*, which "views" or takes an impression of all objects within its range or field of vision, and transmits an image of such object through the right-angle prism, *B*, which turns the image so that it appears some distance down the tube, say, for purposes of description, at *C*. If a piece of ground glass were held at the focus of the objective lens at *C*, the image could be seen. The lens *D*, located farther down the tube, in turn now "views" the image and transmits it still farther down the tube, where it is turned through the right-angle prism, *E*, and where the image is again turned into an erect position. A piece of ground glass located at *F* would show the image in the same manner as an image is shown on the ground glass of a camera. The magnifying eyepiece *G* magnifies the image so that distant objects appear of natural size.

Other figures show a periscope as made by the Officina Galileo in Florence, Italy. This firm makes periscopes with binocular eyepieces. The success of any periscope depends upon the character of the material used in the lenses and prisms and the accuracy of the workmanship. This firm, which is probably the oldest optical manufacturing house in the world, said to have been founded by Galileo himself, turns out instruments of the most beautiful workmanship. The flange of the instrument is bolted to the top of the conning tower, or deck, and a gate valve is arranged between the deck and the eyepiece so that in case the tube should be carried away the gate valve can be closed and thus prevent water from entering the vessel. A hand wheel arranged below the binocular eyepiece permits of easy rotation of the instrument. Provision is made for introducing dry air; this prevents condensation forming on the lenses or prisms within the tube.

Owing to the fact that there is a certain loss of light in transmitting the image through the various prisms and lenses, it is customary to magnify the image so that it appears to be about one-quarter larger than when viewed by the natural eye. This has been found by experience to give, when viewed through the periscope alone from a submerged vessel, the impression of correct distance.

Previous to 1900 there was no instrument which would give through a long tube normal vision and a correct idea as to distance. At this time I took up with various opticians the question of producing such an instrument. They all contended that it was impossible to produce an instrument that would give through a long tube a field of vision equal to the natural eye or that would convey a correct idea as to the distance of an object when viewed through a long tube. The camera lucida which Mr. Holland and others had used in the earlier submarines simply threw a picture of the object on a bit of white paper, usually located on a table. This did not give to the observer any more idea of the correct distance of an object than a photograph would. Believing, however, that a solution could be found, I then purchased a variety of lenses and started making experiments.

Without any special knowledge of optical science, one day quite by accident I secured the desired result and found that it was possible to secure practically normal vision through a tube of considerable length. About the same time, Sir Howard Grubb, of England, brought out an instrument in which he accomplished the same result. I then continued in my experimental work and brought out an instrument which was designed to give a simultaneous view of the entire horizon.

This instrument was called an "omniscope." It was first called a "skalomniscope," which was a word coined with the idea of describing the function of the instrument and which, translated, means "to view and measure everything." A scale was used in connection with this instrument which would convert it into a range finder by measuring the image of an abject of known dimensions, such as the length of a ship or the height of its smokestack, and give simultaneous reading as to its distance.

For a time it was necessary for us to manufacture our own sighting instruments, but later, when the optical houses understood the principle of the periscope, they took up the matter of manufacture and have so greatly improved them that it is now possible to secure instruments of great accuracy and fine definition.

The periscope, however, is faulty, in that it is only an instrument for day use. As soon as dusk comes on the periscope becomes useless. The passing of the image down the tube and through the various lenses and prisms reduces the brilliancy of the image to such an extent that, even though it is finally magnified to above normal, the image is so thin at night that it cannot be seen. This forces the submarine to become vulnerable in making an attack at night, as it is necessary for the conning tower to be brought a sufficient distance above the surface of the water to permit the commanding officer to secure natural vision.

With the powerful searchlights and rapid-fire guns, the submarine would have little opportunity to approach a surface war vessel at night without great danger of being discovered and destroyed.

THE VOICE AND EAR OF THE SUBMARINE

A Fessenden oscillator, before being installed. The flange of the oscillator is riveted to the shell of the ship and its diaphragm is caused to vibrate by the sound waves, which pass through water more distinctly than they do through the air. To send out signals it is caused to vibrate mechanically by electrical apparatus.

Invisible Conning Tower.—For night observation it has been proposed to use transparent conning towers built of clear glass, in which the commander takes his station and just sticks his head above the crest of the waves in order to direct his vessel against the enemy. This has not as yet come into general use because of the difficulty of securing sufficiently clear glass in the desired form. Experiments have been made, however, which show that quite a large transparent conning tower cannot be seen on a submarine at rest even when within a couple of hundred yards; the application of these conning towers will greatly increase the submarine's efficiency for night work.

Submarine Sound Receivers.—All modern submarines are fitted with devices which enable the commanders of submarines to communicate with each other when running under water even when considerable distances apart. One of these outfits consists of a signal bell and a powerful receiver with which sounds may be transmitted and heard. Conversations may be carried on by the Morse and other codes for distances of ten or twelve miles.

TORPEDO TUBES ASSEMBLED READY FOR INSTALLATION IN A SUBMARINE BOAT

Left view, the breech end of the tube. Right view, the outboard doors, which must first be opened before the torpedo is expelled from the tube by compressed air. When the torpedo is expelled it starts a compressed-air engine supplied with air stored at high pressure within the torpedo, and will run several thousand yards under its own power.

A later device, called the Fessenden oscillator, will transmit or receive sounds a distance of twenty miles. The principle of its operation is that of setting up wave vibrations by very large transmitters; these vibrations are carried by the water and taken up by receivers on other submarines. It has been found that the human voice will set up vibrations in the Fessenden transmitter so clearly that wireless conversation may be carried on under water for several hundred yards. I discovered in my earlier experiments that when a submarine was lying submerged, with all machinery shut down, the noise of the machinery in an approaching ship could be detected quite a distance off without the use of any special kind of receivers. In this way the commander of a submarine can always note the approach of an enemy simply by shutting down his own machinery. The warning thus given him comes long before he could sight the enemy ship were he on the surface. After a little experience one can tell the type of ship approaching from the sound, as every type of ship has sounds peculiar to her class. The smash of paddle wheels, the deep, slow pound of the heavy merchant ships or battleships, the clack and the whir of the higher speed machinery on destroyers or torpedo boats, are all easily recognizable when one becomes familiar with them. At the present time all the larger submarines are fitted with wireless outfits on their decks which they may use when on the surface to communicate with other submarines or with their base.

Torpedo Tubes.—These are used to start the automobile torpedo on its course toward the enemy. In simple form they are tubes about eighteen inches in diameter and seventeen feet long, placed in line with the axis of the vessel. They are fitted with doors both internal and external to the submarine. The inboard door of the tube opens into the interior of the vessel and permits the loading of the torpedo. When the torpedo is to be discharged the inboard door is closed and securely fastened. The outer door is then opened, and through the operation of quick-opening valves compressed air is admitted back of the torpedo and the torpedo is driven out of the tube in the same manner that the bullet is driven out of an air rifle or the cork out of a pop-gun. Some of the larger modern submarines carry several torpedo tubes firing in line with the axis of the vessel both forward and aft. Some carry torpedo tubes on their decks which may be made to train to fire broadside on either side of the vessel.

A WHITEHEAD TORPEDO

Courtesy of the Scientific American

The forward end of the torpedo is the war head filled with guncotton or trinitrotoluol. A detonator is screwed into the end of the war head to set off the main charge on contact. An air flask forms the middle portion of the torpedo. Aft of this is the depth-control mechanism, in which a diaphragm controls the diving rudder by the pressure of the water against a spring set for the desired depth. A pendulum controls the levelling mechanism and a gyroscope its direction in the horizontal plane, tending to keep it on the course by its control of the vertical rudder.

REAR END OF THE WHITEHEAD TORPEDO

Courtesy of the Scientific American

Showing compressed air engine and twin propeller with their control gear.

Automobile Torpedoes.—These are the projectiles which are used to destroy the enemy's ship. They are called automobile torpedoes because they will, on being ejected from the torpedo tubes, continue running in the direction in which they are aimed, from power and mechanism contained within themselves. They are wonderful pieces of mechanism and cost several thousand dollars each. They are virtually miniature submarine boats. The essential features of the automobile torpedo are the airflask, the warhead, the depth control, and steering and propelling machinery. The airflask forms the central section, which is a steel tank containing compressed air stored at high pressure; about twenty-five hundred pounds per square inch is the present practice. When the torpedo is expelled from the torpedo tube this air is automatically turned on to run the engines. It passes through reducing valves and heaters to drive either a multiple cylinder or a turbine engine, and revolves two propellers, running one clockwise and the other counterclockwise, set in tandem at the stern of the torpedo. The propellers, running in opposite directions, thus enable the torpedo to be more easily steered by the delicate automatic steering machinery. A diaphragm operated by the pressure of the water operates control mechanism which regulates the depth. An instrument called the "Obry gear" steers it in the horizontal plane. The essential feature of the "Obry gear" is a gyroscope which is started when the torpedo is ejected from the tube. It is instantly speeded up either by a powerful spring or an air turbine to about fifteen thousand revolutions per minute. The peculiarity of the gyroscope is that it has a tendency to hold the direction in which it is started. Hence, if the torpedo starts swerving either to the right or left from the direction in which it is aimed, the gyroscope causes certain valves to function which will automatically set the steering rudder to bring the torpedo back into its original course. The "Gyro" will continue this control until the torpedo has completed its course, which in some of the latest types is said to be about five miles.

The warhead is the forward portion of the torpedo and contains usually wet gun-cotton, which is a safe high explosive and can be exploded only by a detonating charge of the more sensitive explosives. This detonating charge is placed in a tube screwed into the forward end of the torpedo. Extending out from the forward end of the tube is a small propeller, the purpose of which is to set the firing mechanism after the torpedo has run a certain distance from the vessel from which it has been fired. This is a safety device to prevent the torpedo from being exploded near its own ship. The torpedo running through the water causes the propeller to revolve, which turns a shaft. After the shaft makes a certain number of revolutions it sets a firing pin, and then if it hits an object it will explode. Many modern torpedoes are loaded with trinitrotoluol. This is a much more powerful explosive. According to experts, the explosion of two hundred and fifty pounds of T-N-T, as it is called, will destroy any battleship ever built.

RAPID-FIRING GUNS

Courtesy of the Scientific American

Rapid-fire disappearing guns may be quickly elevated above armored turret when the submarine rises to the surface.

Divers' Compartment.—Some submarines are fitted with a divers' compartment, from which compartment mines may be planted, either when on the surface or when submerged. This compartment is fitted with a door which opens outwardly in the bottom of the boat. It is shut off from the living and machinery rooms of the vessel by an air lock and heavy pressure-resisting doors. The divers' door may be opened when the vessel is submerged and navigating on the bottom, and *no water will come into the vessel when the door is opened.* This is accomplished in the following manner: The members of the crew who wish to go outside the vessel first go into the diving compartment. They close the door which shuts them off from other parts of the vessel. They then turn compressed air gradually into the compartment until the air pressure in the compartment equals the water pressure outside. If the depth is one hundred feet the air pressure in the compartment would need to be 43.4 pounds per square inch; if the depth is two hundred feet, twice that, or 86.8 pounds per square inch, etc. When the air pressure in the compartment equals the water pressure outside, at any depth, the door in the bottom may be opened and the water will not rise up into the compartment, because the air pressure keeps it out. Tests have been made which show that it is safe for divers to go out from compartments of this kind in depths up to two hundred and seventy-five feet.

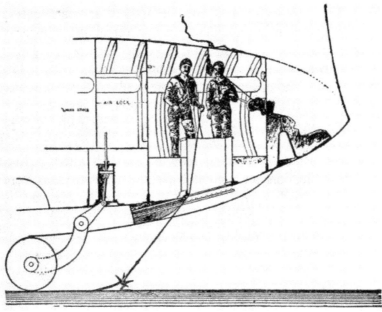

DIVING COMPARTMENT

This view shows the diving compartment being used for the purpose of grappling for the electric cables controlling fields of submarine mines. Operating in this manner, the diving compartment becomes a veritable travelling diving-bell, and when the air pressure in the diving chamber is made to balance with the water pressure outside the diving door may be opened and yet the water will not enter the working chamber.

Dangers.—Years of painstaking development work have eliminated most of the dangers connected with the operation of submarines in times of peace. The experienced designers have learned the importance of having great submerged stability, so that no modern craft is likely to make an unexpected headfirst dive into the mud, hard sand, or rocks on the bottom. This was a common occurrence not many years ago. Another danger to be avoided is that of asphyxiation by the escape of noxious gases from the engines. The blowing up of the vessel by the ignition of hydrogen fumes from the battery is another risk to be guarded against. In the latest vessels the noxious gases from the engine are not permitted to escape into the engine-room; gasolene is rapidly giving place to heavy-oil engines which do not use an explosive fuel, and the hydrogen gas given off during the charging of batteries is pumped overboard as rapidly as it is generated. Consequently modern submarines, when navigating on the surface, are as safe as any surface ship. In fact, they are safer, from the fact that they are so much more strongly built and that they are divided into compartments. Any one of these compartments could be filled by water in an accident and the remaining compartments would keep the ship afloat. In submerged peace-time navigation the dangers are those of collisions with surface vessels, uncharted rocks, or sunken ships. The danger of collisions with surface ships may be avoided by keeping below the depth of keel of the deepest draft surface ship, when long under-water runs are being made, and always stopping machinery to listen for the sound of surface ships before rising to the surface. If running near the surface where periscopic vision is possible, constant vigilance must be maintained, as there are no rules of the road or right of way which may be claimed by the submarine commander, owing to the fact that the lookout on the surface craft, in all probability, cannot see his little periscope in time to avoid collision.

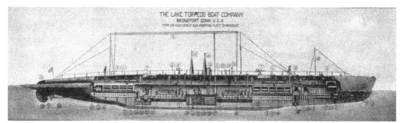

A MODERN SUBMARINE CRUISER, OR FLEET SUBMARINE (LAKE TYPE)

The parts indicated by numbers in this illustration are as follows: 1, main ballast tanks; 2, fuel tanks; 3, keel; 4, safety drop keel; 5, habitable superstructure; 6, escape and safety chambers; 7, disappearing anti-aircraft guns; 8, rapid-fire gun; 9, torpedo tubes; 10 torpedoes; 11, twin deck torpedo tubes; 12, torpedo firing tank; 13, anchor; 14, periscopes; 15, wireless; 16, crew's quarters; 17, officers' quarters; 18, warhead stowage; 19, torpedo hatch; 20, diving chamber; 21, electric storage battery; 22, galley; 23, steering gear; 24, binnacle; 25, searchlight; 26, conning tower; 27, diving station; 28, control tank; 29, compressed-air flasks; 30, forward engine room and engines; 31, after engine room and engines; 32, central control compartment; 33, torpedo room; 34, electric motor room; 35, switchboard; 36, ballast pump; 37, auxiliary machinery room; 38, hydroplane; 39, vertical rudders; 40, signal masts.

How the Submarine Works.—Reference to the diagrammatic view of a modern submarine will probably make clear the following explanation of the operation of a submarine. We will assume that our submarine leaves her own harbor with fuel, stores, and torpedoes on board, wireless and signal masts erected. She is bound to a station farther down the coast, but receives word by wireless that an enemy fleet has been seen approaching the coast in such a direction as to indicate an attack on New York. She receives instructions to return and take up a station fifteen miles off Sandy Hook, the entrance to New York Harbor, and also that she is to coöperate with the smaller harbor-defense submarines that are permanently located in New York. She therefore puts back to the station designated. All deck fittings and lines are stowed except the ventilators and the deck wireless outfit; the latter is left standing so as to keep in touch with the scout ships and destroyers which are reporting the approach of the enemy. Shortly after arriving at her station, the commander notes smoke on the horizon and orders are given to "prepare to submerge." Each member of the crew then proceeds to his particular task; the wireless masts and ventilators are quickly housed, and all hatches are closed and secured. The quartermaster and submerged-control man who controls the steering and hydroplane operating gear take their stations in the control department. The engines are uncoupled by means of the rapid operating clutch, the electric motor is coupled, the hydroplanes are unfolded, the valves are opened, and the word is passed to the commander, "All ready for submergence!" All this is done in a modern vessel in less than two minutes.

The command is then given: "Fill main ballast!" Quick-opening valves are opened and the water rushes into the ballast tanks and superstructure at the rate of fifty or sixty tons per minute. The order is then given: "Trim for submergence!" Sufficient water is then admitted into the final adjustment and trim tank to give the desired buoyancy and trim, and the vessel is now ready to submerge on signal from the commander, who now takes his station at the periscope. The gunners have also taken their stations at the torpedo tubes to prepare to load the tubes as soon as the torpedoes already in the tubes are discharged. The whole time consumed from the time word to "prepare to submerge" until the vessel is running under water has probably not been over two or three minutes. In the meantime the enemy has been rapidly approaching and her superstructure is already above the horizon. The commander of the submarine notes that if the enemy holds its course it will be advantageous to change his position to intercept the oncoming fleet. He therefore gives word to submerge to the desired depth and gives the quartermaster the course, and the vessel proceeds, entirely submerged, to get nearer the enemy's line of approach. The commander then brings his submarine to rest before extending his periscope above the surface. As soon as the enemy is found to be coming within range he manœuvres his ship so that his torpedoes will bear the proper distance in advance of the ship he selects to destroy. To make a hit it is necessary to fire in advance of the oncoming ship to allow for the time the torpedo takes to reach the point where the enemy will be. Range finders, torpedo directors, and rapid calculators enable the commander to calculate this to a nicety. If the distance is only a thousand or fifteen hundred yards, a hit is pretty certain to be made, but the greater the distance the less the chance of success and the greater the opportunity for error.

CHAPTER II

COMEDY AND TRAGEDY IN SUBMARINE DEVELOPMENT

One of the first queries which laymen usually direct at the submarine navigator is, "Are you not afraid that the boat will never come up?" and other variants on the same theme. Most people are surprised and many are very sceptical when they are informed that there is no sensation at all connected with the act of going under water in a boat except that due to one's own imagination. The fact is that if one were going down inside the vessel in some of the modern submarines he could not readily tell whether the vessel was running on the surface or navigating in a submerged condition.

I remember the time when it was first decided to give a public exhibition of the *Argonaut* in 1897. Various newspapers were permitted to send their representatives to make a submerged trip in the vessel. Quite a large number of newspaper men were present, and among the reporters was one young lady representing a New York newspaper. This being the first time that the newspaper fraternity had been given the opportunity to make a submarine trip, speculation ran rife as to the outcome of the venture. So great a number of reporters came that all could not be permitted to board the vessel. Lots were therefore cast as to who should go. The lady claimed the privilege of her sex, and all agreed that she should be one of the party. When the lots were drawn, one of those who had drawn a lucky number suddenly recalled that he was afflicted with a very diseased heart, and he did not feel it wise to go. Another discovered that his life insurance had just expired, and he gave up his opportunity to a friend. Finally the party was made up and the boat started away from the dock. They were all invited down into the cabin, where a general conversation ensued as to the possibilities of submarine navigation proving a success, upon the sensation of going under water, and other related subjects; I had given the signal to submerge, in the meantime, several minutes before they had finished visiting with each other. Soon one of them asked me when I expected to submerge. They were all greatly surprised when I informed them that we had already been under water for several minutes, and they would hardly believe it until I took them into the conning tower, where they could see the dark green of the water through the glass of the eye-ports. Two of the party promptly discovered that they had each a bottle of champagne concealed about their persons. It was their opinion that it was time to drink to the health of the lady and to the success of the *Argonaut*. After we had rummaged around and finally found an old rusty tin cup, this was done.

All first experiences, however, have not been so pleasant as that of the *Argonaut's* trial. The submarine *Hunley* (page 150) suffocated and drowned four different crews during her brief career. Twice she was found standing on end with her bow stuck in the mud in the bottom of the river, with a crew of nine men dead in her fore part, where they had been thrown when she dived to the bottom. In these two instances the men were suffocated, due to lack of air, as no water was found in the boat when she was raised. The gradual exhaustion of the air and final unconsciousness which overtook these brave volunteers can only be left to the imagination.

When experimenting with the *Argonaut*, I received a visit from the late Col. Charles H. Hasker, of Richmond, Va. He had volunteered as one of the party to try the *Hunley* after she had suffocated her second crew. On the trial, for which Mr. Hasker volunteered, she started away from the dock in tow of the gunboat *Ettawan* by a line thrown over the hatch combing. She had been trimmed down so that she had very little freeboard, and as she gained headway she started to "shear," due to her peculiar flatiron-shaped bow. Lieutenant Payne, who was in command, attempted to throw the towline off the hatch combing, but got caught in the bight of the line. On his struggle to free himself he knocked a prop from under the tiller of the horizontal diving rudder, which had been set to hold the bow up. As soon as the prop was knocked out the tiller dropped down and inclined the horizontal rudder to dive, and the vessel dove with her hatches open. Lieutenant Payne freed himself, and Colonel Hasker managed to get partly out of one of the hatches before the vessel sank, but the inrushing force of the water closed the hatch door, which caught him by the calf of his leg, and he was carried with the vessel to the bottom in forty-two feet of water. However, he maintained his presence of mind, and when the vessel became full it balanced the pressure so that he could release himself from the hatch cover. He was a good swimmer and escaped to the surface. Two men escaped from the other hatch. The other five members of the crew were drowned in the vessel.

Notwithstanding that this was the third time she had sunk and killed a number of men, she was again raised and a crew of nine other brave men was found to man her. Under command of Lieutenant Dixon, on the night of February 17, 1864, she was brought alongside of the United States battleship *Housatonic* and sank her, but Lieutenant Dixon and his crew went down with the *Hunley* at the same time. Thus, in the various attempts to operate this vessel in a submerged condition, a total of thirty-two lives were lost.

The New Orleans submarine boat was also built by the Confederates during the Civil War. A friend who took the photograph of this vessel told me the following story as related to him by a Southern gentleman who was familiar with the history of the boat. It appears that this submarine was the conception of a wealthy planter who owned a number of slaves. He thought that it would add considerable interest to the occasion of her launching if, when the vessel left the ways, she should disappear beneath the waves and make a short run beneath the surface before coming up. So he took two of his most intelligent slaves and instructed them how to hold the tiller when the vessel slid down the ways, and in which way to turn the propeller for a time after she began to lose her launched speed. He told them when they got ready to come up they should push the tiller down and the vessel would come to the surface to be towed ashore.

A great crowd assembled to see this novel launching. "When things were all ready," said the old Southern gentleman, "sure enough, them two niggers got into the boat and shut down the hatches; and do you know, suh, that at that time them niggers was worth a thousand dollars apiece." Well, it seems that the boat slid down the ways and disappeared under the water just as had been planned. The crowd waited expectantly, but the vessel did not reappear. Eventually they got into boats and put out hooks and grappling lines, but she could not be found. The designer of the craft stated as his opinion that "he might have known better than to trust them pesky niggers anyway," and he was willing to bet that they had taken the opportunity to steal the vessel and run away. He asserted that very likely they would take the boat up North and give it to the Yankees, and that they could expect to hear of the "Yanks" using it to blow up some of their own (Confederate) ships.

Her disappearance remained a mystery for a great many years—until long after the war closed, in fact, and the incident had been forgotten. Years afterward, during some dredging operations to deepen the harbor, the dredge buckets one day got hold of something they could not lift. A diver was sent down to investigate, and he reported that there was some metal object buried in the mud which looked like a steam boiler. They set to work to raise this, and putting chains around it they lifted it on to the wharf. The old gentleman, in closing the narrative, remarked, "And do you know, suh, when they opened the hatch them two blamed niggers was still in thar, but they warn't wuth a damned cent."

One amusing experience that I had occurred in the Chesapeake Bay in 1898, a few miles below the Potomac River. We were bound from Baltimore to Hampton Roads, and a part of the journey was made on the bottom of the bay. We found this exceedingly interesting, as we could sit in the divers' compartment and view, through the open divers' door, the various kinds of bottom we were passing over, rake up oysters and clams, catch crabs with a crab net, and amuse ourselves in trying to spear fish.

The *Argonaut* at this time had a double pipe mast fifty feet in height, through one of which we got air to run our engines. The other was to provide for the exhaust. We carried a red flag on top of this mast as a warning to surface vessels to keep clear. One afternoon we had been submerged about four hours, running on the bottom in depths varying from twenty-five to forty-five feet; night coming on, we decided to come up and seek a harbor. When we came to the surface we noticed a "bugeye" (a small schooner) "hove to" about fifty yards to the leeward. I blew the centre tank, which brought our conning tower up out of the water, opened the hatch, and hailed the skipper of the bugeye to ask our location and the nearest harbor. He did not wait to answer, but as soon as I yelled he squared away "wing and wing" for the shore. As there was a stiff breeze blowing, it did not take him long to make it, and he ran his vessel right up on the sandy beach, where we saw him and another man—who composed the crew—clamber out over the bow and start to run inland as fast as they could

47

go, leaving their boat without so much as lowering their sails. We finally located ourselves as just north of the mouth of the Rappahannock River, and saw that there was a good harbor very near, so we put in there for the night. After supper, as we were in need of fresh provisions, we went ashore and learned that there was a store a couple of miles down the peninsula. We walked down there and found the store full of natives who were obviously curious as to our identity and business. Finally the storekeeper gathered up his courage and asked us who we were. When he learned that we were down on an experimental cruise in the submarine boat *Argonaut*, he burst into laughter and told us that we had solved a mystery which had stirred up the entire community. He then explained that just about dark one of his neighbors, who never had been known to drink and whose reputation for veracity was excellent, had rushed into the store, followed by his mate. Both were pale from fright, and sank on the porch completely exhausted. They then related a weird tale of seeing a red flag moving down the bay *against the current* on a buoy. When they went alongside of it they heard a "puff-puff" like a locomotive—that was the exhaust from our engine coming up out of the pipe—and, furthermore, they stated that they had smelt sulphur distinctly. Just then, they claimed, the buoy commenced to rise up and a smokestack —our conning tower—came up out of the water and "out stepped the devil"—myself, who at that time had on a rather brilliant red cap. Then they had "moseyed" for shore as fast as they could go. The storekeeper said that they had put the honorable captain to bed, and implied that he would be "right smart mad" when he learned how he had deceived himself. We went back to our boat and got an early start in the morning, as we did not know but that the "guying" of his neighbors might "rile" the captain considerably—and these Virginians are usually pretty good rifle shots.

One of the greatest dangers in submarine navigation is that of being run down by surface vessels when the submarine comes to the surface after a deep submergence. I mean by a deep submergence when the vessel goes down so far that the water covers the top of her periscope and the commander gets out of touch with surface vessels. All submarine commanders have probably had narrow escapes from this danger; it is one of the chances that go with the business. I myself have had several very close calls. The first was with the *Protector* manœuvring in rough weather in Long Island Sound off Bridgeport in

1903. The weather was exceedingly rough, the wind blowing a halfgale and blowing the spume from the white-caps into spray. Some of our directors were in a large towboat at anchor and we were manœuvring in their vicinity, running back and forth, submerging, etc., so that they might observe how steadily she could run in a rough sea. Finally, upon submerging, we observed a sloop in distress; part of her rigging had been carried away, and she was half full of water. The sea had broken the cabin windows and she was on the verge of sinking. We observed this through the periscope, so we came up and got a line to her and took her into Bridgeport. There were several young men aboard her, and when they first saw us standing on our conning tower they thought we also had been wrecked and were on top of a buoy.

As the *Protector* had functioned beautifully and we had in addition saved a shipwrecked crew, I felt quite proud of the day's performance, and was greatly surprised, therefore, when I reported to the directors, who had preceded us into the harbor, to have one of them "call me down" for taking such a foolhardy chance in submerging just in front of the steamer *Bridgeport*. He was astonished when I told him that I had never seen the steamer, and then he informed me that I had submerged just under her bow, and as she was going very fast they all expected us to be hit. The white-caps and spray had prevented us from seeing the steamer, as our periscope was a short one and only gave us intermittent views in the rough water. I was curious to learn whether the captain of the steamer had seen us, but I was told by him that he had not. The rough water had prevented the captain from seeing the wake of our periscope, just as it had made it impossible for us to catch a sight of his vessel.

At another time of close escape I was in the channel leading from the Gulf of Finland into Cronstadt, Russia.

We were requested to conduct some manœuvres for the purpose of familiarizing the Russian officers and crew with the method of handling the boat. Admiral Rodjevensky's fleet was outfitting off Cronstadt, preparing to start for the Orient. As the officers of the battle squadron had never seen a submarine in operation, we were requested to conduct our manœuvres in their vicinity. One of the high Russian admirals, whom I afterward met at the officers' club in Cronstadt, said to me: "Mr. Lake, I do not like your submarine boat. One can never tell where it is going to bob up, and I think if you were

49

my enemy I should slip my anchor and run." After manœuvring around the fleet at anchor we took a run out in the channel. Captain Alexander Gadd, the officer who was to command the *Protector*, was in the sighting hood. Our periscope had gone "blind" because one of the crew did not make up a joint properly. Water had entered and dropped on the lower prism, which destroyed our ability to see. We were anxious, however, to continue our manœuvres, and Captain Gadd had volunteered to "con" the vessel from the sighting hood and give us our steering directions. We were thus able to make submergences of short duration. In leaving the port we appeared to have a clear passageway down the channel. After running for a few minutes we brought the sighting hood above the surface, upon which Captain Gadd became very much excited and cried out in German—which I had no difficulty in understanding—that a big ship was coming right toward us. I was puzzled to know what to do, so I pulled the commander away from the sighting hood, got a look myself, and discovered a big white ship headed directly for us. The only thing to do under the circumstances was to blow the centre tank, give the signal to back up, and to blow our whistle, as there was hardly sufficient time to turn out of our course. Blowing the centre tank relieved us very quickly of sufficient water to bring the conning tower above the surface. Fortunately we were observed, and both vessels reversed and went full speed astern, thus preventing a collision which only could have been disastrous to us, because, as there was not sufficient depth of water in the channel to permit the large ship to pass over us, the small boat would have been crushed like an egg-shell. By looking at the chart I saw that we had sufficient water on either side of the main channel to carry on our work of instructing the crew, so I instructed the quartermaster, in English, to change his course. Captain Gadd, not understanding English, was not aware that I had changed the course, and I did not know that mines had been planted for the defense of Cronstadt and Admiral Rodjevensky's fleet, so the next time we came to the surface Captain Gadd once more became very much excited, finally making me understand that we were in a mine field. It seems that the Russians feared the Japanese might by hook or crook, during the night or at a time of fog, which at that time of the year occurred frequently, get hold of some vessel, equip her with torpedoes, and make a raid on the fleet at anchor. Consequently they had mined all except the principal channel, which could be watched. We immediately stopped the

Protector, blew tanks, and proceeded with caution back to the main channel and returned to Cronstadt. I felt that we had had sufficient manœuvres for that day at least.

Another experience which came very close to a tragedy was brought about by the spirit of mischief of one of the trial officers while conducting the official trials of the *Protector* in the Gulf of Finland. One of the trial conditions set by the Russian Government was that we were to be able to run the *Protector* under her engine with her decks submerged and conning tower awash, I standing in the open hatchway with the *Protector* running under these conditions, ready for instant submergence, her conning tower being held above the surface by setting her hydroplanes up. By pulling the hatch cover down and inclining the hydroplanes downward the vessel could be almost instantly submerged—submergence not occupying over fifteen seconds. I had so much confidence in the safety of the *Protector* running in this condition that I did not hesitate to leave the depth-control mechanism for considerable periods of time.

During this official trial in the Gulf of Finland we ran through a school of small fish, and, leaving the hydroplane control gear, I went out upon the deck of the conning tower and watched the fish, which could be plainly seen as the *Protector* passed through them. At this time there was about three feet of water over the decks, and the deck of the conning tower was about a foot or eighteen inches out of the water. All at once the *Protector* started to go down. I jumped down inside the conning tower, pulling the hatch after me, and I am free to confess that my hair stood on end. I then observed that the *Protector* had gone back to her normal condition, and saw at the same time that the senior Russian officer, a very tall man who had to stand in a stooping position in the conning tower, was shaking with laughter. Captain Gadd then explained to me that the other officer—I shall not mention his name, because he is now a high admiral—had "set" the hydroplanes a little down for the purpose of seeing if he could frighten me. He frightened me all right, and I assure you that I never ran the *Protector* afterward in that condition, because I came to the conclusion that, while it might be possible to make a submarine fool-proof, one could never make reasonable calculations which would eliminate danger from the actions of the practical joker. It was only a few weeks after this incident that I read the account of the A-8, one of the diving type of boats in the British Navy, making the fatal dive when running on the surface with the hatch open, even though she had, according to the testimony of the officer, who was standing on the top of the conning tower at the time she went down—and drowned her crew—as much as six or eight tons reserve of buoyancy.

Some of the early boats of the diving type were fitted with fixed periscopes through which one could see in one direction only, and that straight ahead, and with a limited field of vision. In order to get a complete view of the horizon it was therefore necessary for the commander of a vessel equipped in this way to turn the boat completely around. This was the cause of the first serious accident and loss of life in the British submarines of the A type. The A-1, running in the English Channel with her periscope extended above the surface, did not see a steamer following her at a speed exceeding her own; the lookout of the steamer did not see the periscope, and ran the A-1 down, drowning her entire crew. The foolishness of having a periscope that could see in one direction only was demonstrated by some of the officers in the Austrian Navy. Our company had built the first two boats for the Austrian Government, U-1 and U-2. Another type of boat had been built later which had only a fixed periscope of the type described. One day, when this submarine was running along with her periscope above the surface, which gave her commander no vision back of him, some officers approached in a speedy little launch and left their cards tied to the periscope without the knowledge of the commander of the submerged vessel. This demonstrated perfectly that it is essential, both in war and peace times, for the commander of the submarine to know what is going on in his vicinity on the surface. With the noise of machinery running it was difficult in the early boats for the commander to tell whether there was any other power boat in the vicinity of the submarine. That fact led to the practice of running mostly with the periscope above the surface, and eventually to the introduction of two periscopes, one to con the course of the ship and the other to keep watch of the surrounding water to see that other ships do not approach the submarine unawares. That is now the usual practice in peace-time manœuvres.

At Hampton Roads, on one occasion, after a submarine run, we came up under a small launch and picked her up bodily on the deck. We had not seen the boat until we heard her bump against the conning tower and heard some of the ladies scream. We submerged quickly and lowered them into the water again. Another time we came up under a large barge, but all the damage incurred was a broken flagstaff. The best mode of procedure at such times is to bring the vessel to rest while submerged and stop all machinery, then listen for the sound of the machinery of surface vessels. These noises can be heard for a considerable distance under water. If no sound is heard it is then safe to come up. Even in this case there is some possibility of coming up under or just in front of a sailing vessel. One has to take some chances, and I do not consider this taking any greater chance than is taken by the navigator of a surface vessel in running in a fog or in a snow storm.

The question of air supply was at one time one of the most difficult problems to solve on paper with which early experimenters with submarines had to contend. There was no exception in my case. I thought it would be possible to remain submerged only a short time unless I provided some sort of apparatus to extract the carbonic acid gas and restore oxygen to the air after breathing and exhaling the air in an enclosed space like a submerged vessel. I took up the question with various physicians and with a professor of physiology at Johns Hopkins University, and, according to their information and text-books, it would be a very difficult matter to carry sufficient air to remain submerged without change of air except for a very short time. Their text-books stated the quantity of free air that should be allowed per individual. This varied from fifteen hundred to three thousand cubic feet of air per individual per hour. It would be impossible to provide this amount of air in a submarine. What it was essential to discover was *how little* air a man could live on without suffering ill effects. I then built a box containing twenty-seven cubic feet of air space. I entered this and was hermetically sealed within it. At fifteen-minute intervals I lighted matches to note how freely they would burn. At the expiration of three-quarters of an hour the matches still burned brilliantly at the top of the box, but went out when lowered to about the level of my waist. This indicated that about one-half of the oxygen had been consumed and converted into carbonic acid gas. I was surprised to find how distinctly the line was drawn between the air containing oxygen and that containing the heavier carbonic acid gas. I concluded from this experiment that from fifteen to twenty cubic feet of air per individual per hour was sufficient to maintain life for short periods of time without injury.

On completing the *Argonaut* in 1897 we amplified these experiments, five men remaining hermetically sealed in the *Argonaut* for a period of five hours without admitting any air from our air storage tanks, and later on in the *Protector* eight men remained submerged for twenty-four hours, no fresh air being admitted during the first twenty hours. As the volume of air space in the *Protector* was about three thousand cubic feet, this averaged about eighteen cubic feet per man per hour. Without the definite knowledge of my previous box experiment it is very doubtful if the crew would have consented to remain submerged so long without renewing the air supply, so great is the effect of imagination.

In our first test to determine a practical time of submergence in 1897 we had been submerged for nearly two hours when I noticed some members of the crew showing signs of distress. After a time they got together in the after part of the boat and appointed a spokesman, who came to me and asked if I had not noticed that breathing had become very difficult. They urged that we should go up immediately. By this time two of the men were breathing with evident exertion, and beads of perspiration were on their faces. I told them they were suffering from imagination, and explained my experiment with the box. I then took a candle and proved to them that it burned freely in all parts of the boat. We measured the height of the candle flame at the floor of the boat and found it one and five-eighths inches high. In the twenty-four hours' test on the *Protector* the men became frightened in the same way, but after an explanation had been made and the candle demonstration had been shown them they lost their fear and in a few minutes all were breathing as normally as ever.

I have always had some little sympathy for the sensations or fears which those without a knowledge of natural physics might experience on going down into the water; but I have had little sympathy for those who by their education should know and understand the principles of submarine navigation, when operating with a properly designed boat with an experienced crew.

Now, one of the features which the *Argonaut* possessed, which was new in its application to submarine boats at that time, was the use of a diving compartment and air-lock connected with the main hull of the vessel, which would permit divers to leave the vessel when submerged by opening a door in the bottom of this diving compartment after first filling the compartment with compressed air corresponding to the pressure of the water outside of the vessel, which varies in accordance with the depth of submergence.

Every schoolboy is taught the principle of the diving bell, which can be illustrated by the use of a tumbler or glass. If a tumbler is turned upside down and forced into water, the water will not rise to fill the tumbler, owing to the fact that the air, being the lighter, will remain in the tumbler and the water will simply rise, compressing the air to the same pressure per square inch as the pressure surrounding it. Now if you push a tumbler down into the water a distance of thirty-four feet the tumbler would be about one-half full of water and one-half full of air, which corresponds to one atmosphere in pressure. Now if an additional tumbler full of air was compressed to the same pressure and released in that tumbler it would force the water out, and there would be a double volume, or two atmospheres of air, in the tumbler, or just twice what there would be on the surface and under normal atmospheric pressure. This is the principle on which the diving compartment in the Lake type boat operates, it being only necessary to admit air into the diving compartment until the pressure equals the outside water pressure; then a door opening outwardly from the bottom may be opened to permit ready egress or ingress, and so long as the air pressure is maintained no water will rise in the boat.

A professor of physics in the University of Pennsylvania visited the *Argonaut* in Baltimore during some early experiments with her, and in discussing the features of the diving compartment with which, from his position as a professor of natural physics, he should have been entirely familiar, expressed some doubt as to its practicability. He said he understood the theory of it all right, but thought there might be some difficulty in carrying it out in a practical way as I had explained. I invited him into the diving compartment and told him that I would submerge the boat and open the door for him for his benefit, so that he could explain to his students that he had actually seen it done. He turned pale and said, "Oh, no; I would not put you to that trouble for the world"; but by that time I had the heavy iron door closed between the diving compartment and the main hull, and had already started to raise the pressure of the air in the compartment, and assured him that it was not the least trouble in the world; on the contrary, it was a great pleasure. By this time beads of perspiration were standing on his face. When one undergoes air pressure for the first time considerable pain is ofttimes experienced in the ears, due to the pressure on the Eustachian tubes and ear-drums not becoming equalized. To equalize this pressure it is necessary for divers or those undergoing pressure to go through the movement of swallowing, which has a tendency to relieve the unequal pressure and stop the pain. I noticed that the professor was experiencing quite a little pain and consequently told him to swallow, and it was really amusing to see the rapidity with which he worked his "Adam's apple" up and down. He then asked if there was any danger. I answered him that there was none, except to those who were troubled with heart-disease. He immediately put his hand up over his heart and said, "Well, my heart is quite seriously affected," but by that time we had secured the necessary pressure to enable me to open the diving door at the bottom, so I released the "locking dogs" and allowed the door to open, and when he saw the water did not come in, his face cleared and he said, "Well, you know I never would have believed it if I had not seen it," and then he added that he would not have missed seeing it for the world.

Another interesting incident in connection with undergoing pressure occurred while at Hampton Roads, Va. One day I received a visit from a professor of mathematics and his wife at the Hampton Institute, each of whom held a professorship in the college. They stated that the *Argonaut* had been discussed before the faculty and that they would like very much to go down in her and see the diving door opened, which I was very glad to show them. Just previous to going into the diving compartment Professor S—— explained to me that his wife was deaf in one ear, that she had been under a physician's care for about two years, and he wanted to know if undergoing pressure was likely to have an injurious effect upon her. Not being a physician or knowing what might occur, I advised against her undergoing pressure; but she insisted on going into the compartment, promising that if she felt any ill effect from the air pressure she would tell me and I could let her out. I was reluctant to have her go in, and when we entered the compartment I allowed the air to come in very slowly, in the meantime giving a general description of the vessel, and occupying as long a time in the procedure as possible. I noticed almost at once that she was in pain. Although she turned her back to me, I could tell by her clenched jaws and hands that she was probably suffering agony. I then stopped the pressure and suggested to the professor that he had better let his wife go out, but through clenched teeth she still protested, "No, go ahead; I can stand it!" Finally we got the pressure on and opened the door, but, while the professor seemed delighted, his wife made no remark. She simply stood with her hands clenched and I was afraid she was going to faint. Then all at once she screamed; but immediately after her face lighted up with a smile and she exclaimed, "It is all gone!" When she came out of the compartment, after the experiment was over, I noticed her put her hand up to one ear, and she said to her husband, "Do you know, I can hear as plainly out of that ear as I ever could!" About a year afterward I saw Professor S—— and he told me that apparently the experiment had cured his wife of deafness where physicians had failed to help her; that to date it had never returned, and that she could hear as well as she had ever heard. In discussing this matter with an ear specialist some time afterward, he explained to me that the lady had probably been suffering with a disease which caused the small bones connected with the ear-drum to freeze fast, so that the ear-drum did not vibrate. He stated that it is a very common cause of deafness and can seldom be cured; that the bringing of the uneven pressure on the Eustachian tube or other parts had broken away the secretion which had cemented these small bones together and permitted the ear-drum to vibrate as it should, and probably that was the only way in which she could have been helped. I am publishing this incident in the hope that it may lead to the construction of scientific apparatus for the cure of deafness in cases where the deafness is caused by trouble similar to that of the professor's wife.

After our experiments with the *Argonaut* in the Chesapeake Bay and on the Atlantic coast, she was enlarged and otherwise improved and in the winter of 1899 I brought her to Bridgeport, Connecticut, which offered excellent harbor conveniences and deep water, as well as providing the necessary manufacturing facilities for continuing my experimental work.

While there the request was made of me to let some of the newspaper people and some prominent men of the town witness her trials; I therefore invited them to take a trip out into the Sound. I remember that we extended in all twenty-eight invitations to the Mayor, to the press, and to some other prominent citizens, expecting that perhaps three or four of the number would accept. Very much to my surprise, twenty-nine appeared, and only one of those who had received the invitation failed to come, while two others brought their friends with them. Among the number was John J. Fisher, at that time quite a noted singer for the American Graphophone Company. I had planned to cook and serve a dinner for the party on board, and we intended to be back about two o'clock in the afternoon, but when we got out on the bottom of the Sound all the different members of the party wanted to see the bottom, so we travelled out over some oyster beds and clam beds and I opened the diving door and let the party all see the bottom of the Sound and pick up clams and "jingle" shells, in depths varying from twenty-four to thirty-odd feet, while running along the bottom. The air-lock was small and we could take only two at a time through it into the diving compartment. In the meantime a meal had been cooked for the others and served. Mr. Fisher amused the company by singing "Rocked in the Cradle of the Deep" and other songs appropriate to the occasion.

We did not arrive at Bridgeport until after four o'clock, and then found the wharf black with an excited populace, largely composed of friends of those who had taken the trip. Tugboats had been engaged, and the editor of one of the afternoon papers gave me a very severe "dressing down" for having kept the party out so long, as the whole city was excited and every one feared that we had been lost. The afternoon editions of the papers had all been held up awaiting our return, and the editor of the paper in question informed me that they were just telegraphing New York for a wrecking outfit to come and raise us, as they had sent a tugboat out and the captain had reported that we were submerged off Stratford Point Light and that our red flag, which extended from the top of the mast, was above water, but that we were not moving at that time and hence they thought that all hands must have perished.

Working under water from a submarine boat is very interesting work. The *Argonaut* was built with the idea of demonstrating the practicability of conducting explorations under water, locating and recovering beds of shellfish, in addition to locating and recovering wrecks and their cargoes. This line of work is the most interesting of the submarine work in which I have been engaged, and offers, in my judgment, great opportunities for the benefit of the human race. A submarine boat is a rather expensive craft, however, for conducting such operations, and there are certain disadvantages in operating around wrecks in a submarine without any surface connections, as there is always a possibility of the vessel becoming entangled in the wreckage of the sunken ship. I remember in one case we had located a sunken wreck and had gone down alongside of her with the *Argonaut*. This sunken wreck had an overhanging guard and was quite strongly built. The tide carried the *Argonaut* up against the side of the sunken wreck, and after our divers had come in and made their report in regard to her we attempted to come up to the surface, but the Argonaut could not come up, because the current had carried her in under the guard, and it was necessary for us to wait until the tide turned to enable us to get away from the obstruction.

At another time we were operating alongside of a wreck in which we were demonstrating the practicability of removing cargo from the sunken wreck to a small experimental cargo or freight-carrying submarine. This freight-carrying submarine was practically a tank, and was built purely for demonstrating purposes. It was nine feet in diameter and twenty-five feet long, with conical ends (see illustration, page 278). It had wheels underneath so that it could be towed on the bottom by the *Argonaut*. The *Argonaut* had gone down alongside of a sunken wreck loaded with coal, with the freight submarine alongside opposite to the wreck. The *Argonaut* had a centrifugal wrecking pump mounted on her deck, driven by a shaft extending through a stuffing box, and to fill the little cargo-carrying submarine it was necessary for the diver only to place the suction pipe connected with the wrecking pump into the sunken coal barge and the discharge pipe into the hatch of the cargo submarine, start the pump, and transfer the coal from the sunken wreck to the cargo-carrying submarine. We made several successful demonstrations of this, and actually transferred fifteen tons of coal from the sunken wreck to the cargo submarine with a six-inch pump in nine minutes. It was then necessary for the diver only to close the hatch of the freight-carrying submarine, admitting compressed air into the interior which blew the water out through check valves in the bottom of the freight submarine, and then the freight submarine would come to the surface with her cargo, which could be towed into port on the surface by surface tugboats. One day, when down on the bottom repeating this experiment, the diver came back into the diving compartment and said that he wanted the *Argonaut* moved ahead about twenty feet. The divers, having become familiar with the operation at this time, were a little careless. There were three of us in the diving compartment at the time, and it was "up to me" to go back into the machinery compartment and move the boat forward twenty feet; we could tell the distance by the revolutions of her wheels over the bottom. I told them to close the bottom diving door, and when I left the diving compartment they were in the act of doing so. As I looked back through the lookout window in the air-lock door I saw that the diver had taken off his helmet and was smoking his pipe—this being the first thing a diver always wants to do when coming out of the water. I then started to move the boat, assuming that the diving door was closed, but the boat did not move. Having been at rest there for some time, I assumed that she had probably taken in through a leaky valve some additional water, and I decided that it was necessary to lighten her somewhat, so I called on the telephone and asked them if everything was all right in the diving compartment and they replied that it was. I then pumped and tried her again; still she did not move, so I pumped out a little more from the forward end of the boat for the purpose of lightening her burden some more. All at once she left the bottom with a rapid rush and ascended to the surface. There was something which held her down, I do not know what it was, but it was not released until we had given her a partial buoyancy of perhaps two or three tons. I submerged her again quickly and went back through the air-lock into the diving compartment and then observed that the diver was taking off his diving suit; he was pale and appeared to be very much excited. I asked his helper, who was laughing, what the matter was. To this question the diver himself replied, "I will tell you a funny story when we get ashore." The tender then explained to me that they had not closed the door entirely, but had left it open about four inches, and when the boat rose, the air, rushing out of the compartment with a noise like a thousand locomotive whistles, had scared Captain S—— half to death. The tender had been with me in the diving compartment once before when a similar accident occurred and consequently he was used to it. As soon as we got alongside of the dock the diver referred to jumped ashore and said, "The funny story I am going to tell you is this: I will never set foot in your d—— boat again."

Another amusing situation occurred on the *Argonaut* which might have proved very serious. After we had completed our experiments with the *Argonaut* and started to build the *Protector*, not having any immediate use for her, the *Argonaut* was anchored in the river off the place where we were conducting our building operations. Our engineer, W——, received a visit one day from a friend of his who had visited Bridgeport on his wedding trip and had left his wife in the depot between trains while he ran up to see his old friend, our chief engineer. The chief took him out on board the *Argonaut* to show him through, and in explaining the boat to him the two men went into the diving compartment. Now the Argonaut had been shut up for some months, but the chief found that there was still sufficient air in the air tanks to enable him to admit the air into the diving compartment and show his friend how the door could be opened. The door, which opened downward, was quite heavy, weighing something over four hundred pounds, and was raised by block and tackle. He got the air pressure on all right and opened the door; the boat was near the bottom, and when the door opened downward the lower end of it settled into the mud. In attempting to lift it again the rope, which had become rotten, due to dampness, broke, and consequently he could not lift the door. In the meantime the tide was falling and the diving door was forced farther into the mud. As no one at the works knew that the chief had gone on board the *Argonaut*, when night came everybody went home and it was not until eleven o'clock that night that the watchman went down to the end of the pier and heard some one tapping on the *Argonaut*. Thinking this somewhat strange, he got into a boat and rowed out alongside. He still heard the tapping at regular intervals, and was astonished to see a small boat alongside; then he struck the *Argonaut* with his oar and immediately got a rapid tattoo in response. Feeling sure now that somebody in distress must be down in the *Argonaut*, he got a lantern, went down inside the boat and forward to the diving compartment. There, on the other side of the lookout window, he saw the face of the engineer. The chief had made the mistake of closing the forward air-lock door, so that when he got the pressure on in the diving compartment and the diving door open he could not close it again. There was no way for him to relieve the pressure and open the air-lock door without flooding the whole boat; while, had he closed the first or inner door he could have gone through into the air-lock, closing and securing the forward door behind him. He could then have released the air from the air-lock and escaped, in the meantime leaving the pressure on in the diver's compartment and the divers' door open. When the watchman appeared the chief wrote a note and put it up to the window, instructing the watchman to close the inner air-lock door. This was done, and then he and his friend got out. It was nearly midnight when they were released; and, feeling a natural curiosity in the circumstances, I asked the chief if his friend found his bride still waiting for him at the station. He replied that after they had managed to get out his visitor would not even speak to him, and that he had never heard from him since the occurrence.

I have described above how I ran grave risks while navigating in Russian waters, and it was in connection with the construction and delivery of these same boats for the Russian Government that I met with still other interesting experiences.

THE LAUNCHING OF THE "PROTECTOR"

Built in Bridgeport, Connecticut, in 1901-1902. Sent to Vladivostock, Russia, during the Russian-Japanese war, and was the only Russian submarine in full commission during that war. She was the forerunner of the German U type of boat, with her large flat deck, light-weight watertight superstructure and hydroplane control.

At the time of the Russo-Japanese War the *Protector* was being tried out in Long Island Sound, and representatives of both warring countries sent officers to witness her perform and to make propositions for her purchase. Russia secured her, however, and it then became a problem to get her out of the country without evading the neutrality laws. We discovered that we were being watched by spies, and had reason to believe that if it became known that Russia had purchased her, and that we were planning to take her out of the country, an injunction would be secured against us. We had secured high legal advice that if she were shipped incomplete we would not be evading the United States laws, but that she might, notwithstanding this precaution, be captured on the high seas or held in this country by injunction as contraband. We therefore removed her battery and sent it to New York, ostensibly for repairs; from there it was later shipped to Russia *via* steamer. The agents of the Russian Government then chartered the steamer *Fortuna* to carry a cargo of coal from Norfolk, Va., to Libau, Russia. While loading coal, heavy timbers to form a cradle on the deck were also shipped on board, and while coming up the coast this cradle was assembled and the *Fortuna's* decks strengthened sufficiently to carry the *Protector*, which had been stripped down to about one hundred and thirty tons by the removal of her battery. The plan was that the *Fortuna* should come into Sandy Hook at midnight on Saturday and proceed to Prince's Bay, a cove back of Staten Island. There the *Protector* was to be picked up by the powerful floating derrick, the *Monarch*, and the *Fortuna*, with the *Protector* on her deck, was then to get outside of Sandy Hook before daylight and pass the three-mile limit on Sunday morning. None of my crew was in the secret that an effort was to be made to get the *Protector* out of the country before legal proceedings could be taken to prevent her going; and, as she had no batteries on board, they were much surprised to be informed on Saturday—the morning of the day set to make the attempt—that they were to bring their suitcases and a change of clothing with them, as I was going to give the *Protector* a trial under her engines alone and we might be away a day or two. When we left Bridgeport I headed the *Protector* away from New York, and our men thought we were bound for Newport, but as soon as we got out of sight of the shore, in which we were assisted by a fog, I ran over under the Long Island shore and headed for New York. We remained in hiding during the day and passed through Hell Gate, the entrance into the East River, at about nine o'clock, and reached Prince's Bay according to schedule; but the *Fortuna* did not appear until eight o'clock on Sunday morning. Fortunately for the enterprise, a very heavy rainstorm came up and shut out all view of us from the shore until the *Protector* had been loaded and was out to sea. Before she sailed I called my crew together and told them that the *Protector* had been sold to a foreign country, and that, although I could not tell them to whom or to what port she was bound, I should like some of them to go with me to assist me in training the foreign crew to operate her. Every man volunteered and was anxious to go, so I selected those I wanted and they took their suitcases on board the *Fortuna*. It was seven years before some of these men returned to America.

The *Protector* was covered with canvas and she was sighted but once on her way across. To prevent suspicion I returned to Bridgeport for a few days and then took the fast steamer *Kaiser Wilhelm II* to Cherbourg and was met by the Russian Ambassador in Paris, who gave me Russian passports under the assumed name of Elwood Simons, as the Russian Government did not wish it to become known that it had purchased the *Protector* or that the builder was coming to Russia to instruct their officers and men in the use of submarines. This travelling about under an assumed name brought about some amusing complications and experiences later.

I arrived at Libau by train the morning the *Fortuna* and *Protector* arrived off that port, but the government had decided to send her on to Cronstadt, the principal naval station and defense of St. Petersburg, now called Petrograd, so orders were given accordingly. On the way up the Baltic the coverings over the *Protector* had been removed, and a Russian torpedo boat, seeing her, made off at full speed, soon to return with another torpedo boat and a larger gunboat and beginning to fire blank shots for the *Fortuna* to stop. The captain did not stop quickly enough, and then they fired solid shot just in front of the *Fortuna's* bow and she was forced to stop. It developed that one of the officers had recognized the *Protector* from having seen the pictures of her, but, not knowing that she had been bought by his own government, suspected that the Japanese Government had purchased her, and that she would probably be launched somewhere in the Baltic and attack the Russian fleet. He then sent an armed prize crew on board the *Fortuna* to take her into Cronstadt as a prize—which incidentally was where she was bound, anyhow.

On arriving at Cronstadt we were met by a number of officers of the Russian Navy, among whom were Captain Becklemechief and

Chief Constructor Bubonoff, who were the joint designers of the Russian submarine *Delphine*, which had recently been completed. While sitting in the *Fortuna's* cabin exchanging congratulations upon the safe arrival of the *Protector* a telegram was brought in to Captain Becklemechief which, I noticed, caused his hitherto cheerful face to assume a grave aspect. He handed it to Constructor Bubonoff with a word in Russian which I could not understand. A little later, on our way to Petrograd, he informed me that the *Delphine* had sunk and drowned twenty-three officers and men, a number of whom were in training to be transferred to the *Protector* to make up her crew upon her arrival. We passed her on our way into Petrograd. She lay just off the Baltic works dock, and divers were then recovering the bodies.

THE "DELPHINE"

Russian submarine, which drowned 23 of her crew the day the author arrived at Cronstadt.

It appears that thirty-five men, all told, were on board, and that her conning tower hatch was closed by a lever arm connected to a nut which travelled on a threaded shaft operated from down inside the vessel, and it is believed that the officer in command gave the order to fill certain tanks which were usually filled previous to closing the hatch, not taking into consideration the fact that there was so much more weight on board than usual, due to so many more men—eight being the usual crew—and at the same time giving the order to close the hatch. Just then a steamer came by and a sea broke into the hatch, which frightened one of the men so that he tried to get out, and succeeded in getting one shoulder and his head out of the hatch. His body prevented the man down below from closing the hatch before the vessel had sunk with all hands; but after she sank either the man at the closing mechanism or some one else must have had sufficient presence of mind to open the hatch again, as twelve of the men were carried up out of the boat, presumably by the air bubbles which must escape from any enclosed airtight vessel before it can become entirely filled with water. This phenomenon may be observed by taking a bottle and forcing it down under water; the water will rush in and compress the air, and then the compressed air will overcome the pressure of the incoming water and rush out, carrying some of the water with it. Two of these men and Captain Tillian, who escaped, were afterward members of the *Protector's* crew. Captain Tillian told me that he was in the after part of the boat when she sank, and the last he remembered was being in water up to his breast and that one of the sailors asked him to kiss him good-bye. The captain was picked up on the surface unconscious. Another of the men said that he was carried to one end of the boat on the first inrush of water and then he felt himself being rapidly carried back to the centre of the boat and heard a sharp hissing sound like the rush of air. The next thing he recalled was coming to on the dock.

The *Alligator* was the first of the large cruising type of submarines which we built for the Russian Government. These vessels were five hundred and thirty-five tons submerged displacement, which was about twice that of the displacement of any submarines which had previously been built; and I was very anxious to get a trial of her before the winter season came on in the fall of 1907. As the winter closes all navigation in the Gulf of Finland for six or seven months, and as there were a number of new features to be tried out in this boat, I knew that unless I succeeded in getting a trial before the winter shut down I would have several months of worry as to whether or not the boat would function satisfactorily when submerged. Delays occurred, so that we were not able to get our trial as early as expected. The action of the weather indicated that navigation was likely to be closed within a day's time, as frequently occurs in those northern latitudes. We had not received the periscopes or lights, and the boat was not entirely completed, but was sufficiently far advanced to make it safe for me to try her on a submerged run. Consequently we arranged with the commandant of Cronstadt to supply us with a seagoing tender and went out for a trial in the open gulf, where we could get sufficient water to navigate such a large boat. It was very rough and stormy, and it took us some little time to get our final adjustments to enable us to submerge completely. We found that we did not have sufficient ballast to enable her to be submerged by filling the usual water ballast tanks, so we had to let some additional water in her motor-room, being careful not to let it rise high enough to saturate the windings of our dynamo-motors. In the meantime the storm had been increasing in velocity and a very rough sea had arisen. I had observed through the sighting hood that the tender was making very bad weather of it; the last I saw of her she was pitching and jumping out of the water to such an extent that at times I could see her keel from the stem to nearly one-half her length. When we got under water we became so much interested in the operation, which was entirely satisfactory, that we did not come to the surface again for about fifteen minutes. Then we simply rose for a look around and submerged again, giving no thought to the tender. The seas were so high that we could not see any distance from our sighting hood, and supposed she was somewhere in the vicinity. We continued our tests, alternately submerging and trying her out on the turns and at different speeds of motors until our battery was nearly run down, then we blew tanks and came to the surface just at dusk, expecting to find the tender to lead us back to Cronstadt. We had no lights or compass at this time, but fortunately we were able to catch sight of one of the lightships off the entrance to the channel leading to the harbor of Cronstadt, sufficient to set our course for port. By this time it was blowing a gale; in fact, it was the north storm which preceded the close of navigation, which followed a day or two later. Finally it set in to sleet and rain, and shut off our view of the light. We had nothing to guide us, but took a chance on the general direction. Fortunately we had no mines to fear, as the war had closed and they had been removed. Finally it "cleared up" sufficiently for us to make out the lights again, and we got into Cronstadt in the early hours of the morning. On our arrival at the dock we found the commandant of the port and a number of officers who had been informed of our arrival when we came through the war harbor gateway. We found the officers and men of the tender which had escorted us, all under arrest, and the commandant of the port asked me with very great seriousness if I would like to have them sent to Siberia. It seems that they had waited about an hour after they saw us disappear, and had come to the conclusion that we were lost. The commander of the tender said that if he had remained out any longer he thought that he himself would have been lost, as the storm was so severe. It broke loose nearly everything he had in the boat, washed all of his portable deck fittings overboard, and he feared his vessel would founder. I explained to the commandant of the port that under the circumstances, and from my observations of the way the boat had jumped around when we submerged, as well as from the fact that the commander of the tender could not see us, he was justified in coming into port. I also said that I would be very greatly obliged to him—the commandant of the port—if he would release the captain and crew from arrest, with my compliments; and this, I am glad to say, was done.

A number of submarine vessels with their crews have been lost in peace-time manœuvres. The cause of loss has not always been easy to determine. In numerous cases it was undoubtedly due to faulty design, especially in boats of the diving type, where they lacked sufficient static stability and plunged headfirst into the bottom. Numerous lives have been lost by the explosion of either gasolene fumes or hydrogen gas given off by the batteries, and some by asphyxiation, caused by the escape of the products of combustion from the engines, the accumulation of carbonic acid gas or chlorine gas generated by salt water getting into the batteries.

These accidents are usually brought about by the carelessness of some member or members of the crew. I had been fortunate in not having any loss of life on any of my boats up to the beginning of the war, but ignorance and carelessness have, in several instances, caused injuries, and might as readily have caused loss of life.

I have had a commander, after being coached as to proper procedure, to attempt to submerge his submarine vessel without checking up to see that hatches and ventilators were closed.

When we were enlarging the *Argonaut* at Erie Basin, in Brooklyn, I went down into the boat one day and found a strong odor of gasolene and saw numerous kerosene torches burning. Upon investigation I found that two machinists who were dismantling the engine had broken the gasolene supply pipe and allowed the gasolene in the pipes to run out on the floor of the engine-room—about a half-gallon,

I should judge. I ordered the men all out of the boat and blew out the torches, even taking the precaution to pinch the wicks. Upon going up on the deck, a sub-foreman in charge of the men declared that there was no danger and ordered the men back to work. I objected, and went up to the main office to report that they were doing a dangerous thing, and to see if I could not get the superintendent to order a blower sent down to blow the gas fumes out of the boat. But before I could get his attention I saw the ambulance drive by, and learned that as soon as I had left the deck a couple of the men said I must be a d——— fool to be afraid of a little gas, and they had then gone down in the boat and struck a match to relight one of the torches. By this time an explosive mixture had been formed, and I can only hope that the explosion which occurred, as well as the following weeks which they spent in hospital, have now convinced them, as well as some of the other doubters, that a little gasolene in an improper place is exceedingly dangerous.

Another more serious explosion occurred on one of our large cruising submarines at the New Admiralty Works in Russia, which was due to a combination of both carelessness and ignorance. In this instance, gasolene had been sent down to the Admiralty dock for conducting dock trials of the engines. When the fuel arrived, the boat was full of workmen, carpenters, pipe-fitters, machinists, etc., but, notwithstanding the fact that there were rules posted that all men should leave the boat when taking on gasolene—except an inspector, who should check up to see that the proper valves were opened and everything tight—the quartermaster in charge of the labor crew, without notifying anyone in charge or anyone aboard the boat, connected up with the supply system and started pumping the gasolene into the boat. The engine was then running and charging batteries. Now it appears that one of the naval officers had—also without notifying the engineer—ordered a section of the filling pipe taken down for the purpose of having a branch pipe connection made in order to carry some additional fuel in the centre ballast tank— something we did not approve of; so, when the gasolene was pumped into the boat, instead of going into the proper tanks it ran out on the floor of the conning tower, then down through some openings for electric wires that had not yet been sealed, over the switchboard, and collected in a large puddle on the floor. One of the Russian electricians, who had been aft adjusting the dynamos, finally noticed this gasolene running down over the switchboard and cried out in Russian, "Quick, leave the boat for your lives!" and in his excitement he pulled the switch through which the dynamos were charging the batteries. This created a spark, which was all that was needed to create an explosion. Fortunately, this was a large boat and she had three exit hatches, all of which were open. A number of men were just in the act of going through the hatches; they were blown up into the air twenty-five or thirty feet, according to some observers, two of them falling into the water, from which they were rescued. Many of the men were seriously burned, but none fatally. Those most seriously injured were those near the hatches, as the flash of flame rose toward the hatches, the openings being the line of least resistance for the compressed air and gases. The men in the ends of the boat were not injured, while those midway between the hatches had about six inches of the bottom of their trousers burned to a crisp, which shows that the heavy gasolene fumes had not yet become thoroughly mixed with the air.

I had been on board this vessel only a few minutes previous to this explosion and at that time everything was in proper order, but I had left to keep an appointment with the Minister of Marine. Before reaching his office, however, one of our office men overtook me and notified me of the explosion. On my return I found great excitement, as it was reported that many men had been killed. The explosion had set fire to a lot of shavings and the wooden deck covering over the batteries, as well as some joiner work which was in process of erection. Some of the yard officers had ordered the hatches battened down, but the engines were still running, receiving sufficient air through ventilators to supply combustion. It was reported that several men were missing, and it was believed they had been killed by the explosion and were still on board. In the meantime the Minister of Marine and other officers had arrived, also a couple of fire companies, and I requested them to open the hatches and see if they could not put out the fire and get out the bodies if any were there. The officers objected on the ground that if any water were put on board it probably, upon coming in contact with the batteries, would create a lot of hydrogen gas and cause a further and perhaps more disastrous explosion. Finally I procured a couple of flasks of carbonic acid gas and let that into the boat over the battery compartment where the fire was, which smothered the flames, and then borrowed one of the firemen's smoke helmets and went down into the vessel, expecting to find some of the bodies of our missing men. The fire had burned the rubber insulators off the wires and some of the asphaltum insulators around the batteries, and the smoke was so thick that it was impossible to see anything, even with an electric lamp which I carried, but the heat was not very intense, as the flames had been put out by the carbonic gas and I found no bodies, so I ordered the hatches open, blowers put in, and a few buckets of water, which put out the embers. Our missing men were later found in the hospital, where they had been rushed before their names had been taken. Seventeen of the men were injured so badly that they had to go to the hospital, but the burns were mostly superficial, only the outer skin and hair being burned, and this was due to the instantaneous flash of the gasolene. They all eventually recovered.

The following day I held an investigation and learned the above facts regarding the delivery of the gasolene on board, the breaking of the pipe, etc. Several of the Russian workmen saw the gasolene leaking down into the compartment; one whom I interrogated said it had been leaking in for about five minutes before the explosion. I asked him if he knew it was gasolene. He said, "Yes." I asked him if he knew it was dangerous, and he said, "Yes." I asked him then why he did not report it, and his reply was characteristic of the Russian "moujik." He said, "I was sent down there to clean up the shavings after carpenters and not to look after the gasolene, as to whether that was being put on board in a proper manner or not, and I know enough to attend to my own business and do only what I am told to do."

The evidence further shows that about a quarter of a barrel of gasolene had been pumped into the boat before it was discovered that the pipe had been disconnected.

From the fact that the trousers of the men standing between the hatches were burned only about six inches up from the bottom, it shows that the gasolene fumes were still lying close to the floor, owing to the fact that the fumes of gasolene are heavier than atmospheric air. Had the explosion come a few minutes later, when the gasolene fumes and the air had been more thoroughly mixed, the explosion would have been more powerful and would probably have killed every man on board, as it did in the Italian submarine *Foca*, when twenty-three men were killed by an explosion due to a leaky gasolene tank.

There have been many other explosions, resulting in fatalities, in almost all of the navies using gasolene boats, especially where the fuel was carried in tanks built within the main hulls of the vessel, as it seems impossible to so "caulk" a seam in a tank that the fumes of gasolene will not leak through. The fact that it first settles to the floor makes it not easy to detect by the nostrils. When gasolene fumes become sufficiently mixed with air to rise up to the height of one's nostrils I always consider it an explosive mixture and would not think of striking a spark, as experiments show that a proper mixture of air and gasolene or hydrogen and air at only atmospheric pressure in an enclosed vessel will exert an explosive force of about ninety pounds per square inch, which will cause practically instant death. The above case, in regard to the Russian vessel, was undoubtedly due to carelessness or thoughtlessness of the officer who ordered the pipe to be disconnected, and the ignorance of the "moujik" who failed to give warning when he saw the gasolene coming into the boat; also to the further thoughtlessness of the electrician who pulled the switch which made the spark.

Among other accidents that have happened in peace times, causing loss of life, are several in the British Navy in vessels of the diving type; the *Farfadet* and *Lutine* in the French Navy, due to lost control in diving; also the *Pluviose*, which was run down and cut in two as she was coming to the surface; the *Fulton*, during an experimental cruise, and the F-4, E-2, and F-1 in the American Navy. In war time there have undoubtedly been many submarine vessels and entire crews lost, with none to tell the story of their passing.

CHAPTER III

EXPERIENCES OF PIONEER INVENTORS OF THE SUBMARINE

The experiences of the pioneer inventors of the submarine, if known in detail, would undoubtedly afford many amusing incidents as well as some tragic ones. Some of these have been treated in the previous chapter on the comedy and tragedy of submarine development. Cornelius Debrell must have been either something of a joker or else he was much further advanced in the art of revitalizing the air than are any of our modern scientists. His experiments attracted much attention during the reign of King James the First, and, according to the accounts published at that time, he must have been quite a court favorite, for it is reported that King James made a trip with him from Westminster Bridge to Greenwich. The accounts assert that he could remain under water for long periods of time by simply pouring out a few drops of some secret liquid from a bottle which he carried with him. The celebrated Ben Jonson, in one of his works, refers to Debrell and his celebrated boat in a humorous passage from one of his plays, "The Staple of News," acted by "His Majesty's Servants" in 1625.

P. Jun.—Have you no news against him, on the contrary?

NATH.—Yes, sir. They write here, one Cornelius-son hath made the Hollanders an invisible eel, to swim the haven at Dunkirk and sink all the shipping there....

P. Jun.—But how is't done?

CYM.—I'll show you, sir. It is an automa, runs under water, with a snug nose, and has a nimble tail, made like an auger, with which tail she wriggles betwixt the costs (ribs) of a ship, and sinks it straight....

P. Jun.—A most brave device, to murder their flat bottoms.

(*Act* II, *S.* 1.)

Of course, there are no authentic plans of Debrell's boat in existence, but from the descriptions which were published in regard to it I am under the impression that probably he did succeed in submerging below the surface of the water and propelling her with the tide for some distances. The description tells of some very ingenious arrangements for submerging the boat, in which he used goatskins sewed together in the form of bags. The mouth of each bag was nailed over an orifice opening from the interior of the boat into the sea. These goatskins were placed between planks, with a sort of a Chinese windlass arrangement for squeezing the planks together. When he wished to submerge the boat he allowed the planks to open out, and the water, rushing into the goatskins, increased the vessel's displacement so that it sank. When he wished to come to the surface he simply drew the planks together and squeezed the water out of the goatskins, thus restoring the vessel's buoyancy. According to description, the boat was propelled by oars extending through ports opening into the sides of the boat. Goatskins sewed in the form of cones prevented the water from entering the vessel, the base of the cone being nailed to the sides of the boat, the apex of which was cut off and bound around the staff of the oar. This gave sufficient flexibility to feather the oars and row under water.

Nearly one hundred years after Cornelius Debrell's experiments an Englishman by the name of Day built a small wooden submarine and descended in it under the water. This experiment gave him sufficient confidence to undertake the construction of a large vessel, and he proposed to make a profit from its use by making wagers that he could descend to a depth of one hundred yards and remain there for a period of twenty-four hours. He built the vessel, placed his wagers, and descended. He won his wagers but never returned to the surface to claim them.

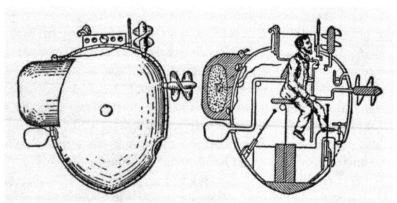

BUSHNELL'S SUBMARINE, THE "AMERICAN TURTLE"

During the Revolutionary War Dr. David Bushnell, a resident of Saybrook, Connecticut, devised a submarine vessel called the *American Turtle*. He aimed to destroy the British fleet anchored off New York during its occupation by General Washington and the Continental Army. Thatcher's *Military Journal* gives an account of an attempt to sink a British frigate, the *Eagle*, of sixty-four guns, by attaching a torpedo to the bottom of the ship by means of a screw manipulated from the interior of this submarine boat. A sergeant who operated the *Turtle* succeeded in getting under the British vessel, but the screw which was to hold the torpedo in place came in contact with an iron strap, refused to enter, and the implement of destruction floated down stream, where its clockwork mechanism finally caused it to explode, throwing a column of water high in the air and creating consternation among the shipping in the harbor. Skippers were so badly frightened that they slipped their cables and went down to Sandy Hook. General Washington complimented Doctor Bushnell on having so nearly accomplished the destruction of the frigate.

If the performance of Bushnell's *Turtle* was as successful as this, it seems strange that our new government did not immediately take up his ideas and make an appropriation for further experiments in the same line. When the attack was made on the *Eagle*, Doctor Bushnell's brother, who was to have manned the craft, was sick, and a sergeant who undertook the task was not sufficiently acquainted with the operation to succeed in attaching the torpedo to the bottom of the frigate. Had he succeeded, the *Eagle* would undoubtedly have been destroyed, and the event would have added the name of another hero to history and might have changed even the entire method of naval warfare. Bushnell's plans did not receive any encouragement, however, and were bitterly opposed by the naval authorities. His treatment was such as to compel him to leave the country, but, after some years of wandering, under an assumed name he settled in Georgia, where he spent his remaining days practising his profession.

Doctor Bushnell was also the inventor of the submarine mine, with which he blew up a schooner anchored off New London, Connecticut, and attempted to sink some British men-of-war in the Delaware River off Philadelphia by setting them adrift with the tide, expecting them to float down, strike against the sides of the ship, and then explode. Fortunately for the ships, none of them happened to strike, but the fact becoming known that torpedoes were being set adrift in the river caused great consternation among the British shipping people. When some wag set a lot of kegs adrift, which floated down the river, it caused tremendous excitement, the English crews firing at the kegs as they came floating down the river. This has been recorded in that humorous poem called "The Battle of the Kegs," by Francis Hopkinson, one of the signers of the Declaration of Independence.

Fulton's Attempt.—Robert Fulton, the man whose genius made steam navigation a success, was the next to turn his attention to submarine boats, and submarine warfare by submerged mines. A large part of his life was devoted to the solution of this problem. He went to France with his project and interested Napoleon Bonaparte, who became his patron and who was the means of securing sufficient funds for him to build a boat which was called the *Nautilus*. With this vessel Fulton made numerous descents, and it is reported that he covered fifty yards in a submerged run of seven minutes.

In the spring of 1801 he took the *Nautilus* to Brest, and experimented with her for some time. He and three companions descended in the harbor to a depth of twenty-five feet and remained one hour, but he found the hull would not stand the pressure of a greater depth. They were in total darkness during the whole time, but afterward he fitted his craft with a glass window, one and a half inches in diameter, through which he could see to count the minutes on his watch. He also discovered during his trials that the mariner's compass pointed equally as true under water as above it. His experiments led him to believe that he could build a submarine vessel with which he could swim under the surface and destroy any man-of-war afloat. When he came before the French Admiralty, however, he was met with blunt refusal, one bluff old French admiral saying, "Thank God, France still fights her battles on the surface, not beneath it!"—a sentiment which apparently has changed since those days, as France now has a large fleet of submarines.

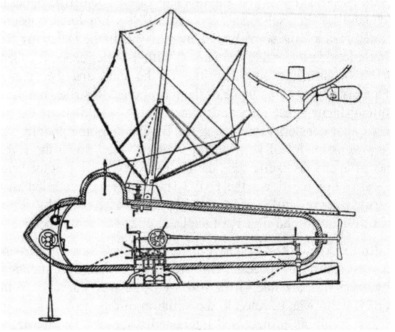

ROBERT FULTON'S SUBMARINE

After several years of unsuccessful efforts in France to get his plans adopted, Fulton finally went over to England and interested William Pitt, then Chancellor, in his schemes. He built a boat there and succeeded in attaching a torpedo beneath a condemned brig provided for the purpose, blowing her up in the presence of an immense throng. Pitt induced Fulton to sell his boat to the English Government and not bring it to the attention of any other nation, thus recognizing the fact that if this type of vessel should be made entirely successful, England would lose her supremacy as the "Mistress of the Seas," a prediction which seems now somewhat verified, judging from the work of the enemy submarines in the past few months.

Fulton consented to do so regarding other European countries, but would not pledge himself regarding his own country, stating that if his country should become engaged in war no pledge could be given that would prevent him from offering his services in any way which would be for its benefit.

The English Government paid him $75,000 for this concession. Fulton then returned to New York and built the *Clermont* and other steamboats, but did not entirely give up his ideas on submarine navigation, for at the time of his death he was at work on plans for a much larger boat.

Tuck, the inventor of the *Peacemaker*, had an unhappy lot. He spent a considerable portion of his wealth upon his experiments, and it is reported that his relatives, thinking he would spend all of his money in this way, and consequently leave nothing to them, had him adjudged insane and incarcerated. Some years ago I met a diver who had been employed by Tuck in his submarine boat experiments. This diver related to me an incident that nearly caused them to lose their lives. It appears that the boat had been first submerged in shallow water to find out if it was tight, which it was under a moderate pressure. They then took it out in the Hudson River, but on reaching a greater depth, water started to come in around the gasket of the hatch, the hatch not being constructed in a manner to increase its tightness as the pressure on the same increased. The water came in so fast that they could not rise. He said they tried to caulk the leak by stuffing their handkerchiefs in between the hatch covering and the combing, but they could not stop it. Finally one of the men became so hysterical that it was necessary for the diver to take up a hammer and tap him on the head with it and threaten to brain him unless he became quiet and did as he was told. The diver told me that he became satisfied that the only chance for their lives was to allow the boat to fill, then hold their breath as it was filling, until the external pressure on the hatch was equalized, and then open the hatch and swim to the surface. They followed this plan and escaped safely.

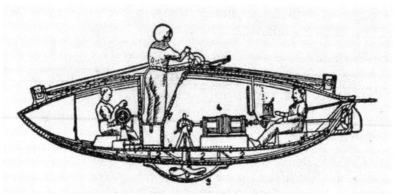

TUCK'S "PEACEMAKER"

Holland's Achievements.—While Mr. John P. Holland and I worked in adjoining rooms at the Columbian Iron Works, in Baltimore, in the years 1896 and 1897, at the time he was building the *Plunger* and I the *Argonaut*, and saw each other almost every day, we never became sufficiently intimate to exchange personal experiences. I am therefore indebted to his son, Mr. John P. Holland, Jr., for the loan of notes left by his father and compiled by himself regarding his father's early and later experiences. I quote from the notes:

On the southwest coast of Ireland, a few miles from the famous cliffs of Mohar, and overlooking the river Shannon, stands the village of Liscannor. Here was born on February 24, 1841, John P. Holland, later to become famous as the inventor of the Holland submarine. He was the second son of John and Mary Holland, who had long been residents of the place. His father was a coast guard, and from him little John heard the stories of the sea that inspired in him the love he had for it in later years. His elder brother, Alfred, was a strong, healthy boy of great intellect. When John was six years old he was sent to the Irish Christian Brothers school at Ennistymon, in the same county. He always credited the Irish Christian Brothers with giving him the early education that made him capable, later, of achieving results that scientists of to-day can hardly credit as being true.

In 1853 the family moved to Limerick, causing John to be transferred to the schools taught by the Christian Brothers at Sexton Street, that city. He was a very studious boy and made great progress in his studies. He loved to tell how he was in the habit of rising early in the morning and going into the fields, where he would climb a tree and there study his lessons for the day. The family had not resided long in Limerick when the father was taken from them very suddenly. He had been suffering from some slight ailment, and mentioned the fact to a friend. The friend advised that he take a home remedy, composed mostly of potash. He took the prescribed dose and died within a few hours.

On the death of his father John was compelled to give up school and seek employment in a tobacco shop. In 1858 he left the position and became a teacher in the Christian Brothers schools. In 1860 he showed signs of failing health; accordingly the Brothers transferred him to one of their schools in Waterford, in the hope that the climate there would prove more beneficial to his impaired health. However, after residing in that town for a time it was seen that the looked-for improvement did not materialize, and he grew worse instead of better. During the following twelve months he was assured by the best medical advice available that his health would not permit him to continue his studies, and that in order that it be restored he would do well to live in some place having a mild and dry climate, such as is found in the Madeira Islands. For several reasons this was impracticable, so he went to Cork to wait until he could find a suitable climate in which to live. While staying in Cork he lived at Ashburton, at the western end of Clanmire Hill, for about one year. While here he improved greatly in health and strength.

The War of the Rebellion in the United States had started a few months before he came to live in Cork. Toward the end of November, 1862, he read in the Cork *Examiner* an announcement of the first combat between armored ships that had occurred about two weeks previously; that is, the battle between the *Monitor* and *Merrimac* at Hampton Roads, Va., in which the little *Monitor* defeated the *Merrimac*, of twice her bulk and power, after a short contest. Just before the remarkable duel the *Merrimac*, ignoring the guns of her opponent, the wooden ship *Congress*, sank her by striking her with her massive iron stem. The *Cumberland*, another ship like the *Congress*, lying in the water near her, did not wait to be similarly rammed, but made haste to run aground on the nearest shallow place. But this did not save her, as the *Merrimac* attacked her and set her on fire with her heavy guns, while ignoring her fire, which did very little harm. This epoch-making contest in Virginian waters astonished naval authorities the world over, especially in England, whose main reliance for the maintenance of their power was placed in the "wooden walls," and in the bravery and skill of their seamen. The English nervousness was due to the demonstration at Hampton Roads that wooden ships could be no more of a hindrance to an armorclad than the *Cumberland* and *Congress* were to the *Merrimac*, and that if the Yankees built a few more monitors and sent them across the Atlantic quickly, they could come to London by water absolutely unhindered and destroy London and all the English navy within reach. All the English naval depots could, with practically no hindrance, be treated similarly within a few months, and an end made of English oppression from which it could never recover.

That this is no wild dreaming will be evident to everybody, when the action of the English Parliament regarding a proposal made there by a Lord of the Admiralty was considered and acted upon favorably in rapid order. A certain Lord Paget, who commanded an English ship at the bombardment of Sebastopol, proving that he was not without experience in justifying the assertion, told them that if all the five hundred and eighty English warships then in existence were sent into the Cork harbor; and if the little American *Monitor* were to get in there, too, at the same time; and also if a suitable chain boom were fixed so as to enclose the whole lot, that the same little *Monitor* could send them all to the bottom within a few hours without being compelled to fire a single shot. Lord Paget made these assertions in support of a motion he made before the House of Commons, proposing that the unspent part of an appropriation of about $75,000,000 designed to build forts to defend harbors in the South of England for the protection of their fleets against the French and Yankees should be immediately applied to the construction of armorclad ships. Without any delay a bill was passed making the required change in the appropriation bill. Very shortly after the Admiralty proposed the construction of four ironclads, which proposal was immediately adopted.

Four large battleships were taken and razed and covered with armor-plate. They were followed later by many much more powerful vessels designed especially to carry armor, *until at the present day the English Navy is competent to engage all the European navies together*. Mr. Holland, reflecting upon the result of the duel at Hampton Roads, foresaw this result clearly, because he knew that

England possessed the necessary materials, money, and mechanical skill required to provide ships enough to maintain her claim to her assumed title, "Mistress of the Seas," and to enable her to terrorize the greatest nations of Europe that had persistently shown lack of wisdom by their neglect to properly provide themselves with the only weapon that could resist her; that is, a sufficiently powerful navy.

They trusted, to their undoing, to great armies, forgetting that England had already proved her ability to cause combinations of her former enemies against any one of them.

But, having carefully noted the development of armored ships in the American, English, and French navies since the first duels of armorclads at Hampton Roads, Mr. Holland conceived the notion that it would be possible to build a vessel that would utilize water cover as a protection against an enemy's projectiles and thus be capable of ramming her enemy without exposing herself to attack. The study of the possibility of designing a practicable submarine boat to encounter English ironclads in this manner became the most interesting problem that he had to solve for a considerable time afterward. He further relates the physical difficulties that had to be overcome; bad health and hard work hindered consideration of the problem for a long time, until one day he happened to see in a newspaper an account of the experiments made with a submarine in New York harbor.[1] The description of its performances appeared to be incredible when he remembered the physical difficulties that had to be overcome, as his former study of the subject revealed them. Reflecting later that it was foolish and unfair to ridicule and laugh at a project which was described only by a short notice in the newspaper, and that described only its success in overcoming the physical difficulties in its operation, he started on a thorough study of the question in connection with a design roughly sketched on a sheet of paper; giving due attention to the essential points concerned in using a submarine boat so that it would be practical to live and work while completely submerged even in rough water; so as to propel it, first, at an even or any required depth; second, to be able to steer it with certainty in any required direction; third, to have an ample supply of compressed air on board, as well as the necessary apparatus to renew it when exhausted.

Fortunately he had sufficient engineering knowledge to determine the thickness and weight of a spindle-shaped steel shell competent to endure the external water pressure due to a submergence of two hundred and fifty feet depth, which was probably the greatest pressure it would ever be compelled to endure when in action. He was also competent to provide for a change of trim and for regulating the degree of submergence, as well as to provide for a slow or a rapid rise to the surface as circumstances might require. After completing his design, however, he found there was no one with confidence enough in the idea to give him backing. He was regarded as a second Jules Verne; in a word, a dreamer. He accordingly locked his plans in his trunk and for the time being forgot all about them.

A few years later his mother came to the United States and he decided to follow her. He landed in Boston in the winter of 1872, and in the middle of typical New England weather as found at that time of the year. Everything was covered with ice and snow, quite different from the mild winters he had known in the little "Green Isle." One morning after his arrival he was walking through one of the streets of the "Hub," and, not being possessed of the agility of a mountain goat —so necessary for a man to navigate one of our American streets during an icy spell—he had not gone far before he fell and broke his leg. Passersby helped him home, and he was assured by the physician who set the fracture that he would not be able to move about for at least two months. Finding himself with so much idle time on his hands, he decided to get out his forgotten plans and study them again. The result was that by the time his convalescence was over he had drawn a new and much superior design.

But it was not until 1876, when he was teaching school in Paterson, New Jersey, that he succeeded in securing financial backing for his first boat. A friend at that time raised the necessary capital, about $6000, and the building was done at the Albany Street Iron Works, corner of Albany and Washington Streets, New York, in 1876, in the shop owned by Messrs. Andrew and Ripley. To their courteous superintendent, Mr. Dickey, he was indebted for many suggestions toward rendering the boat practical and useful. Early in 1878 she was removed to Todd and Rafferty's shop in Paterson, New Jersey; he, being a resident of that city at that time, could complete her outfit more easily there. Toward the end of July, 1878, she was taken to a point where she could be more easily launched, about one hundred yards above the Falls Bridge, on the right bank of the river. She was taken there late one fine afternoon and launched from the wagon on which she was moved. Mr. William Dunkerly, the engineer in charge of the operation, fastened a strong line on her bow to bring her to when she was afloat; but she did not float long, for the wagon wheels sank in the made ground where they launched her, the greater part of the wagon being submerged, as well as nearly one-half of the volume of the boat, leaving the boat with the stern considerably elevated. After hard work on the part of Messrs. Dunkerly and John Lister, the owners of a boathouse above the bridge she was pulled off the wagon and floated for a few minutes, amid the cheers of mill operatives who lined the banks and covered every available spot on the bridge. But the cheering suddenly ceased when the boat backed a little out in the river, for she settled deeper in the water and finally sank, to the great disappointment of the crowd, who expressed their feelings in loud yells until Messrs. Dunkerly and Lister moved the wagon out of the way, took hold of the boat's painter, and pulled her out of the water high and dry on the spot previously occupied by the wagon. It is no exaggeration to say that the natives were much astounded to see a little iron boat weighing four tons pulled by two men from the bottom of the Passaic and left standing high and dry on the bank.

The next day the accidental submergence was explained by the absence of two five-eighths inch screw plugs from the bottom of the central compartment in which the operator would be seated while the boat was in operation. By opening a stop valve while the boat was in operation under water a sufficient quantity of water would enter, surround the operator in his diving suit, and render the boat and its contents heavier than water, so that it would sink as it did after having been launched with the plug holes open. The reason that it did not sink, and that it was so easy a matter to pull it ashore, was because the total weight on board on that occasion was much more than it was designed to carry. The central space then carried water equal to the weight of the diver and his suit of armor, as well as the additional quantity that would fill the space around him, as well as that which would be due to the distention of the suit by air pressure while it was in action during diving. The actual practicability of being able to handle the boat under these conditions was the first important point proved by experiment on the day following the launch.

"We proved conclusively, a few weeks after, that our estimate of the quantity of fresh compressed air required to support life comfortably in the operator was probably a little excessive. The quantity of compressed air, as well as the pressure required to force all water out of the boat and to cause her to float light on the surface, was ample. A few days after the launch, the engine having been given a slight test, the boat was towed up the river to a point opposite the old Pennington house. In the launch that towed her were Mr. Dunkerly, Captain John Lister, and three men prominent in the 'Fenian' movement."

What happened when the boat reached the point for the test is best told by Mr. Dunkerly: "We fastened ropes to the bow and stern," Mr. Dunkerly said; "Mr. Holland climbed into the submarine, closed the hatch, and started the engine. The bow went down first, and before we realized the fact the boat was under twelve feet of water. The ropes were a safeguard in case the compressed air should not prove sufficient to expel the water from the ballast tanks. Holland was also given a hammer with which to rap upon the shell of the boat should he find himself in difficulties. After being submerged one hour, Holland brought the boat to the surface, to the great relief of all who were witnessing the test. As soon as the boat came up the turret opened and Holland bobbed up smiling. He repeated his dive several times, and then he invited us to try it, but we preferred to 'stick to the ropes.' About the third trip we made up the river a stranger was seen hiding behind the rocks on the river road. He had a powerful field glass, and it was said that he was an agent of the British Government. His presence caused a commotion for a time." From here we will continue in Mr. Holland, Senior's, own words:

"Continuous submergence trials for various periods were next undertaken. We had one serious setback that caused no greater trouble than shortening our experiments by compelling us to omit all running trials and to confine ourselves to testing matters of essential importance. This was due to the failure of the misnamed Braton engine that was installed in the boat. The builders assured me that it was a Braton engine, but they had improved on Braton's designs by employing two double-acting cylinders, having both ends of each supplied with charges from one central combustion chamber. On trial in the boat this engine failed to develop any noticeable power, so we were compelled to employ Mr. Dunkerly's launch, supplying her engines with steam, which was conducted from the boiler of his launch by way of a hose to the engine of the submarine, which was now employed as a steam engine. This entailed a considerable loss of steam, due to condensation, but it produced enough power to propel the submarine, having Mr. Dunkerly's launch alongside so as to allow free vertical movement, as when diving, so that we could test the efficiency of the boat's horizontal and vertical rudders. The vertical rudders, those that controlled horizontal motion, proved to be very effective, but the horizontal rudders, placed on the level of the centre of buoyancy, proved to be useless. We proved that the boat should move three or four times more rapidly before they could produce a useful effect. This experiment showed the folly of attempting to control the degree of submergence of the boat by the employment of central horizontal rudders, a method on which so much importance was placed by some of my predecessors and successors, in attempts at submarining, and, strange to say, some of them still believe in it, very evidently because they have never tested them. A good many submarine and other inventors are satisfied with designs on paper and do not bother to make experiments. We determined some other very evident matters that it was necessary to prove by actual experiment; that is, that it is not practical to cause a boat to lie still at any given depth without the employment of complicated machinery that should have no place in a submarine boat. Several other important points regarding the design, construction, and management of submarines, which still cause difference of opinion and design, were determined fairly well. For instance, the modern craze for 'good, big boats,' as well as for large, high conning towers, was proved to be absurd. Even though our views on these and other matters were exhibited to the Navy Department Ordnance Bureau, practically no notice was taken of them. I disliked the idea common among politicians that my failures to get a government contract was owing to political influence or 'pull,' but, judging by my short experience in Washington, I concluded that there was another, and much more serious, hindrance to the adoption of my ideas.

"The history of the efforts I made to induce the government to consider the claims of the first submarine boat proposed to them by me in 1875, as well as the results, reflects no credit on the officials that had anything to do with it, as can be clearly seen from what follows.

"The first proposition was made in 1875, through a friend of the late Secretary of the Navy Robeson, for his consideration. It was referred by him for a report to the late Admiral Sampson, at that time commander of the torpedo station at Newport, Rhode Island. The Admiral reported in good time that the project was practically impossible, owing mainly to the difficulty of finding in what direction to steer the boat under water, and the attempt to do so would be an aggravated case of trying to find one's way in a fog. Very evidently he had no notion of the possibility of steering by compass under water. The same incredulity was expressed by a distinguished Swedish officer whom I afterward met in New York.

"After having determined the correctness of my ideas regarding submarines, and adding a few points revealed by the experiments made on the Passaic River, my financial supporters, the trustees of the Fenian Skirmishing Fund, determined to build a larger boat that could be employed for breaking blockades.[2] Toward the end of May I started to design a new boat of about nineteen tons displacement; in other words, one small and light enough to be carried on ship's deck and launched overboard whenever her services would be required. Only three men were required for her crew.

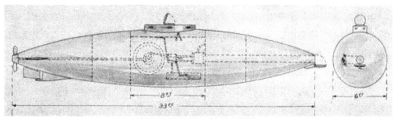

THE "FENIAN RAM"

The first Holland power-propelled submarine boat (built 1881). Sketch made by the author after measuring the boat at New Haven, Connecticut, in 1915.

"She was built at the shops of the Delamater Iron Works, at the foot of West Thirteenth Street, New York, and launched in May, 1881. During her construction my curiosity was excited by the apparent incredulity of some of the engineers in the shop regarding the practicability of such a boat. Many objections were urged against her, especially by men who should have known better, but the trouble with them was almost the same as I encountered later among the staff officers of the navy, viz., because they were, almost without exception, of English, Welsh, or Scotch descent, experienced in all kinds of shipbuilding. They appeared to know by intuition that the project was absurd. They proposed many difficulties that were not solved for them. I also noticed that many of the men appeared to take a deep interest in the progress of the work, even though they never made any inquiries to my knowledge, yet they observed everything, because there was no way of preventing them. I also noticed what appeared to be consequences of this curiosity of foreigners regarding an American machine.

"During the following twelve months many visitors came to look over the submarine, mostly Swedes, Russians, Italians, and Germans. I was much pleased to meet two of them who apparently had no idea of the jealousy with which some people guard their military secrets, viz., Ali Ritza and Hassan Effendi. But, very clearly to me, they had no idea of the importance of what was expected from the machine, or, much more likely, they had been persuaded by their acquaintances of English connections that the project would never amount to anything because it did not originate in England. The fact that English opinion in naval matters governed the opinion of every American was made quite clear to me later on.

"This nineteen-ton boat was launched in 1881. She was thirty-one feet long, six feet beam, seven feet four inches in depth, and was propelled by a Brayton petroleum engine. Her crew consisted of three men—the pilot, engineer, and gunner. She laid at the Morris & Cummings Dredging Company's dock in Jersey City until July 3, 1883, during which time many interesting experiments were made with her.

"The first run on the surface and while submerged was made in the basin, or passage, east of the Lehigh Valley Railroad. The first tests made were the surface runs to test the engine, clutch, gearing, etc. These proved very successful, and the next in order was to submerge the boat at the dock and determine whether the seams were all right, and also to test the efficiency of the compressed-air tanks for supplying oxygen for breathing and giving impulses for expelling water from the ballast tanks.

"Accordingly Richards, the engineer, and myself entered the boat and closed the hatch. This shut us off from the air, and our breathing now depended entirely on the compressed-air reserve. After waiting a few moments and finding no ill effects from the compressed air, I decided to submerge. I drew back the little iron levers on either side of my head (these operated the Kingston valves in the bottom, through which water was admitted to the ballast tanks). Almost immediately the boat began to settle, giving us the suggestion of slowly descending in an elevator. I now looked through the ports in the superstructure and observed that the bow had entirely disappeared and the water was within a few inches of the glass. A second or two later everything grew dark and we were entirely submerged, and nothing could be seen through the ports excepting a dark-green blur.

"Our next suggestion was a slight jar when the vessel struck the bottom. It might also be mentioned here that we had no light except the glow that came through the conning tower. This just about sufficed to read the gauges, but was too poor to be of much interest to the engineer. The engine was not needed at that time, however, but we decided to carry a small lantern, to be used when any adjustment was necessary, but not otherwise, as it consumed too much of our precious oxygen.

"Richards having made an examination and found everything tight, I decided to blow out the ballast and come up. Accordingly I opened the valve admitting air to the ballast tank, and at once heard a hiss that told me that the air was driving out the water. The green blur on the ports in the conning tower grew lighter as I gazed through them until suddenly the light of full day burst through, almost dazzling me. After blinking my eyes a few times I looked out again and saw the familiar surroundings of the 'Gap.' I now opened the hatch and stood on the seat, thus causing my head and shoulders to protrude from the tower. As soon as I was observed doing this a cheer burst from the crowd of observers on the dock, among whom opinion was equally divided as to whether we would ever emerge alive from our dive or not. We had now demonstrated the fact that our boat was tight, that our air was sufficient for breathing, and that our ballasting system was perfect.

"Our next test was to prove that we could dive with our engine running. Many were the gloomy prophecies advanced as to what would happen when we attempted to force our exhaust outboard against the water pressure found at eight or ten feet depth. For this occasion Richards and I entered the boat, I taking my place in the conning tower, while he went forward to start the engine. After a little kicking and sputtering he succeeded in getting it started. We then let in the clutch and the boat started forward. When we reached the far side of the basin I turned her around and threw out the clutch, causing the boat to slow down and stop. Closing the hatch, we then made sure that everything was tight, and opened the Kingston valves. When the water reached the observer's ports in the conning tower, I closed them again. We then proceeded along awash; that is, with only the little tower showing above the surface. I found that from this position I could observe objects quite a distance ahead, and my vision was obscured only occasionally when a wave washed against the glass. I next threw forward the lever on the right side of my seat (this was connected with the diving, or vertical, rudder by a lever action). Immediately the nose of the boat went down, and before I realized it our gauge showed a depth of about ten feet. I now drew the lever back to centre, and the boat straightened out on an even keel. There was very little or no tendency to buck or be cranky; in a word, I had no difficulty in preventing her nose from rising or dipping down.

"After running about one hundred yards submerged I steered the boat up, and in a few seconds the superstructure of the boat was again above water. I then opened the air valve and expelled my ballast, causing the boat to rise and assume her normal position. This dive was practised for some time in order that we might gain facility in handling the diving and steering gear.

"Captain John Ericsson was at that time preparing to build his *Destroyer* in the same part of the shop in which my boat had been built. Somebody in Delamater's described my boat to Captain Ericsson and explained the purpose of a nine-inch tube placed in the axis and having a breech and bow cap. The object of this fitting was to permit the insertion of a six-foot torpedo that could be shot out at a target while the boat was under water by air at a heavy pressure contained in steel flasks connected with the breech of the gun by a balanced valve. After the torpedo was ejected the breech and muzzle were closed, and the water contents of the tube were permitted to flow into two tanks to correct the position of the centre of gravity.

"Not having any torpedo models ready for experiment when the boat reached Jersey City, Captain Ericsson very kindly sent me word that I might build a few like those he proposed to use in his *Destroyer*. I therefore deferred building any on my own ideas, and decided to use his, should they prove suitable. The Delamaters built me two on his models and sent them to Jersey City for trial. For the trials of Ericsson's torpedo models the boat was set awash in the water, with the axis of the torpedo placed horizontally and about three and one-half feet below the water surface. Because there was a new floating dock lying in the water about one hundred and fifty yards from the submarine, and in a direct line with it, the firing pressure was reduced to about three hundred pounds on the square inch. When the firing valve was opened the projectile passed out and travelled about six or eight feet beyond the muzzle of the gun, then it turned upward and arose in the air to perhaps sixty or seventy feet; then it fell point foremost in the water and buried itself so deeply in the mud that we could never find it again. For the second shot the boat was depressed a few degrees and was swung to port so as to avoid butting the floating dry dock. It travelled about twice as far as its predecessor, then rose fifteen feet in the air and passed over the wall limiting the basin, striking a pile that projected above it, and frightening a fisherman who was dozing thereon. He was in no danger, however, as the pile and string-piece of heavy pine afforded him ample protection.

"While the boat lay at Gorky's repair shop at the point called the 'Gap,' a test was made of the efficiency of the apparatus provided for using the boat as a diving-bell, viz., a watertight hatch placed over a hatchway on the bottom, with valves leading from air-chambers, through which air under pressure was permitted to flow and fill the space occupied by the operators.

"When employing the boat as a diving-bell everything was closed tight and air was admitted to the central space until the external water pressure was exactly balanced, and when the lower hatch might be opened without any risk of water entering. The first man to make a test was Mr. George M. Richards, of Erie, Pennsylvania, my engineer. He sank the boat at high water while she lay at the dock. When she rested on the bottom he opened the test valves to make certain that the external water pressure was balanced by the internal air pressure, admitting an excess of water equal to his weight to hold her on the bottom. This operation did not consume more than a minute. He did not actually go out of the boat, but only dropped his feet on the bottom, passed his hands under the boat, one on either side, and lifted the boat slowly and with little exertion about one foot from the bottom. Had I provided the boat with a diver's outfit he could have gone out and come back again without trouble or risk. On July 3, 1883, we left the 'Gap' in Jersey City in order to do some diving in the deep water of the Narrows.

"The boat went out under its own power, unaccompanied by anybody save a small colored boy who had managed to drop on the turret when we were leaving the dock. The first intimation I had that we were carrying a passenger was shortly after we had passed Robbins's Reef Lighthouse. Then I found my view of Staten Island and Bay Ridge became obscured by what seemed to be a pair of brown rags hanging on either side of the turret and blocking the vision through the side lights. When we passed Robbins's Reef the water became a little rougher, so that the water passed up on the hull and washed over the turret. After the windows had been wet a few times I heard noises that plainly indicated that we were carrying an uninvited and unwelcome passenger. Fearing that the waves would wash him off, I headed the boat upstream, opened the hatch, and invited him to come inside, as I feared running through rough water with him on top. He politely refused my invitation, assuring me that he was 'puffectly safe' where he was, and that he would 'hold on like grim death.' This unfortunate circumstance spoiled my chances of diving in deep water that day, so we were compelled to abandon it. This interruption by the young colored gentleman wasted so much time that it was after sunset when we headed for the Bay Ridge shore, with which I was unfamiliar, to look for a landing place. Seeing through the twilight unmistakable signs that the shore was rocky, I ran the boat out about one hundred yards and then headed her up toward the Bay Ridge Ferry landing, with the intention of leaving her there until daylight the next morning. Before starting north we noticed two boys in a rowboat approaching us from the shore. We stopped until they came alongside and inquired: 'What is this thing?' They came on board and inspected her at our invitation, and expressed great astonishment at the strange boat they had picked up. But what was much more to the purpose was that when they found we had no particular landing place in view they very kindly offered us the hospitality of Mr. Vanderbilt Bergen's dock at Bay Ridge for as long as we wished to stay there for experiments.

Then they took our 'painter' and towed us into his dock on the site of the present Crescent Yacht Club station. The two young gentlemen, Tunis Bergen and his cousin Harry Midgley, also contracted to take care of our material and help us out during our stay at their dock. What was of great importance to us was that we learned from Mr. Vanderbilt Bergen, Tunis's brother, that the place we had happened upon was by far the most suitable of any within miles for diving and experiments. We left the boat there over two months, making experiments to determine the value of our devices and to improve them wherever possible.

"Every time we went out we took two or more dives of various lengths, most of these quite across the Narrows, a little below Stapleton. During these dives I always made certain that there was no ship of twenty-five or thirty feet draught passing. Ordinarily we ran at a depth of not less than twenty feet, so that we could afford to ignore excursion steamers, fishing boats, and small yachts. The paddles of excursion steamers we could hear a long distance away, so that we never had any difficulty in avoiding them by changing our course or running at a greater depth until they had passed. We had a rather exciting experience on one occasion when we started to run submerged from Stapleton to Bay Ridge. At starting there was no large vessel in sight, but when about two hundred and fifty yards from shore I distinctly heard the paddle of a steamer. I instantly changed the vessel's course from directly across the Narrows, heading her upstream and running to twenty feet depth so as to eliminate any danger of a collision. Running along I listened for the sound of paddles, but could hear nothing, so I concluded that the steamer must have passed beyond the range of hearing or else had changed her course. Therefore I thought it would be safe to come within fifteen feet of the surface and listen again. I did so, and, hearing no sound, brought the turret above the surface to look around, but I could see no steamer. I then resumed my course back to Bay Ridge. On approaching Mr. Bergen's dock I saw three or four men jumping around and acting as if demented, so on landing I asked Bergen the cause of their hilarity. 'Oh,' he said, 'you frightened the d—— out of the *St. Johns*, the Long Branch steamer. You remember having come near the surface shortly after you started across and then diving? We didn't see you again until you rose three hundred yards out at this side.' I said that I remembered it. 'Well, when you went down that time your propeller shot a great mass of water out backward, just as big as, or bigger than, any whale could blow. The *St. Johns* was about two hundred yards astern of you, and she stopped instantly, not being able to tell what the trouble was ahead of her. After a while she started up and headed into the Staten Island shore, keeping on until I thought she would run ashore. She ported her helm and kept close along shore until she passed the Quarantine anchorage, then she headed straight for New York.'

"Experimental runs were made almost every day during the months of July and August, and continued until September, when we returned to the 'Gap' in Jersey City. During our experiments we were never without a considerable crowd of witnesses, sometimes numbering hundreds, especially in our runs from the 'Gap' up the Hudson and return. One morning in July a very patronizing gentleman, who announced himself as a reporter from the *New York Sun*, requested permission to go into the boat and examine it, but, much to his surprise, I was compelled to refuse him permission. The next morning there appeared in his paper a long report describing the performances of the *Fenian Ram*, a new name to which I had no objection excepting its incorrectness. Because public curiosity was aroused, the same Mr. Blakely Hall seldom missed reporting every run or experiment we made while at Bay Ridge. He explained to me that I was foolish in not wishing to advertise my invention, because the Government would certainly wish to acquire boats of the same type, as he could see by the newspaper reports that they were already preparing to build them in France.

"Shortly after our return to the 'Gap,' an amusing incident took place which is well worth recording. A number of friends and myself decided to take a trip up the Hudson. There were eight or ten in the party, and, as the submarine could accommodate only four, a small sloop was hired to carry the overflow. When we got under way, the submarine towing the sloop, we found the going rather hard, owing to cakes of ice floating down the river. When we were off Hoboken I slowed down to allow a steamer to cross our bow. This, of course, slackened the towline, with the result that when I got under way again said line fouled the propeller, held for a second, and then broke, sending the sloop adrift among the cakes of ice. The crew of the derelict bark shouted to attract my attention, but I had the hatch closed and could not hear them. I proceeded about a mile upstream from the point of the accident before I discovered that my tow was missing. I turned back and found my unfortunate mariners had been picked up by a passing boat and towed back to Jersey City.

"In November, 1883, while returning from a run through the Narrows, we dove to a depth of sixty feet, remained on the bottom for an hour, and came to the surface with no more trouble or inconvenience than if we dove only eight or ten feet. Shortly after this the *Ram's* career ended in a rather odd way. I have no intention of advancing any excuses for the incident, as no official explanation was ever made to me concerning it. As a result, I never bothered again with my backers nor they with me, but before recording the more solemn incident I would like to mention a rather amusing one that has just come to mind.

"One morning, on going down to board the boat, I was surprised to find no boat there. I was puzzled for a minute, but, on inquiry of the bystanders, I found that my engineer, Richards, had decided to take the boat out for a run by himself. He had proceeded down stream, but that was about all the witnesses could tell me. I therefore walked along the wharves until I came to a crowd of men standing on a pier and pointing out into the river. My attention was called to a point on the surface about two hundred yards off the pier head. There a great deal of air was coming to the surface in countless little bubbles. The man told me that the *Irish Ram* had just gone down there, owing to the fact that the conning tower was open when it passed close to a barge and tug. The wash from the tug passed over the little boat, flooded the hatch, and came near catching Richards below. He happened to be just below the hatch, however, and was blown out by the escaping air when the boat went down. He floundered around in the water for a few minutes and was finally picked up by the crew of the tug. A few minutes later Richards appeared, still a bit pale from his rather startling experience. It cost my backers about $3000 to raise the boat and put her in shape again.

"The final history of the boat is told in a few words. She was taken one night from her slip in the 'Gap' and towed to New Haven, Connecticut. During the trip she was in charge of Breslin, one of the trustees of the fund. I received no notice of the contemplated move then, nor was I notified after. I am told that when they arrived in New

Haven they attempted to make dives, but handled the boat so awkwardly that the harbor master decided that she constituted a 'menace to navigation' and demanded a bond if any further trials were to be made. As a result she was hauled out of the water on the property of Reynolds, another member of the committee, and there she still is. There is also a rumor that they have tried to sell her to the Russian Government, but failed, as on investigation the prospective buyers found that title to her was not clear.

"After the *Ram* was taken from me, I had no means of experimenting further or building another boat. After a time I secured a position with the Pneumatic Gun Company as a draughtsman. While employed there I managed to interest some members of the company and some friends of theirs in a design that I had drawn immediately after the loss of the *Ram*. I allowed these men to examine my plans, and they, approving of them, set about to organize a company, known as the Nautilus Submarine Boat Company.

"During the organizing of the company I became acquainted with Captain Zalinski, U. S. A., an expert on heavy artillery. Through Captain Zalinski I met many influential men, who not only helped me with the project in hand at the time, but were largely instrumental in having my boat adopted by the United States Navy.

"At the suggestion of Captain Zalinski the boat was built at Fort Hamilton, as he was stationed there at the time, and, being on the army active list, could not be away from his post of duty. During the time of her construction everything was under his supervision. The boat was fifty feet long, six feet beam, and the hull was constructed of wood. In 1886 the boat was launched. The launching ways ran down from the fort wall to the water's edge. This part of the program was in the hands of a young engineer who had either an insufficient knowledge of the subject or lacked the ability to put his knowledge to practical use. The result was, that when the heavy boat started down the launching ways they suddenly collapsed and she crashed into some piling near the water's edge, tearing out the greater part of her side and bottom.

"On investigation it was found that the cost of repairs would exceed the amount of money still on hand in the company's treasury. Accordingly the wrecked boat was broken up where she lay, the engine and fittings removed and sold, and the proceeds used to partly reimburse the stockholders for the money they had invested. This accident discouraged my company from any further attempts at submarine construction. Had this boat been successful, submarines would have become an accepted success years before they did. This unfortunate incident held me back at least ten years, as it was that long before I was able to secure backing to construct another boat.

"About this time the United States Navy Department was mildly interested in the performances of submarines in France, where they had attained some slight degree of success. The designs for these boats, I am sure, were based on certain fundamental points of my *Fenian Ram* design. As I have said previously, there were a number of foreign officers present at Delamater's Yard from 1879 to 1881, while the boat was in course of construction, and it is hardly to be expected that they failed to take notes. However, the knowledge they secured did them very little good, because, while they secured a lot of valuable data, their inexperience caused them to disregard the most vital points, with the result that their boats never attained any degree of success. However, I do not wish to convey the impression that the United States Navy Department was at this time considering building submarines as the results of the French experiments; far from it. Had it not been informed of the success of my *Fenian Ram*, which was far more interesting and wonderful than anything the French had done, and still remained unconvinced? I was totally sick and disgusted with its actions, and was seriously tempted to abandon all further attempts to convince and awake it from its lethargy. About this time I wrote an article, "Can New York be Bombarded?" with the intention of bringing before the public the pitiable condition of our fleet and coast defences, and showing how a few submarines would place us in a position to ward off an enemy's attack from mostly any point on our coast as effectively as if we had an adequate shore defence and a fleet equal to Great Britain's."

The article referred to treats of other types of ships. This is not of interest now, but we quote what he says concerning

"THE SUBMARINE, OR DIVING BOAT

"This boat has a speed of eight miles per hour; she can remain under water for two days, or longer, without having any connection with the surface. She can be steered by compass when under water, and her course may be laid and corrected without obliging her to remain more than a few moments on the surface. This can be done without ever appearing over water. She can move at any required depth, and is more thoroughly under control when completely submerged than when on the surface. Her horizontal and vertical motions are controlled automatically or by the pilot.

"The torpedo, carrying a one-hundred-pound charge, can be projected in a straight line to a distance of eighty or ninety feet, according to the power employed in expelling it. The method of attack will probably be as follows: The diving boat, with only her turret above water, moves toward the ship. When she gets so close that her presence may be discovered, say half a mile, she descends a few feet under the surface. Once or twice, after the bearing of the ship is observed by means of a telescope projected for a few minutes over the water, corrections are made in the course for deviations owing to currents.

"When near the vessel she goes deeper, so as to bring her stem ten or fifteen feet beneath the surface. Netting can thus be avoided. She can now discharge her torpedo, to explode on contact. As soon as this strikes, the explosion occurs and a large hole is torn in the ship's side. The ship will now become unmanageable, and with assistance may be captured. Experience has shown that in a seaway she rolls or pitches very little, apparently following the wave slope in large waves. In short, sharp ones, she seems to rise and fall bodily with very little tendency to pitching.

"A notion seems to prevail that the proper duty of a diving boat would be to carry a diver, who could come out and fasten a torpedo to a ship at anchor, then retire into his boat and move away; also, that it would be useful in placing and removing stationary mines. It is very evident that if a diving boat can attain a speed of ten or twelve miles per hour, fire torpedoes at ships moving at full speed, and keep to sea for days together, her sphere of usefulness would be greatly extended. In fact, there is no insuperable objection to the employment of such vessels for coast defence and operations against ships. Submarine mines are not so effective against them as vessels on the surface, because they can pass them unobserved. They can enter a harbor that may be thoroughly defended, should it be necessary to destroy vessels inside the defences. If those on the fleet become aware of their presence it is more than probable, judging from the action of the French fleet in 1877-78, that the moral effect of the discovery will be that they will feel convinced of the foolishness of awaiting an attack when the time so employed may be more wisely expended in moving to a safe distance, and in getting there at full speed. Thus, in 1886, did I try to show by comparison the superiority of the submarine over the torpedo boats and gunboats, the two arms of defence on which the Navy placed all its confidence at the time."

From the above words concerning John P. Holland's various efforts to secure recognition of his inventions, and his years of strenuous endeavor to devise a weapon capable of providing a means of defence, there is no question but that it is due to his initiative, perseverance, and success that the diving type of boat was ever brought to be manageable and adopted by the United States and England.

Mr. Holland's health broke down in his later years, said to have been caused by the treatment which he received from some of his associates.

The testimony which Mr. Holland leaves among his notes, and the opinion given me by his son, would indicate that his name and services were used to enable others to make large financial gains, and that he himself received little, if any, benefit from his life's work. His son is authority for the statement to me that such competence as he was able to leave for his family was derived from his other business outside of that of his submarine work, and that his connection with submarine matters undoubtedly affected his mind and health in later years and probably shortened his life.

An appeal found among his papers, addressed to the chairman of the Committee on Naval Affairs of the House of Representatives under date of February 8, 1906, would appear to bear out this statement. I quote:

"APPEAL OF JOHN P. HOLLAND, INVENTOR OF SUBMARINE
BOATS, TO THE COMMITTEE ON NAVAL AFFAIRS OF THE
HOUSE OF REPRESENTATIVES, NOT TO LEGISLATE IN
THE INTEREST OF THE ELECTRIC BOAT COMPANY'S

38 Newton Street,

NEWARK, NEW JERSEY,

February 8, 1906,

HON. C. E. FOSS,
Chairman Committee on Naval Affairs,
House of Representatives.

DEAR SIR:

I am the inventor of the Holland submarine boat, now in use in the United States Navy and in Europe. My old patents, to the number of about twenty, are owned by the Electric Boat Company. On June 16, 1900, I entered into a contract with that company to serve as their engineer for five years, dating back to April 1, 1899, and expiring April 1, 1904. Since the expiration of my contract with the Electric Boat Company I have devoted myself to remedying the defects in my old inventions, and perfecting designs by which the low speed of the present Holland boats can be increased three or four times. Having perfected these inventions until I was sure I could obtain about 25 knots per hour submerged, and after making numerous other alterations, greatly improving the efficiency over my submarine boats now in use in the Navy, I procured the organization of a company, "John P. Holland's Submarine Boat Company," May 18, 1905, with sufficient capital to build a boat under my new plans and inventions, and was about to start to work, when the Electric Boat Company filed a suit against me in the Court of Chancery of New Jersey, applying for an injunction, and claiming substantially that I had agreed to assign to them all my inventions and patents during the term of my natural life. Two other suits have been started, one against my new company in the United States Circuit Court to enjoin the use of the name "Holland"; the other against me personally, alleging a verbal contract never to compete with the Electric Boat Company, was commenced in the New Jersey Court of Chancery. My contract with the Electric Boat Company to act as their engineer, and to give them my patents and inventions, was for the five years during which I acted as engineer, and no longer, and expired April 1, 1904, as stated above.

These suits have had the effect of frightening off the capital that I had enlisted, and I have not as yet been able to get the capital to build my new boat, by reason of these suits. The only object of these suits was to prevent me from building a boat and going into competition before the Navy Department with the submarine boats now being built by the Electric Boat Company under my old patents.

The Electric Boat Company makes the allegation in their last bill of complaint that by threatening to discharge me from their employ and break their contract with me and stop my salary, that I agreed to a contract which prevents me from using my brains and inventive talent in building submarine boats for the balance of my life. This allegation is absolutely false, even though under affidavit by Mr. Rice, and would be, if true, most inequitable on account of duress and on account of want of consideration. This alleged agreement was not reduced to writing; the only evidence the Court has is the sworn statement of Mr. Rice; and when the fact is considered that Mr. Rice, formerly a professor of law at Columbia University, and having the assistance of Mr. Frost, also a lawyer, failed to have such an important agreement reduced to writing and signed by me, the whole proposition appears ridiculous and silly. The further fact that this bill of complaint containing these allegations, has been printed and distributed at the Capitol would seem to indicate that the principal object of this suit is to frighten away the capital I had enlisted, and prevent the consideration of my new patents and claims by your honorable committee.

My attention has been called to the bill (H.R. 10070), entitled "A Bill to Increase the Efficiency of the Navy." It must be apparent to every member of your committee that this bill is drawn solely in the interest of the Electric Boat Company monopoly. The clause in it that "The Secretary of the Navy shall purchase or contract for said submarine boats within four months of the completion of the contract trials of the submarine boats now building for the Navy" is against all public interest, and is something extremely unusual. If the Electric Boat Company should not complete its contract for a year or two years or never, the whole business of the Navy Department in this line would be held up. The bill excludes me, the inventor of the Holland boats and who constructed and built the original *Holland*, which is now in the service of the Navy, from submitting my plans and models to the Navy Department for consideration, for it would be useless to do so if the Secretary is deprived, by the proposed law suggested by the Electric Boat Company, from adopting them, though considering them superior in efficiency and economy to the plans upon which the present boats are being built.

I have recently had my models tested in the government tanks at the Navy Yard in Washington by the United States officers in charge, and their official reports will show that I can get a guaranteed speed of 22 knots per hour submerged, and the same speed on the surface, and this speed can be obtained in vessels of the same or greater tonnage as those now being built by the Electric Boat Company.

I hardly think, Mr. Chairman, that your committee, in making an appropriation for submarine boats, will exclude the Navy Department from any consideration of the plans made by me when I say to you that these plans have the approval of some of the most expert officers in the Navy on the question of submarine boats, and that the boats can be built at one-third less than is now being paid the Electric Boat Company for boats of two-thirds less submerged and more than fifty per cent. less surface speed.

If I am prevented by the suits filed against me by the Electric Boat Company from obtaining capital with which to build my boats, which will have three times the submerged speed of the present boats, and a vast improvement in other directions, then I want the law so framed that I can present a proposition to the Secretary of the Navy to cause my plans and new inventions to be thoroughly examined by a board of experts, and if favorably reported on, that the government may build the same in its yards under my supervision, and pay me a reasonable royalty. That is all I ask your committee to do, and to not frame a law that will exclude me, the inventor of the present submarine boats, from having my improvements considered by the Secretary of the Navy, and pass one in the interest of the Electric Boat Company under its monopoly now of the business of the department under my old and obsolete patents.

The title of the bill (H.R. 10070) should be: "A Bill to Prevent the Increase of the Efficiency of the Navy, and Prevent Economy Being Considered."

If your committee is desirous of increasing the efficiency of submarine boats for the Navy, and at the same time reduce the cost to the government at least one-third, if not one-half, of the prices now being paid for submarine boats, a clause in the Naval Appropriation Bill on the following lines would effect the object:

"The sum of _____ Dollars is hereby appropriated for submarine boats, and the Secretary of the Navy is hereby authorized to contract for or purchase or build in a navy yard of the United States these submarine boats, whichever in his judgment will increase the efficiency of the Navy and will be in the interest of economy to the department."

I consider my old patents assigned to the Electric Boat Company as obsolete; they are ten years behind the age.

I can build in the Navy Yard at Brooklyn boats under my new patents, designs, and inventions, in six months, and guarantee a submerged speed of 22 knots per hour.

Admiral Bowles testified before the Senate Committee on Naval Affairs at its hearing on submarine boats. He was at that time chief of the Bureau of Construction and Repair of the Navy Department, and his statement at that time is entitled to the serious consideration of your committee, because it was that of a government expert, and is true in every respect. This hearing before the Senate committee is printed and the hearing took place on May 29, 1902. Admiral Bowles's testimony can be found in Senate Document 395, 1st Session, 57th Congress, page 82. He said that the Holland boats ought not to cost more than $89,489, and in this sum he said he had allowed an ample profit, and in addition had included $11,000 for experiments and tests. Admiral Bowles is now president of the Fore River Shipbuilding Company, and is building the submarine boats that the Navy contracted for last year, and they are now being built under my old plans and patents, so alleged.

If your committee will call upon the present Chief of the Bureau of Construction and Repairs, he will undoubtedly inform you that he can build in the Brooklyn Navy Yard my submarine boats as quickly and as expeditiously as they can be built by the Fore River Shipbuilding Company.

I am a poor man, while the Electric Boat Company has among its principal stockholders three or four millionaires, including August

Belmont, Isaac L. Rice, and others. The capital stock of that company is ten million dollars. They have deprived me, by their flimsy lawsuit, from getting capital to build a boat under my new inventions and patents, and are now asking Congress to pass a law which will prevent the Navy Department from adopting my new plans and inventions, even should the entire department consider that they are far superior in every way to the plans now being used by that department.

I do not believe that your committee will commit itself to this monopoly which is against the interest of the government.

I am advised by my attorneys that as soon as the suits of the Electric Boat Company can be reached and tried the Court will undoubtedly dismiss them, but in the meanwhile they act as an injunction against me, as they prevent my enlisting capital which is timid and dreads a lawsuit.

Very respectfully,

Mr. Holland and I worked on entirely different lines in the development of our respective types of boats, he being a consistent advocate of the diving principle. He contended for many years that a submarine boat should be built small in size and with little statical stability, so as to dive quickly, while I have stood for great statical stability and for methods of submerging the vessel bodily on a level keel instead of diving at excessive and dangerous angles. I have never refused to accede to him the credit of having been the man who first made the diving type of submarine practical, and to acknowledge his genius and attention to detail which overcame the difficulties which caused the failure of many of his predecessors who attempted to build boats of the diving type.

He died on August 12, 1914, just at the beginning of the present European war, and consequently did not live to see the fulfilment of his prophecy that the submarine would prove the superior of the battleship if they ever became opponents in actual warfare.

My own experimental work began when I was a mere schoolboy. I had become interested in the submarine by reading Jules Verne's "Twenty Thousand Leagues Under the Sea." Shortly afterward I took up the study of natural physics and became interested in the use of the diving bell. Being an excellent swimmer and fond of boats, I spent most of my vacation times on or about the water. I remember building a canvas canoe from a description published in *Golden Days*. This canoe was very "cranky," being only about eighteen inches wide and the sides eighteen inches high. The only way I could learn to sit in the canvas canoe was by ballasting her with pig iron and gradually reducing the ballast as I became more expert, until finally I learned how to keep an equilibrium and maintain the canoe upright. There was only one other boy I remember in the village of Toms River, where I lived at that time, who could ride this canoe, consequently some of the boat men, when they saw it one day drifting bottom side up down the river, came to the conclusion that I had been dumped out and drowned. When they came alongside and righted the canoe they were much surprised to find me in it. I had turned the canoe upside down and crawled up into it, the air pressure keeping the water from rising into it. I had crawled in there for the purpose of finding out how long I could live on the volume of air contained within the canoe; in the meantime it was drifting down the river.

Strange to say, the design of the submarine boat which I made at that time, when I was only about fourteen years of age, contained most of the elements which are being used successfully in the Lake type of boat to-day: the use of the hydroplanes for control of depth, bottom wheels for navigation over the bottom, and a diving compartment with an air-lock so that the crew could enter or leave the vessel when submerged. These plans were shown to my father at that time, who rather discouraged me in the matter on the ground that submarine navigation was something that great engineers had given a lot of attention to, and that I had better give more attention to my regular school studies than to fooling around with experiments of that nature —which was good advice.

Consequently I did nothing further in the matter until 1892, when my attention was called to an advertisement of the United States Government for inventors to submit designs of submarines to the Navy Department. Then I prepared plans which, in my judgment, would meet the Department's requirements. I was still a youngster, and knew nothing about the difficulties met by outsiders in getting hearings before government officials in Washington. On the appointed day, in

June, 1893, on which the bids were to be opened I appeared in Washington with my plans and specifications under my arm, and was directed to the room adjoining the Secretary's office, where a large number of people were assembled. At this time I knew nothing of anyone else's experiments in submarines, and thought that I was the first and only one. I was consequently much disturbed to see so many people present. I sat down on a lounge, and a young man a little older than myself sat down on the lounge alongside of me and said to me, "Well, I suppose you are here on the same errand as the rest of us; I see you have some plans, and I suppose you have designs of a submarine boat which you are going to submit." I said, "Yes, and I guess there are going to be a good many plans submitted, judging by the number of people who are here." The gentleman then said, "No, I only know of two others who are going to submit plans: there is Mr. J. P. Holland, the gentleman standing over there, and my father, Mr. George F. Baker, of Chicago."

He then explained that he was the son of Mr. Baker, the man who had built the Baker boat, and whose experimental work was responsible for the appropriation of $200,000 by the government for building a submarine. I then said to him, "Well, then, who are all these other gentlemen present? "He knew most of them and obligingly pointed them out to me, saying, "There is Senator So-and-so and Congressman So-and-so, and Mr. So-and-so the great lawyer," etc. I then said to myself, "Well, Lakey, it looks as though you were not going to have much of a show here." I submitted my plans and specifications, however, and returned to Baltimore and to my other business. I was much surprised, therefore, to receive, some time afterward, a telegram from the editor of the *New York Tribune*, a Mr. Hall, stating that he had received information from Washington that my plans were looked upon most favorably by the majority of the Naval Board and that they were going to adopt my type of boat. He asked for an interview and a description of the boat. I did not go over to Washington, expecting to receive notice in good time that the award had been granted—which is proof positive that I was still young and ignorant. Nothing further was heard of the matter until I saw a notice in the paper that it had been decided not to build any submarines at that time, and that the matter had been postponed indefinitely. Some years afterward I met the late Admiral Mathews, and he informed me then that he had been a member of the board, and that four of the five members of that board were in favor of adopting my type of boat and of having the government start the development of a submarine on those lines, but that the constructor of the board opposed it on the grounds that when the boat was running on the bottom on wheels she might run off from a precipice and go down head first, and reach so great a depth as to be crushed, evidently not realizing that her great static stability and the use of her hydroplanes would prevent this from happening. Anyway, they did not arrive at a conclusion, and any action was postponed for the time being.

In the meantime Mr. George F. Baker, who had moved to Washington in the full expectation of getting the contract, had died, and the Holland Torpedo Boat Company had offered to build, under guarantee of its performance, a boat to meet the department's desires. As I had no company back of me, and, being only a youngster, was without capital of my own, the department decided it was better for them to place a contract under a definite guarantee of performance than to undertake to develop a submarine themselves. I did not name any price for building the boat at the time I submitted my plans, but expressed the desire to coöperate with the government in any way that they wished. My youthful hopes at that time were that if they considered my general plans worthy of adoption I should be taken into the navy and given some sort of a commission to work out the details of the boat. When I saw some mention in the paper that the matter was to come up for consideration again, I did, however, make a visit to the Navy Department, and assuming, from my observation of the Senators, Congressmen, and representative men who were present at the time of the first opening of the bids, that it was necessary to have some sort of a standing, I secured a letter of introduction from the governor of my native state, New Jersey, who at that time was Mr. Leon Abbott, introducing me to the gentleman who at that time was acting Secretary of the Navy, for the purpose of finding out, if possible, whether I had any chances, and the proper procedure to pursue in getting further consideration of my invention. Presenting myself in the Secretary's office, I sent in my letter of introduction, and the word came back that the Secretary would see me in a few minutes. I waited in the ante-room for a couple of hours, but no word came from the Secretary. Finally he appeared in the doorway and said, "Now, gentlemen, I am going to my lunch, and will be back at half-past two." I Went out to my lunch and was back in the waiting room a little before half-past two, shortly after which the Secretary came into the room, passed around, shook hands with every one, and talked a minute or two with some of his visitors. When he came to me he shook my hand, and I explained to him that I had sent in a letter from Governor Abbott and had been awaiting an opportunity to see him. His reply was, "I will see you in a few minutes." He returned to his office; at four o'clock he appeared at the door again and said, "Gentlemen, I will not be able to see any of you again to-day, as I must now sign my mail."

I was on hand again the following morning, and notified the colored man that I was still waiting for the interview which the Secretary had promised me. The word came back that he would see me in a few minutes. I waited all the morning; the noon hour came, and the Secretary then stated that he was going out to lunch and would be back at half-past two. Every one else who had appeared in the morning the day before had been granted his interview and a new crowd was waiting. I was the only chap who had "stood pat." By this time I was pretty much disgusted. As I went out into the hall the Secretary came out of his door and, putting his hand on my shoulder, said, "I am sorry to have kept you waiting, but as soon as I have finished my lunch I will take up your matter." You may be sure I was on hand, and after he returned he sent for me. He called a colored man and said, "I want you to take this young man down to Captain Sampson (afterward Admiral Sampson, who was at that time head of the Bureau of Ordnance), and tell Captain Sampson that Mr. Lake comes with a letter of introduction from the governor of my state, and I want him to listen to what he has to say about submarine boats, and report to me." This colored man, instead of taking me to Captain Sampson, turned me over to another colored man, and did not report the message which the Secretary had given him. This second colored man took me to Captain Sampson's clerk, and finally I was ushered into the Captain's presence and started to tell him about my boat and its possibilities. He immediately assumed a bored expression, turned his back to me, put his feet up on a chair, and said, "Well, go ahead, but make it brief." I admit that I was pretty much tongue-tied by this time, and I do not flatter myself that I impressed him in the least degree, as his manner had the effect of a cold douche upon my enthusiasm. I remember that as I walked out of the Navy Department I vowed never to return until I was sent for, and I never did.

I now started making experiments on my own account, and built the *Argonaut, Jr.*, and later the *Argonaut*; and I did not return to Washington until I was sent for by a telegram from the late Senator Hale, at that time chairman of the Senate Navy Committee, asking me to come to Washington and submit a proposition for building submarine boats for the United States Government. I was never able to account for my treatment in Washington until some time afterward, when I had an office in New York. The former Acting Secretary had at this time left the Navy Department and was practising his profession of law in New York, where I believe he is still engaged.

Having some legal business at that time which I thought he might be able to handle because of his experience in the Navy Department, I called upon him in regard to it. He stated that, as he was then free, he could handle it for me, and when I recalled my visit to him when he was Secretary of the Navy he said he remembered it very well. He laughingly remarked that I may have thought him a little slow in receiving me at that time; and then explained that, previous to his accepting the portfolio as assistant secretary of the navy, he had been the attorney for a rival submarine boat company; that he knew all about their boats, and the fact that they had expended large sums of money in the development of submarines; and that, although he had resigned as attorney for the company before he became acting secretary, perhaps his former association with them had led him to give less consideration to my proposition than he otherwise might have done.

As I believed the submarine to have great possibilities commercially as well as for war, I gave up my other business and came to New York, opened an office in the old Cheeseborough Building, and tried to secure capital to build a commercial submarine. I advertised in the papers and visited a number of capitalists in the effort to interest them, but usually, after obtaining an interview, as soon as I asserted that it was possible to navigate over the bottom of the ocean as readily as it was over the land, and that when on the bottom I could open a door in the boat but that no water would come in; and, further, that divers could very readily pass in and out of this open door, I observed in most cases a look of dread in their eyes and their hands would slide over and push a button. An attendant immediately came to the door and reminded Mr. "Blank," whoever he might be, that he had a very important engagement or that some other visitor was waiting to see him. Unfortunately for me, this was about the time that a madman had attempted to bomb Russell Sage in his office.

The result was, that after spending six months and all of my savings I had not raised a dollar. I then decided that it was necessary to get some engineer of national prominence to endorse my project, so I went to Charles H. Haswell, author of "Haswell's Handbook," and former chief engineer of the United States Navy, and explained to him that I wanted him to give me a professional opinion on the practicability of my boat. I offered to submit him my plans of the boat —of which I also had a model in the tank of water in the Cheeseborough Building which I would like him to see, as I thus would be better able to explain to him its method of navigating on the surface and submerging beneath the surface and on the bottom itself. And I then asked him how much he would charge me. He stated that he should want $1500 for the investigation and opinion. By this time I had expended my savings and hardly had $15—let alone $1500. I explained the situation frankly to him, and he said, "Well, I will go down and look it over and give you a report anyhow, and you can repay me at some future time when you are able." He did so, and gave me a very excellent endorsement, but I found that even his endorsement was not sufficient to induce capitalists to invest their hard-earned money in any such crazy scheme as mine appeared to them. I finally decided to build a small experimental boat myself to demonstrate the two principal features over which almost every one seemed to be sceptical. These were the ability to navigate over the bottom of the ocean and the ability to enter and leave the boat while submerged without any water coming in and foundering her. I therefore gave up my office and moved down to Atlantic Highlands, where, with the financial assistance of my uncle and aunt, Mr. and Mrs. S. T. Champion, I was able to build the *Argonaut, Jr.* She was built of yellow pine planking, double thick, lined with canvas laid between the double layers of planking, the outer seams caulked and payed. She was a flat-sided affair and would not stand great external pressure. She was propelled when on the bottom by a man turning a crank on the inside. Our compressed-air reservoir was a soda-water fountain tank. The compressed-air pump was a plumber's hand-pump, by which means we were able to compress the air in the tanks to a pressure of about one hundred pounds per square inch.

My diving suit I built myself by shaping iron in the form of an open helmet, which extended down as far as my breast; this I covered with painted canvas. I used the dead-light from a yacht's cabin as my eyeglass in front of the helmet. I tied sash weights to my legs to hold me down on the bottom when walking in the vicinity of the boat. A cousin, B. F. Champion, accompanied me on my first submerged run with the *Argonaut*, which was in Blackfish Hole in the Shrewsbury River. We submerged the boat alongside of a dock and started across stream in the river. The first time we went under water a stream of water came through a bolt-hole which had not been plugged and struck "Bart" on the back of the neck. He said, "Ugh!" and made a dive. The *Argonaut* had a little port-hole in one end about six inches in diameter, and "Bart" said afterward, "I made a dive for that port-hole, but came to the conclusion that I could not get through, so I stopped." It was a simple matter, however, to drive a plug in and stop the water from coming in. On our first trip we ran across the river and back, and, although there was a strong current in the river, she "backed" right back to her starting place, having rested on the bottom firmly enough to prevent the current from carrying her down stream.

"ARGONAUT, JR.," 1894

A small experimental boat built by the author to demonstrate the practicability of wheeling over the bottom and of sending divers out from the boat without water entering the vessel. She was propelled by hand over the waterbed; she had an air lock and diver's compartment which permitted egress and ingress of a diver when submerged.

Later we took the boat up to Atlantic Highlands and had a lot of fun running around on the bottom of New York Bay picking up clams and oysters, etc. We finally decided to organize a company and build a larger boat; so one day we invited the mayor of Atlantic Highlands, the president of the bank, and a number of other prominent people of the little community to witness our trials. A number of the men wrote their names on a shingle, which was tied to a sash weight and then thrown off the end of the Atlantic Highlands pier in about sixteen feet of water. My cousin and I got into the boat, submerged her, wheeled her forward to where the sash weight had been thrown overboard, picked it up, and had it back on the dock again in five minutes.

The performance of the *Argonaut, Jr.*, becoming known, she

received no little newspaper notoriety. In looking over my old clippings I find that there was a vein of scepticism and sarcasm running through most of these early accounts of her performance. I just quote briefly from one of the papers describing her, the *New York Herald*, of January 8, 1895:

THIS BOAT CRAWLS ALONG THE BOTTOM. AT LEAST THAT'S WHAT IT WAS TO DO, BUT IT ESCAPES AND ASTONISHES FOLKS IN OCEANIC, N. J.

DRIFTS UP THE SHREWSBURY

IT WILL CRAWL FIVE MILES WITHOUT COMING UP TO BREATHE WHEN INVENTOR LAKE COMPLETES IT.   FUN FOR MERRY MERMEN.

"RED BANK, N. J., Jan. 8, 1895.—Strange things come in with the tide in the ungodly hours of the night, and in the stillness of the night strange things follow them, but the strange thing which came up the North Shrewsbury a day or two ago, and which lies high and dry on Barley Point, is a 'new one' on the good folk of Oceanic. Now that they have fairly discovered it, they are sorry that it didn't wobble ashore in the summer, when Normandie-by-the-Sea below the Point is crowded with curious persons from the city. Any enterprising Oceanic man might have fenced in the queer thing and charged every one a quarter to see it."

The few substantial persons who had witnessed the *Argonaut's* experiments provided the capital for the construction of the *Argonaut First* and enabled me to complete her, and she was launched on August 17, 1897. I had called the little experimental boat the *Argonaut, Jr.*, because it was born before its mother, although the mother (the *Argonaut First*) had been conceived and designed first. I did not have sufficient capital to go ahead with her construction, and even the design of the *Argonaut* itself was cut down to correspond to the size of the subscriptions that we had been able to secure.

The raising of capital to most inventors is a serious problem; it has always been so with me. I have always been interested in mechanical accomplishments, but always dreaded the necessity of trying to raise capital to carry on those experiments. I have never valued money for itself or felt the need of it except when I did not have it. I think this is the case with most inventors, which is the reason why so many of them go to unscrupulous promoters who rob them of their inventions, or else often tie them up so that they themselves are incapable of continuing their development work.

Having made an initial success by my experiments, like most unsophisticated inventors I also fell into the hands of a promoter of this type. He was introduced to me by an officer of a bank, and, after an investigation of my project, claimed that he could raise all the money necessary to float a project of this kind, which in his judgment had the greatest possibilities of anything he had ever learned of. He said that his friends, the Vanderbilts, "Jack" Astor, and the Goulds, would immediately subscribe large sums upon his submitting the proposition to them. He secured possession of my plans, and took me to his house, which was a handsome brownstone structure standing in beautiful grounds. Another evidence of wealth was that he always had a smart carriage with liveried coachman waiting for him at our various conferences, held frequently in the directors' room of the bank. He had himself made the general manager, myself the president, and Hon. William T. Malster, of Baltimore, the treasurer of the company. At his suggestion we sent out a notification to our subscribers that twenty-five per cent. of their subscriptions was due and payable. Mr. Malster was president of the Columbia Dry Dock and Iron Works, Baltimore, the company with which we had placed the contract for building the *Argonaut*, and as he was a Baltimorean he had kindly consented to serve as treasurer of my company. Everything now looked rosy, and I gave my attention to preparing the detailed plans of the *Argonaut*. One day the general manager came into the room and said, "Now I have arranged for the sale of $100,000 worth of our stock." (He was to get a certain percentage of the stock for selling it to his friends, the Astors, Goulds, etc.) "So," he continued, "I want you to go to Baltimore and get Mr. Malster to sign up a lot of this stock so that we can make immediate delivery of it and get the money, and it would also be advisable for you to have Mr. Malster sign some checks in blank," the checks of the company requiring the signatures of both president and treasurer.

I visited Baltimore and explained to Mr. Malster what our general manager told me, and he said, "Well, Simon, you are a young man, and I think an honest one, and I am willing to trust you. I will sign these certificates, but don't you let them go out of your hands or sign them yourself until you have some definite written obligations on the part of those who are going to purchase this stock that they will pay for it." I returned to New York and told Mr. H—— that I had the certificates, etc., signed, and asked him when he would be ready to deliver the money and receive the stock. He stated that his friend "Jack" Astor was then out of town and he wanted him to be on the list first and would wait until he returned. He said, "I will see him at the first opportunity, but in the meantime you had better sign these certificates in blank and leave them with me, as I will have to fill out the names as he wants them, and I have had to agree to give him the biggest part of my commission to get it started." At the same time he told me that he would like to have a loan of a couple of thousand dollars for a few days (this we had on deposit there in the bank in the company's name). He said, as I had Mr. Malster's signature, I could easily make him the loan and he would return it soon, for he had a large piece of property which he had arranged the sale of, but there were some back taxes due on it which he wanted to clear off before turning over the deed. I told him that I could not make a loan of the company's money. He then became very angry and said, "Well, if I did not trust him to that extent he would not go to his friends or dispose of the stock." He was a very pompous individual, wore gold eyeglasses, and had a large acquaintance, formerly having been a business man of standing.

The fact that he had been introduced to me by an official of the bank led me to investigate him no further, but when he attempted to get the company's funds and its stock in blank I started an investigation, and found that the house that he was living in, and the horses and carriages, had been secured from another unsuspecting individual much older than myself in much the same manner. This individual had been in business for many years, nevertheless the promoter induced him to reorganize his successful business on a much larger capitalization. The promoter made an agreement with this man to sell the stock of the new company, and promised he would interest his friends, the Astors, Goulds, and Vanderbilts. As a partial consideration for this he was to receive this mans beautiful home and a certain percentage of the stock. The man's wife having died, he did not care to live longer in the house, so he agreed that the house should be given as a part consideration, and as a guarantee of his delivery of the house and stock as a part consideration on this promoter's agreement to float the stock of the much larger capitalized new company, he had placed both the controlling stock of the company and the house in escrow, and had turned the possession of the house over to this promoter, who was now our general manager, with the deeds of same to be held in escrow and not to be finally recorded until the Goulds, Vanderbilts, Astors, etc., had come into the new company. Hard times occurred about this time, so he claimed, which prevented promised capitalists from coming in, but, as Mr. H—— held the control of the company by holding the control of the stock, he had himself elected an officer of the company at a handsome salary and still held possession of this most beautiful home without ever having paid a dollar. I merely recite this as a warning to inventors to look out for the plausible New York promoter. I also discovered that Mr. H —— had made application for patents, my own patents not yet having been issued, with the idea of getting me into interference in the Patent Office, and it was necessary for us to threaten him with arrest and bring a suit against both himself and the cashier—whom we now learned had known of his previous experiences and expected to share in his profits this time—in order to get a legal release so that we could proceed with the work.

Many of the troubles of inventors can be traced originally to certain semi-professional men who call themselves patent attorneys. There are two classes of patent attorneys, one class consisting of conscientious, honorable gentlemen, who consider it their duty, when an unsophisticated inventor comes before them with an idea which the inventor considers new, to tell him the truth about his invention and to inform him whether it is really an original invention or not, or merely a slight modification of some old idea on which no protection can be secured. There is another class of attorneys who have been more properly termed patent sharks, who will get a patent on anything brought to them; for by juggling words they are able to get claims which mean nothing, except that they serve the purpose of getting the attorneys their fees. Many an inventor has an idea which is original with him but which may be as old as Bushnell's submarine or entirely impractical. The patent shark will get him a patent on this, and the inventor then thinks his fortune is made. He is very likely then to sell his farm and go to New York and advertise in the papers that he has a valuable invention, there to fall into the hands of some unscrupulous promoter who secures all of his money without letting him know that the patent is worthless; or if he happens to have a valuable invention the promoter will in all probability arrange matters so that he himself gets the cream and leaves the inventor a mere pittance.

Since the war began, and there has been the general editorial demand by the papers of the country for some means to destroy or offset the submarine menace, I have received hundreds of letters asking advice, etc., regarding various devices. I have received visits from a number of people who have come from long distances, some from the West, others from Canada and from the South, to ask my opinion regarding certain attachments to be applied to submarines or on devices to capture submarines. Many of the ideas were old and some of them pitiful in the fact that they showed such ignorance of the laws of nature and of mechanics on the part of their projectors. One man sends me a copy of his allowed patent with a letter from one of these patent sharks acknowledging the receipt of final payment of a considerable amount for his having received an allowance of his patent. I will, without betraying the name, quote in part from his letter:

> I would kindly ask if you would take hearing from me and take notice of my new invention, which is called the Power Transmitting Mechanism. The machine is started by spring or batteries; the first start is the spin of the fly-wheel; the fly-wheel pumps on the handle of the jack: one revolution to the one pound on the fly-wheel drives the handle of the jack back and forth. The jack will throw the crank one revolution with ninety-seven pounds. The jack is the result of multiplying power, and the jacks can be used in the same position as any and all cylinders. This machine will nicely furnish you the power for your undersea liner. No fuel is needed....

Now anyone can see that this proposition is nothing more or less than an impractical proposition mechanically, and that it is on the perpetual-motion order, yet this patent shark mulcts the poor man of a considerable sum to secure him some kind of a worthless patent. He is likely to expend much further sums in trying to get it on the market. A patent lawyer of that stamp should be put in jail for fraud, and should not be permitted to practise in an honorable profession.

I have already recited my own difficulties in attracting the interest of the United States Government to my work, and I call attention to the fact that it required many years of persistent endeavor and the expenditure of vast sums of money furnished by patriotic individuals, and also the recognition of my devices by several foreign governments, before our own government recognized any merit in my work. That has been the experience of almost every American inventor, so far as I am aware. We have seen how Bushnell was derided and driven from his home; and that Robert Fulton received no recognition from his home government, and that the only recompense he ever received for his submarine work was from the British Government. Strangely, the money paid him was not for the purpose of enabling him to develop his invention, but rather to suppress his inventive genius. Ericsson could get no recognition or assistance from the government when he presented his design of the *Monitor*. She was built by private capital, and her builders assumed all the risk, and it is stated that at the time she fought the *Merrimac* and helped to save the United States from being divided internally, she was on a builder's trial and had not been accepted or paid for by the government. All readers of the life of Ericsson are familiar with the lack of consideration he received from the naval authorities of the United States at that time, and that his epoch-making invention was derided as a "cheese-box on a raft." It was strange that he received such little consideration, as at the time of his arrival in America he was an engineer of note and while still a young man had built the wonderful canals of Sweden. I had never really appreciated Ericsson's great engineering ability until I made a journey over these canals, which are virtually carried up over mountains, and offer one of the most interesting European trips a tourist can make. Maxim had to go to England and Hotchkiss to France to get their guns adopted. Sir Hiram Maxim told me of the heartbreaking time he spent in his native country, America—he was born in Maine—trying to get his inventions properly developed, and the lack of consideration he received here by our own government officers, while in England, on the contrary, he was received with open arms. The late King Edward visited him, and the English took up his invention and knighted him.

The Wright Brothers' first recognition and the first dollar they ever received as profits in their years of experimental effort came from France. I remember well when Wilbur Wright came to France with his flying machine and secured the recognition that the Wright Brothers had not been able to secure in the United States, their native country. The Wright Brothers and their and our own European representative, Mr. Hart O. Berg, occupied for a time one of the rooms in our suite of offices in Regent Street, London, as their headquarters, and I am therefore familiar with some of their difficulties in getting recognition in this country.

It has been said that Americans invent and the Europeans develop. This statement seems to be borne out in fact, so far as our military inventions at least are concerned. From the time the Wrights first introduced the flying machine in Europe all the important countries over there have been consistently assisting inventors in improving the construction of the planes and machinery for driving them, while our own country has stood almost at a standstill. Our government gave no aid to foster this American invention so that it could be gradually developed, but rather our authorities made the first requirements so difficult to fulfil that there was no incentive to work; which is a mistake often made by men with a theoretical rather than a practical education. A practical man may evolve something radically new in the arts or sciences, but to get it introduced into the government service it must first be passed upon and approved by men who at the country's expense have received, for the most part, a purely theoretical education; and nine times out of ten these men get some additional theories of their own which they insist must be incorporated in the machine or apparatus, and thus make it impossible of operation or delay its accomplishment. It is probably due to this cause that we are now forced to go to France for plans of our aeroplanes and their driving machinery to enable us to compete with the Germans' machines.

What is the reason for this lamentable state of affairs in respect to American military inventions? I believe that I can partially explain it. I believe it is because our army and navy officers are too busy with the routine of their profession to give the necessary time to a thorough investigation of devices other than those with which they are forced to become familiar by their training. I believe that there is not a single fundamental invention which has emanated from an army or navy officer during his service, although it is true that such men have made some improvements upon devices in their hands, based upon working experience. Their education and routine require them to be well-informed as to the *proved* devices of which they make use in the service. On looking over the volume of text-books, rules and regulations covering in the most minute details all the methods of construction, tests of strength, chemical analyses, etc., with which officers are obliged to become familiar, I can fully appreciate the fact that they are too highly educated in the knowledge of accepted devices to be able to find time to look into the future.

I believe that the present Secretary of the Navy, Mr. Josephus Daniels, in his creation of a civilian board of advisers to the navy to pass upon new inventions of value to the navy, has taken an important step in the protection of this country; the creation of this board I consider one of the greatest achievements of the present administration.

The few inventions which have gained sufficient early recognition and have received governmental aid in their development have usually been forced on the Army or Navy by either political or financial interests. The intrigue and lobbying conducted in Washington to secure exclusive privileges would make volumes of interesting and spicy reading, and it is possible that the knowledge of these well-known intrigues makes officers very chary in recommending or taking up devices that may appear to have merit. The usual answer to inventors of untried devices who offer their plans to the government has been, "Well, if you try it out and it proves successful, we will then consider it"; and in such a case should the inventor have no means or financial backing the invention is lost to the United States and is adopted abroad.

This policy is "penny wise and pound foolish" when it so directly affects the safety of the nation. I was informed by Mr. Otto Exius, the managing director of the great Krupp Works in Germany, that the Imperial German Government has followed a far different method in fostering inventions that might be of benefit to the state. Mr. Exius informed me that when they undertook the development of a new invention for the purposes of national defence the government paid them for the cost of all material used and allowed them a sufficient percentage over labor costs to cover their overhead, plus a fair amount of profit. This probably accounts for the fact that Germany to-day is far ahead of us in her development of engines for the military submarine. There is no gainsaying the fact that the policy of our government has been to make up an ideally perfect weapon and then invite manufacturers to bid for the work. They have thus thrown the burden of development upon individual firms, many of whom have been forced into bankruptcy in their patriotic desire to furnish acceptable devices to the government.

We have the inventive genius in this country to *create and originate* new machines and new methods of manufacture. In most commercial and industrial lines we are able to maintain a leading position, but in devices designed for the national defence we originate, and other nations develop and profit. Had we supported our inventors and held within this country as far as possible the knowledge of their devices, and withheld the secrets of their work from foreign powers, as indeed we should have, the United States to-day would be in a position of military effectiveness very different from that in which we are found. All this is due to the fact that the government does not foster and protect our newly created devices, and to-day we are behind the continental powers in our gunnery, our airplanes, in our dirigibles, and in our submarine engines, as well as in many other auxiliaries necessary to our national protection.

I feel that it lies within the province of the civilian board to correct the mistakes in our governmental policy, provided, of course, that Congress makes suitable appropriations to enable it to carry on investigations in a proper manner and to protect the inventors who submit new and original ideas. At the time Secretary Daniels created the board I wrote him, in part, as follows:

"I notice by to-day's *New York Herald* that you are proposing to appoint an 'advisory board of civilian inventors for a Bureau of Invention and Development,' to be created in the Navy Department, and that you have asked Mr. Thomas A. Edison to be the chairman of said board.

"I wish to congratulate you upon this conception. I believe such a board, if its work is properly systematized, can be made of great and permanent value to the nation.

"Many illustrations could be found in which other nations have been the first to take up and reap the benefit from American inventions. It is doubtful if Morse, Edison, Bell, the Wrights, or any other pioneer American inventors have received any reward whatever from many countries whose own citizens have grown rich and prosperous by taking up and manufacturing American inventions without giving consideration to them.

"When I first submitted my plans of a submarine boat to the Navy Department in 1893 I had no company back of me and did not make a proposition to the department to build a boat. I suggested to them that I would coöperate with the Navy Department in a way satisfactory to them.

"My hope was, at that time, as I was only a youngster, to receive some sort of a commission in the United States Navy and to be placed in charge of the development of the submarine, but the submarine was a discredited machine in those days, and after I had spent several days in trying to interest the authorities at that time in my proposition I failed, and felt very much discouraged, and did not again return to the Navy Department until called there in 1901 by a telegram from Senator Hale, who was then chairman of the Senate Navy Committee.

"Since that time I have been offered a splendid position with very large financial backing if I would take charge of the development of submarines for a foreign government. This I refused to do, because I had a natural desire to receive some recognition in my own country.

"The principal aim and ambition in my life has been to be able to make sufficient money to endow an institution for the protection of American inventors.

"I tried to interest Enoch Pratt in this scheme twenty-three years ago in Baltimore. I have given a great deal of thought to such an institution. It does not look now as if I should be able to carry out my plans. If I had had sufficient financial backing in the early days of my experiments and development of the submarine to have protected myself fully by foreign patents, all of the European countries to-day would be paying me royalties, as they are all using a number of features in their boats which I originated.

"While I regret that the probabilities are that I will not be able to carry out my ambition, your proposition would, if carried out, go a long way toward improving the opportunities of American inventors to secure proper recognition of their inventive genius so far as they could be applied to the protection of the nation.

"I can, however, foresee certain oppositions to this scheme: first, there will be opposition from the vested interests who have held for years control of certain lines of manufactured articles and material used in the service.

"The scheme would also fail unless it would be possible for this board to secure the entire confidence of the American inventors. Very few inventors have had large business experience or know how to protect themselves from the various parasites who thrive upon them.

"A man gets an idea—it may be an old one, but he considers it original—and becomes obsessed with the idea that he has made a great discovery. He may be a farmer, a mechanic, a clergyman, or any other form of good American citizen, but not an experienced business man. In many cases he becomes a prey to people who live entirely upon their wits and the inexperience of others.

"First, if he is unfortunate enough to fall in the hands of an unscrupulous patent attorney, he will get all the money he can out of him by securing him a worthless patent. Probably 75 per cent. of the patents issued are not worth the paper they are written upon. After securing the patents he will then give up his farm or his position, take his savings and go to New York or some other city, and fall into the hands of an unscrupulous promoter, who makes the inventor believe he can place his patents, or, if he has a good invention and falls into the hands of an unscrupulous promoter, the invention is taken away from him, or he is given a mere pittance for it.

"I know of one case where an inventor of one of the most successful typewriting machines on the market, who spent his life in developing it, is receiving the munificent sum of eleven cents from each machine as a royalty. There is a large number of these machines being manufactured, and of course he is receiving a comfortable income even at this small rate, but the promoter who had nothing to do with its origination and who only happened to know the capitalists to go to, and the capitalists, are receiving a princely income.

"So many instances of inventors being deprived of a fair remuneration for their inventions have occurred that as a class it will be found that many of them will hesitate to submit their ideas to the board.

"I have received many letters from inventors throughout the country

124

who had all sorts of schemes for improving submarine boats, for detecting their presence under water, for destroying them, for protecting battleships against them, etc. In some cases they were accompanied by plans and descriptions, and they are usually old ideas, in many cases already patented. In other instances I have received letters stating that they had ideas which they would submit to me if I would pass upon them or coöperate with them in developing or introducing them to the Navy Department. My practice has always been to refuse to consider any device or invention unless the inventor had made application for a patent, as I did not want to be accused of taking another man's ideas, as he might submit to me ideas similar to my own and which I might have already had either patents pending in the Patent Office for same, or had made similar plans upon which I might expect to take out a patent at some future time.

"This feeling of uncertainty may cause inventors to hesitate to send their ideas in, but I think that could be overcome by having certain rules of procedure; that is, any idea submitted must be put into form, sworn to as original by the man who submitted it, which must be attested by witnesses. It could then be sent to examiners—first, to find out if it was an original idea; second, to find out if it was a mechanically operative idea; and, third, to find out if there was any need for such a device.

"I think your naming Mr. Edison as the head of such a bureau will go a long ways toward creating confidence in the mind of the inventors, that they would receive proper consideration. Most every one knows of Mr. Edison's perseverance in his early days in getting his inventions upon the market. A great many people know that he himself has not received a fraction of the reward that he is entitled to because of his great inventions. He is, without doubt, the greatest inventor the United States has produced. While I have never met Mr. Edison personally, I have always been a great admirer of him, because he is the man most responsible for raising the title of 'inventor' from that of crank to that of honor. I was such an admirer of him in my youth that I named my son after him. I do not think you could have made a better choice than he to head this bureau.

"If the bureau is organized, permit me to suggest that there should be some definite inducement held out to the inventors in the way of a royalty compensation or some other form of compensation for such ideas as the government might take up and utilize. The plan which I had in mind for my inventors' institution was to erect buildings, machine shops, laboratories, with a staff of patent experts, draftsmen, and engineers, so that the crude idea could first be investigated to see if it was original, then passed on to the engineers, who would coöperate with the inventor, and they would see that proper plans were made covering the proper kinds and strength of material to accomplish the purpose, and then it would be sent to the shops, all this work being charged up to the invention, or to the inventor if he was in a position to pay for it, at cost.

"The institution would, in consideration of its placing all these facilities available to the inventor, receive a certain percentage for its part of the work. In that way a properly endowed institution would probably be self-supporting. It might be possible to work that idea into your scheme. Take, as an illustration, the submarine boats. Something new and revolutionary might be introduced in the way of propulsive means which would enable submarines to make very much greater speed, both on the surface and submerged. As soon as the submarine has the speed of a battleship, it will be able to drive the battleship from the seas. Without battleships to cover the landing of troops from transports, no invasion of one country by another country, from the sea, can be made. Therefore, no more wars between maritime countries.

"Such a propulsive means, therefore, will become a great and valuable adjunct to any nation. If the government developed such a machine it would be only right for them to pay a royalty to the inventor. On the other hand, this same machine would undoubtedly be very valuable for a great many other industrial purposes. If it was used for other purposes, it would only be right that the inventor pay the government in return a royalty or percentage of his profits in consideration of the government having developed it for him.

"I hope you will not think I am officious in offering these suggestions. Having given so much thought to the matter in the line as above referred to, I felt that you were entitled to have my thoughts for what they were worth.

"I certainly hope you will be able to get the support of Congress, the naval officers, and the inventors in carrying this scheme through to a successful conclusion, which, if done, I believe will be one of the greatest constructive pieces of legislation accomplished in years."

A larger institution along the same lines might well be endowed by a number of America's bright business men who have made fortunes based upon the ideas of some poor, unsophisticated inventor who has not been brought up to worship wealth, but who had an original idea of value to the world and to the individuals who had the business capacity to get the money out of it.

Original ideas are creations, and the creation of ideas may become possible by constant study and research. In this class are all the professional inventors; but many good ideas are spontaneous and occur in brains not educated along mechanical or scientific lines. The establishment of such an institution as above outlined would conserve these spontaneous inventions for the benefit of the nation, as well as assist the professional inventor in his research.

CHAPTER IV

THE EVOLUTION OF THE SUBMARINE

Among the many submarines which were built previous to the beginning of the present century, very few taught lessons of positive value, for the great majority of these experimental craft were total failures. Knowledge of the causes of their failures is important, however, because it teaches us what errors in construction to avoid. Practically all of these early submarines were built secretly; when failures resulted the vessels were abandoned and the results of such trials were not published, consequently the succeeding designers were very apt to make the same mistakes.

It was not until the past decade that any general description of many of the early submarines was published and made available to students of this problem. In looking over the published plans and descriptions of a number of those early submarines, I have been convinced that many lives and much capital could have been saved had the results of the various experiments been openly disclosed for the guidance of later designers.

The desire to navigate in the depths of the sea has possessed the minds of many men since the beginning of history, and even at very early times several crude submarines were devised in the attempt to solve the problem. But, as I have related in the preceding chapter, it was not until the period of the war between England and her American colonists that any important progress was made. Bushnell's little submarine, called the *American Turtle*, was built at that time. It took its name from its shape, which resembled the back shells of two turtles joined together.

From the rather complete description of this vessel contained in one of Dr. Bushnell's letters, it appears to have been propelled by a screw propeller to obtain forward or reverse motion. It was ballasted in such a manner as to give the vessel great inherent stability. It had water ballast tanks which could be filled to give the vessel negative buoyancy, if desired, or to reduce the positive buoyancy so much that the vessel could be readily drawn under water by another screw propeller which was operated by a vertical shaft extending through a stuffing box into the vessel. This submarine carried a mine on its back, and provision was made to enable the operator inside the submarine to attach the mine to the bottom of a ship at anchor. This vessel was regulated in such a way that the mine could be exploded by a clockwork mechanism after the submarine had reached a safe distance from the vessel.

With this submarine a mine was placed under the bottom of the English frigate *Eagle*, anchored in New York Bay, but the mine drifted clear before the clockwork mechanism caused it to explode, otherwise the frigate would undoubtedly have been destroyed. General Washington complimented Dr. Bushnell on having so nearly succeeded in his attempt to sink the ship.

SKETCH OF THE CONFEDERATE SUBMARINE "HUNLEY"
Made after she was recovered and hoisted on the dock years after the war.
(Drawing by R. S. Skerrett.)

This submarine was unquestionably a successful model. It had one important feature that many designers have failed to appreciate, and that was great inherent stability. Great stability in a submarine means the carrying out of the now popular maxim "Safety First." Sufficient static stability is a guarantee that during all the manœuvring evolutions of a submarine she will always remain right side up and not dive into the bottom unless the hull is punctured or flooded at one end or the other.

Bushnell's model was not suited to high speed, but high speed was not essential in the days of the sailing ship. If this design had been developed further, so that several men could have been used to operate the propeller, it should have given a good account of itself.

Robert Fulton's boat, to which I also have made reference in the foregoing chapter, differed from Bushnell's in its method of submerged control, which was by vertical and horizontal rudders at the stern. It also carried a collapsible mast on which a sail could be spread for surface navigation.

A Bavarian by the name of Bauer built a submarine in 1850. Its method of control was by shifting a weight forward to dive and aft to rise. It was a flat-sided and flat-decked vessel with comparatively thin plating and entirely unsuited to resist the pressure of the water at any considerable depth. It collapsed in the harbor of Kiel during one of its trial trips. Bauer kept his presence of mind, however, and when sufficient water had entered and raised the trapped air pressure inside of the boat equal to the pressure outside, he opened the hatch and swam to the surface. This vessel remained partly buried in the mud into which it had sunk until 1887, when it was located during the deepening of Kiel harbor and taken to Berlin, where it is now kept in the Museum of Oceanography as an exhibit of Germany's first submarine.

No further important advance was made in the art of submarine navigation until the period of the Civil War, when the Confederates built several small submarines, called "Davids." One of these was called the *Hunley*, after her designer. During her brief career she suffocated or drowned thirty-two men, including her designer.

During my early experiments with the *Argonaut* in 1898 I received a visit from Col. Charles H. Hasker, of Richmond, Virginia, who explained in detail the method of operating the *Hunley*. She was a cylindrical-shaped craft, about thirty feet long and six feet in diameter, with both bow and stern flattened to form a stem and stern-post, respectively. Water-ballast compartments were located in either end of the vessel. She was propelled by eight men, who turned the cranked propeller shaft by hand. These men sat on benches on either side of the shaft. She had the usual vertically hung rudder aft, and a diving rudder forward to incline her bow down for diving, or to raise her bow to bring her to the surface (see page 150). Unfortunately she lacked longitudinal stability, and during her experimental trials twice dove head first into the bottom. Of her experience I have given an account elsewhere.

The lesson to be learned from the disastrous trials of this vessel was that sufficient statical stability should always be secured to prevent the vessel taking on an excessive inclination due to shifting of water ballast or movement of crew.

THE NEW ORLEANS SUBMARINE
Built by the Confederates during the Civil War.

Another submarine built by the Confederates shows a much safer design. It is shown as the New Orleans submarine. According to the story told by a native of New Orleans, this vessel was built during the Civil War to destroy the Northern ships. The story of her launching has been given in a foregoing chapter.

It is evident that the designer of this vessel miscalculated and made his boat so much overweight that she could not be given sufficient buoyancy to bring her to the surface by the means provided. From a study of the form of this vessel, she should have been very stable, and I am of the opinion that she could have been successfully navigated submerged had she been properly ballasted.

THE "INTELLIGENT WHALE"
Built by O. S. Halstead of Newark, N. J., and sold to the U. S. Government in 1870, now in Brooklyn Navy Yard.

During the years 1863 and 1864, Messrs. Bourgois and Brun brought out for the French Navy the largest and, in some respects, the most completely equipped submarine that was produced during the nineteenth century. This was *Le Plongeur*, a vessel about one hundred and forty feet long, ten feet depth, and twenty feet beam, with a displacement of over four hundred tons. Her motive power consisted of compressed-air engines of eighty horsepower. The compressed air was carried in air tanks at a pressure of one hundred and eighty pounds per square inch. It is reported that the capacity of the air tanks exceeded one hundred and forty cubic metres.

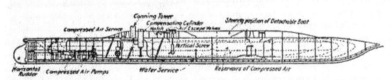

LONGITUDINAL SECTION OF THE FRENCH SUBMARINE "LE PLONGEUR"
This vessel was built by Messrs. Bourgois and Brun in 1864 and was backed by the French Government. She was the largest and the most costly vessel built in the attempt to solve the problem of successful submarine navigation up to about the beginning of the 20th century. (See text.)

Her submerged control system consisted of the usual water-ballast tanks for reducing the vessel's surface buoyancy preparatory to submerging. The final adjustment of displacement was to be effected by means of cylinders which could be forced out through stuffing boxes to increase her displacement or withdrawn to reduce her displacement. It was hoped that by manipulating these cylinders she could be put in equilibrium with the water she displaced, and that she could then be steered in any desired direction by the vertical and horizontal rudders placed at her stern.

Theoretically this is an ideal method for submerged control, but in practice it works out badly, especially when a vessel has little stability, for the reason that there are so many disturbing influences to cause the vessel to take on dangerous angles in diving. If free surfaces exist in the water-ballast tanks, the slightest change from a level keel causes the water to flow to the lower end of the ballast tank. This is apt to augment the inclination still further, and cause the vessel to dive, or, *vice versa*, to broach. The density of the water also varies, especially where freshwater rivers empty into salt water. At times quite different densities are found at various depths. The fresh water and salt water, instead of rapidly mixing, seem to have a tendency to remain in strata which extend, in some cases, considerable distances off shore. Therefore it is practically impossible to secure and maintain a vessel in perfect equilibrium. The movement of the crew forward and aft, or the effect of the sea, which imparts a vertical motion to the water beneath the surface, all tend to destroy both trim and equilibrium to such an extent that many failures have resulted in vessels of this type.

Le Plongeur was no exception to this rule, because it was found impossible to control her depth when running submerged, and she would either dive into the bottom or broach to the surface. One report stated that even in depths of thirty feet she would make progress "by alternately striking the bottom and then rebound to the surface like an elastic india-rubber ball."

One other novel feature introduced in *Le Plongeur* was an "escape boat," which was carried on top of the main hull, to which it was secured by bolts. A double hatch connected the submarine and the escape boat together. In case the submarine became disabled or entangled in wreckage and could not be brought to the surface, the crew could enter through double hatches into the escape boat, secure the bottom hatch, and by turning the securing bolts from the interior release the escape boat and ascend to the surface.

Mr. O. S. Halstead, of Newark, New Jersey, completed, in 1866, a submarine vessel on which the United States Government made a partial payment. This vessel is known as the *Intelligent Whale*, and is now installed as a permanent exhibit on the Green at the Brooklyn Navy Yard, New York. The vessel had a vertical and horizontal rudder at the stern for submerged control. According to official reports, she must have functioned fairly well when submerged.

One of the features of this vessel consisted in its ability to be converted into a diving bell when resting on the bottom. A large trap-door was arranged in the bottom of the vessel. After filling the whole interior of the vessel with compressed air equal in pressure to the pressure of the water at the bottom of the vessel, the trap-door could be opened and the air pressure would keep the water from rising, the same as in a diving bell.

A study of this vessel shows that she must have been a very stable craft and not likely to dive at an excessive angle or to stand on end, as was the tendency of many of the early diving boats. A report signed by Gen. T. W. Sweeny, U. S. A., and Col. John Michal, Col. T. R. Tresilian, and Major R. C. Bocking, engineers, strongly endorsed this vessel.

On the strength of the above-mentioned reports and endorsements, the government, through the Navy Department, appointed a commission composed of Commodore C. M. Smith, Commodore Augustus L. Chase, Chief of Bureau of Ordnance, and Edward O. Mathews, Chief of the Torpedo Board, "to examine, inspect, and report on the merit of said boat." As the report of this commission confirmed the capacity and efficiency of the boat for submarine purposes, the government made a contract for her purchase for the sum of $50,000 (£10,250).

The contract specified certain conditions which were to be fulfilled before the final payment was made, one of which was that Halstead should "write out fully and describe, without reservation, all the inventions, secrets, and contrivances necessary to enable any competent person or persons to operate and manage said boat as contemplated, desired, or designed, more especially the methods of furnishing, managing, controlling, purifying, and renewing the air when and in quantity as needed, so as to enable those in the boat to descend and ascend or remain under water any reasonable length of time; also, to open the doors in the bottom of the boat and keep the water from coming therein at any reasonable and regulated depth." For this information Halstead was to receive such further sum as a board of officers might grant. Halstead was to have the further right to apply to Congress for additional compensation.

In carrying out the provisions of the contract, the government, on May 27, 1870, took over the *Intelligent Whale* and then paid $12,050 (£2,470) on account of the contract. Shortly after this Halstead was instantly killed. Differences then arose between Halstead's heirs and others who claimed an interest in the contract. It does not appear that anything further was ever done with the boat to carry out the terms of the contract. She lay neglected for years on the old "Cob dock" in the Brooklyn Navy Yard, but was recently erected as an exhibit on the Green.

Some years later that famous inventor, Mr. J. P. Holland, brought out a submarine vessel called the *Fenian Ram*. This vessel was about thirty feet long and six feet in diameter. She was navigated, when submerged, by the use of vertical and horizontal rudders located at the stern. The novel feature introduced in the vessel was an under-water air-gun which was designed to fire a shell under water.

Mr. Holland was originally a school teacher in Ireland, from which country he was exiled because of his political beliefs. On coming to the United States he became affiliated with the Fenian movement. Previous to his construction of the *Fenian Ram* Mr. Holland built experimentally a small one-man boat. The money to build the *Fenian Ram* was subscribed by the "Clan-na-Gael" and other Irish patriotic societies, and an associate of Mr. Holland recently informed me that over $200,000 (£41,000) was subscribed to enable Mr. Holland to carry on his experiments. After the collapse of the Fenian movement the *Fenian Ram* was towed up to New Haven, Connecticut, and hauled out on the banks of the Mill River, where it has lain ever since, hidden under a pile of lumber.

One of the former leaders of the Fenians informed me that the scheme was to build a number of submarines of about the size of the *Ram*. They were to have been carried across the Atlantic in a special ship with water-tight compartments extending below the water line,

136

into which the submarines were to have been floated and a sea door closed. On arrival on the English coast, this special ship, which was apparently a harmless merchantman, was to locate the British war vessels in some one of the harbors, sail in and anchor near them; then the little submarines were to be released from their mother ship and proceed to sink as many of the British ships as they could by firing explosive shells into them below the water line. The novelty of such an attack was relied upon to spread consternation among the British fleet and thus enable the submarines to escape.

In 1878 Mr. G. W. Garrett, of Liverpool, took out a patent and constructed a small boat whose equilibrium was to have been maintained by the admission of water into a cylinder and forcing it out by a piston. In 1879, Mr. Garrett brought out a larger vessel, called the *Resurgam*, in which his means of control were forward diving rudders similar to those of the Confederate *Hunley*. The novel feature of this vessel was the installation of a very large steam boiler in which sufficient heat could be stored to enable the vessel to make a submerged run of several miles after the fires were shut down. This vessel was lost during her experimental trials.

Mr. Garrett then interested Mr. Nordenfelt, the inventor of the celebrated Nordenfelt gun, in his boat. Mr. Nordenfelt improved upon Garrett's boat and built vessels for Greece, Turkey, and Russia. His first boat was sixty-four feet in length by nine feet beam, with a displacement of about sixty tons. The method of submerged control, which he devised, consisted of the use of two downhaul screws located in sponsons on either side of the vessel. These screws were operated by bevel gears and were run at sufficient speed to overcome the reserve of buoyancy. The vessel was intended to be always operated with a reserve of buoyancy. To submerge, therefore, it was necessary to run the propellers at a speed sufficient to exert a thrust to overcome this buoyancy and pull her bodily under water. After reaching the desired depth, forward motion was then to be given by the usual screw propeller, and she was expected to make progress on a level keel and in a horizontal plane. The level keel was to have been maintained by the use of a horizontal rudder placed in the bow.

This method of submerged control for submarine vessels of moderate speed seems to me to be an excellent one in principle. I have been surprised that further development has not been made along these lines. I think the final abandonment of the Nordenfelt type of vessel was due to failure in carrying out the details of design rather than to faulty basic principles. A former chief engineer of Mr. Nordenfelt informed me that the heat from the large amount of hot water stored up in the reservoirs—for submerged power—made the interior of the vessels almost unbearable for the crew when the hatches were shut down, and that he did not believe the submarines ever made any submerged runs after being delivered. I also judge, from his description of his experiences with the vessels, that they lacked longitudinal stability and were difficult to hold in the horizontal position, which Mr. Nordenfelt claimed was a *sine qua non* for a submarine boat. I concur in this claim.

In an article on his boats, Mr. Nordenfelt stated that they were very sensitive, and that he had purposely made them so in order that the horizontal rudder might easily maintain the boat in a horizontal position. My experience has led me to prefer great statical stability rather than sensitiveness.

Mr. Nordenfelt's boats had means for discharging the smoke from the fires under the water. This was done so as not to betray the submarine's position to surface vessels. He also seems to have been the first to incorporate torpedo tubes within his hull for the discharge of the Whitehead torpedo.

The Spanish Lieut. Isaac Peral built, in 1887, a vessel in which the motive power was supplied from electric accumulators. It was operated by the usual vertical and horizontal rudders. Its submerged control was bad, but its electric propulsive system worked well.

Mons. Goubet built several small boats during the period from 1885 to 1890 with a propeller which worked on a universal joint so arranged that the direction of thrust could be changed to drive the boat under water or to bring her to the surface when submerged. This propeller took the place of the usual vertical and horizontal rudders.

Prof. Josiah L. Tuck built, in 1885, a vessel called the *Peacemaker*, the novel feature of which consisted of a "caustic soda" boiler for generating steam for submerged work.

In 1886 a Mr. Waddington, of England, brought out a small electric accumulator boat with downhaul screws arranged in vertical tubes. He also used side rudders to assist in control of depth. It is reported that this vessel functioned quite successfully, but she was abandoned, and Mr. Waddington does not seem to have developed anything further.

In 1892 George H. Baker brought out an egg-shaped vessel which he ran submerged by the use of side propellers driven by bevel gears. These propellers were carried in frames so that they could be inclined to exert a thrust downward or upward, or at any desired angle so as to pull the boat downward and drive her forward at the same time. This was an improvement over Nordenfelt's side propellers, which ran on fixed vertical shafts. This vessel functioned fairly satisfactorily at slow speeds, but neither the form nor driving mechanism was suitable for the higher speeds required by modern practice.

A number of other boats were built, but there does not appear to be anything new in principle in them.

This brings us up to 1893, when the United States Government made an appropriation of $200,000 (£41,000) for a submarine boat and advertised for inventors to submit designs. This was the first time that it was officially recognized in this country that there *might* be possibilities in this type of boat. Most of the naval officers, however, were very sceptical of the practicability of such craft, and, from the conservative point of view, they were perhaps justified, as no satisfactory boat had been built up to that time.

A program of requirements, which undoubtedly would produce a weapon valuable for defence, was made up by the Navy Department, and these requirements were designated in the following order of importance:

1. Safety.
2. Facility and certainty of action when submerged.
3. Speed when running on the surface.
4. Speed when submerged.
5. Endurance, both submerged and on the surface.
6. Offensive power.
7. Stability.
8. Visibility of object to be attacked.

This standard of accomplishments is as important to-day as when it was first promulgated.

This first appropriation was brought about by a recommendation to Congress, made by Commander Folger, Chief of Ordnance, who had been much impressed with the possibilities of submarines after witnessing a test of the Baker boat in Lake Michigan. Commander G. A. Converse, president of the Torpedo Board, also made a report certifying that it was his belief that a larger vessel operating on the Baker principles would, with some modifications, prove valuable for defensive and offensive purposes.

France at this date was the only other country which was giving official encouragement to the development of the submarine. She was conducting experiments with the *Gymnote*, a small vessel of the diving type, and had under construction a much larger vessel to be operated on the same principle. This vessel was afterward called the *Gustave Zédé*, but she did not go into commission for some time, as her submerged control was found to be bad. One report of her trials states that, "with the committee of engineers on board, her performance in attempting to keep an even depth line was most erratic, and frequently a thirty-degree inclination was reached before the boat could be brought up. On one occasion she hit the bottom in ten fathoms with sufficient force to unseat the engineering experts."

The *Gymnote* was five feet ten inches in diameter amidships and fifty-nine feet ten inches in length. The *Gustave Zédé* was ten feet nine inches in diameter and one hundred forty-eight feet long. It is very difficult to secure sufficient metacentric height in a boat of the above proportions, which probably accounted largely for their erratic behavior when submerged.

In response to the United States Government's advertisement for designs of submarine boats, only three inventors submitted plans and specifications. These were Mr. George C. Baker, Mr. J. P. Holland, and myself. Mr. Baker submitted designs of a boat sixty feet in length and of about one hundred and twenty tons displacement. This vessel was expected to have a speed of about eight miles per hour. The method of submerged control and known characteristics were the same as have already been described in connection with his boat as built in 1892. Mr. Holland proposed to build a vessel eighty-five feet in length, eleven and one-half feet in diameter, of one hundred and sixty-eight tons submerged displacement, and of one hundred and fifty-four tons light displacement. This gave a surface "reserve of buoyancy" of only fourteen tons, or less than ten per cent. The method of control was by the use of vertical and horizontal rudders on the same principle as was used in his *Fenian Ram*, described above.

In 1897 Mr. Holland published in *Cassier's Magazine* an article on submarine navigation, giving some of his experiences with the *Fenian Ram*. This article explains very well the state of the art of submarine navigation in 1893. One of the early difficulties encountered was how to know the direction one was going when submerged. Referring to his experience in the *Fenian Ram*, Mr. Holland said:

"Experience with submarine boats had been so very limited up to 1881 that more difficulty in steering a straight course by compass while submerged than while moving on the surface was scarcely expected. The writer had no suspicion that his boat could not be steered perfectly until he had tried it after making about half a dozen preliminary dives to adjust the automatic apparatus. Having become doubtful of the reliability of the compass, he had it carefully compensated, and then made a trial submerged run in New York Harbor, heading the vessel toward a point which he knew was about twelve minutes' run distant.

"The boat dived at an inclination of about fifteen degrees, and it was noticed that when she again reached a horizontal position the compass needle swung around a complete circle and vibrated a good deal before coming to rest. The boat was then discovered to be about ninety degrees off her course. It was steered again in the proper direction, and then inclined upward at a sharp angle to find whether the action of the compass would be as erratic while rising as while running downward. One end of the needle dipped to the bottom of the cup when beginning the ascent, and remained there during the rise. When the boat approached a horizontal position, a few feet below the surface, the needle swung around as violently as it had done during the boat's descent, and then came to rest again at a point that indicated the boat to be far off the true course.

"As it appeared quite clear that the run was not made in the direction intended, and that about one mile must have been covered from the start, ten minutes having already passed, the boat was brought to the surface of the water just in time to prevent her from running on rocks that lay about twenty yards straight ahead and sixty yards down from the starting point.

"The boat had been started to run over one mile up stream, and the mile-run ended sixty yards down stream, with the boat heading exactly opposite to her original direction. This erratic action of the compass was discovered to be due to heeling, or inclining from the horizontal position, and that it could not be corrected in that boat on account of the near proximity to the compass needle of considerable masses of iron that were liable to have their position changed while the vessel was submerged."

To overcome the above-mentioned difficulties, Mr. Holland invented a device and was granted a patent (No. 492,960) for a triangular drag, which was expected to keep the vessel on a true course when under water. This triangular drag was the novel feature of Mr. Holland's 1893 design, and was intended automatically to steer the vessel on a straight course when submerged. It was intended to operate on the following ingenious principle:

While the vessel was running on the surface the steering gear was under the control of the steersman. In this condition the compass could be adjusted, as the vessel was on a substantially level keel and the masses of metal remained fixed in their relation to the compass, but when the vessel was caused to dive the masses of metal changed their relation to the adjusting magnets and the compass was thrown out of true. Therefore, on beginning a dive the vessel was first started on the surface on the course it was intended to follow submerged until the triangular drag, being drawn through the water, assumed a direction parallel to the axial line of the boat by reason of the rush of water against said drag, and especially against the rib thereon. As soon as the boat was on her course the steersman was expected to disconnect his hand steering gear and allow the drag to control the rudder to hold her to her original course. Mr. Holland maintained that any departure from a straight line would cause the drag to produce swinging motion of a lever, which was expected to throw the rudder in a reverse direction, thus returning the ship to her original course.

Another automatic steering device operated by the pressure of the water was expected to automatically control the depth of submergence, it being only necessary, theoretically, to move a control lever to a point on a dial corresponding to the desired or predetermined depth of submergence, and the horizontal diving rudder would then be automatically manipulated to incline the bow of the boat down so as to dive until the desired depth was reached and then to be manipulated to throw the bow up or down to maintain that depth.

In further describing his 1893 design for the *Plunger*, for which he received the award based on a guarantee of performance, Mr. Holland describes her as follows:

"The boat now being built for the United States Government satisfies all the requirements detailed earlier in this article. It will have a length over all of eighty-five feet, and diameter of eleven and one-half feet; total displacement, one hundred and sixty-eight tons, and a light displacement of one hundred and fifty-four tons. The guaranteed speed on the surface will be fifteen knots, the speed awash fourteen knots, and submerged eight knots. At full speed the boat will have an endurance of twelve hours and a radius of action of one thousand miles at slower speed. The endurance, when submerged, will be ten hours at a speed of six knots. The boat will be propelled by triple screws, operated by three independent sets of triple-expansion steam engines, capable of developing 1625 indicated horsepower. There will also be electric storage batteries and a motor of 70 horsepower for submerged running. The armament will consist of two expulsion tubes and five Whitehead torpedoes.

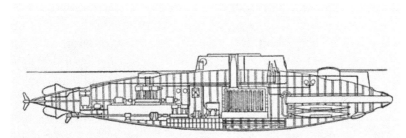

THE PLUNGER (HOLLAND TYPE SUBMARINE), LAUNCHED IN AUGUST, 1897

Machinery not drawn to scale. The engines of 1,600 horse-power, with the necessary auxiliaries, nearly filled the after portion of the vessel.

"Steering on the horizontal plane while submerged is accomplished by an automatic apparatus that performed very well in one of the boat's predecessors. Steering in the vertical plane is also done automatically, and with considerable exactness, while submerged. Steering in both planes can also, at the same time, be controlled manually. There will be a steel armored turret, four feet high, to protect the pilot and smokestack, and the hull will be covered by three feet of water while the vessel runs awash to attack.

"When engaged in harbor defence duty its position will be outside the outer line of harbor defences; that is, beyond the reach of the guns defending the entrance. While performing this duty it will lie awash; that is, with only the top of its turret over the surface of the water. On the approach of an enemy's vessel the smokestack will be shipped and the aperture on top of the turret through which it passed will be quickly closed watertight. She will then run in a direction to intercept the enemy's ship, still remaining in the awash condition, until she comes near enough to be discovered by the lookouts on the ship, when she will go from the awash to the entirely submerged condition. The distance from the ship at which she will dive will depend upon the weather. In rough weather she can come quite close without being observed. Having come within a distance that the operator estimates at two or three hundred yards from the ship, the diving rudders are manipulated so as to cause the top of the turret to come for a few seconds above the surface of the water. During this short exposure of the turret—much too short to give the enemy a chance to find its distance and train a gun on it capable of inflicting any injury—the pilot ascertains the bearing of the enemy's ship, alters his course or makes another dive if necessary. If he finds that the submarine boat is within safe striking distance, say one hundred yards, a Whitehead torpedo is discharged at the ship. A heavy explosion within six seconds after the torpedo is expelled will notify the operator that his attack has been successful, and he may then devote his attention to the next enemy's ship that may be within reach. When the boat is running on the surface of the water, with full steam power, and it becomes necessary to dive quickly, the pilot gives the order, 'Prepare to dive.' The oil fuel is instantly shut off from the furnace, the valves are opened to admit water to the water-ballast tanks, an electric engine draws down the smokestack and air-shaft into the superstructure, and moves a large, massive sliding valve over the aperture on the turret through which the smokestack passes. These operations will be completed in about thirty seconds, when the boat is in the awash condition and prepared to dive. In twenty seconds more it will be running horizontally at a depth of twenty feet below the surface of the water and quite beyond reach of the enemy's projectiles."

I submitted designs of a twin-screw vessel eighty feet long, ten feet beam, and one hundred fifteen tons displacement, with 400-horsepower steam engines for surface propulsion and 70-horsepower motors for submerged work. This design introduced several new and striking features into the art of submarine navigation which have been the cause of considerable scientific discussion. The design called for a *double hull* vessel, the spaces between the inner and outer hulls forming water-ballast tanks; the design also called for twin screws and four torpedo tubes, two firing forward and two aft.

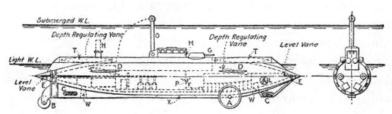

LAKE DESIGN AS SUBMITTED TO THE U. S. NAVY DEPARTMENT IN 1893

Novel features consisted in: (A) wheels for running on the bottom; (B) rudder forming also a steering wheel when navigating on the bottom; (C-C) propellers for holding vessel to depth when not under way; (D-D) depth regulating vanes or hydroplanes for causing vessel to change depth while under way and to accomplish the changes of depth on an even keel; (E-E) horizontal rudders or "leveling vanes" designed to automatically hold the vessel on a level keel when under way; (F) a weight automatically controlled by a pendulum; (P) mechanism to correct trim; (G) gun arranged in watertight revolving turret for defense purposes or attack on unarmored surface craft; (L) propeller in tube for swinging vessel at rest to facilitate "pointing" her torpedoes; (M) conning tower; (N) telescoping smokestack; (O) observing instrument arranged to turn down on deck when under way; (T-T) torpedo tubes, two firing forward and two aft; (W-W) anchoring weights to hold the vessel at rest at any desired depth between the surface and bottom; (X) an "emergency keel" which would be automatically released if the vessel reached an unsafe depth. She was a double-hull vessel, water being admitted to the space between the inner and outer hulls and in trim tanks forward and aft to effect submergence. A diving compartment was also provided to enable the crew to leave or enter the vessel while submerged.

The novel feature which attracted the most attention and scepticism regarding this design was—so I was later informed by a member of the Board—in the claim made that the vessel could readily navigate over the water-bed itself and that while navigating on the water-bed a door could be opened in the bottom of a compartment and the water kept from entering the vessel by means of compressed air, and that the crew could, by donning diving suits, readily leave and enter the vessel while submerged. Another novel feature was in the method of controlling the depth of submergence when navigating between the surface and the water-bed. The vessel was designed always to submerge and navigate on a level keel rather than to be inclined down or up by the bow to dive or rise. This maintenance of a level keel while submerged was provided for by the installation of four depth-regulating vanes, which I later termed "hydroplanes" to distinguish them from the forward and aft levelling vanes or horizontal rudders. These hydroplanes were located at equal distances forward and aft of the centre of gravity and buoyancy of the vessel when in the submerged condition, so as not to disturb the trim of the vessel when the planes were inclined down or up to cause the vessel to submerge or rise when under way. I also used, in conjunction with the hydroplanes, horizontal rudders, which I called "levelling vanes," as their purpose was just the opposite from that of the horizontal rudder used in the diving type of vessel. They were operated by a pendulum-controlling device to be inclined so as always to maintain the vessel on a level keel rather than cause her to depart therefrom. When I came to try this combination out in practice I found hand control of the horizontal rudders was sufficient. If vessels with this system of control have a sufficient amount of stability, they will run for hours and *automatically maintain both a constant depth and a level keel*, without the depth-control man touching either the hydroplane or horizontal rudder control gear. This automatic maintenance of depth without manipulating the hydroplanes or rudders was a performance not anticipated or claimed in my original patent on the above-mentioned combination, and what caused these vessels to function in this manner remained a mystery, which was left unsolved until I built a model tank in 1905, in Berlin, Germany, and conducted a series of experiments on models of submarines. I then learned that the down pull of a hydroplane with a given degree of inclination varied according to its depth of submergence, and the deeper the submergence the less down pull. This works out to give automatic maintenance of depth so long as the vessel is kept at a constant trim on a substantially level keel, and I have known of vessels running for a period of over two hours without variation of depth of one foot and without once changing the inclination of either the hydroplanes or the horizontal rudder.

The capability of this arrangement of hydroplanes and horizontal rudders to control the depth of submergence was questioned and doubted for many years. As late as 1902, nearly ten years after I first submitted this method of control to the United States Navy Department, Naval Constructor L. Y. Spear, U. S. N., testifying before the Committee of Naval Affairs, House of Representatives, in reference to the "Lake even-keel boat" and my use of hydroplanes, said, "As an expert I do not think he will make his hydroplanes work"; and strongly contended that submergence by inclining the vessel itself was the proper method.

Several years later, in 1908, in Paris, I met Captain Lauboeuf, the celebrated French naval constructor, who has perhaps done more toward perfecting the French submarines than any other designer, and he informed me that after the French Government had its sad experience in the loss of the *Lutine* and *Farfadet* with their crews, it had changed all their diving boats into even-keel boats and was now using substantially my method of even-keel submergence with hydroplane control. He also informed me that it had, at that time, thirty-five new boats under construction to operate on the even-keel principle, eighteen of which were of five hundred and fifty tons displacement. Captain Lauboeuf was kind enough to compliment me as having been the first to introduce this method of submerged control.

Commander Murray F. Sueter, Royal British Navy, in his most complete work on "The Evolution of the Submarine Boat, Mine and Torpedo, from the Sixteenth Century to the Present Time," published in 1907, said:

"After scrutinizing all the information available, I am certain that several features of the 'Lake' design will be embodied by most nations in the construction of future boats, the chief of which, perhaps, are 'the even-keel method of submergence' in preference to the 'dynamical dive' of the Holland boats; also the provision of a safety keel and diving compartment. This latter forms a ready means of communicating with the surface should the boat, through some small mishap, find herself on the bottom and unable to rise."

Sir Trevor Dawson, formerly (R. N.) manager of "Vickers," in discussing submarine boats before the Institution of Naval Architects in 1907, said:

"Mr. Lake mentioned the question of the importance of horizontal stability and the use of hydroplanes. I think these have been used by the Holland Company in America in connection with the experiments they made for the American Government. In one of the boats I saw they gave me particulars of such experiments. I know, too, that they have been used considerably in France with satisfactory results, and I think his contention as to the importance of horizontal stability, as things exist to-day, is fully justified."

Captain Edgar Lees (R. N.), who was the officer in charge of the British submarines, said:

"I may say, with regard to the features that Mr. Lake has brought to our notice—the hydroplane, for instance, and getting good freeboard and seaworthy boats—the mere fact that they have been largely copied and that most nations build these submarine boats is, as Mr. Lake contends, a conclusive proof that he has been for years on the right tack. Well, I do not think at the present moment submarine boats are being built in any country without hydroplanes, in order to dive, if desired, almost horizontally."

One of the latest contract requirements of the United States Government, specifying the characteristics of the new boats to be built under the appropriation for submarines for the year 1915, stated:

"The vessel shall make also the necessary trials to demonstrate her ability to effect initial submergence, to maintain submergence under way, and to change depths without exceeding an angle of inclination of one degree." This, in substance, calls for "even-keel submergence" when one considers that it was common for early boats of the diving type to take on an inclination of fifteen to twenty degrees, and inclinations of as much as forty-five degrees were not unknown.

All governments and submarine builders have at present in their latest boats adopted the method of even-keel submergence by the use of hydroplanes, and I am gratified that this method of control has been finally adopted as the standard, as I believe none of the latest modern submarine boats will make the uncontrollable dives to the bottom common in the boats of the diving type, which have been accompanied in many cases by the loss of their crews.

I did not make a proposal to build a boat from my designs as submitted in 1893, but offered to coöperate with the government in developing submarines under my patents, which were then pending, on such terms as the government might desire. Not being fortunate enough, however, to secure the financial assistance of the government in developing my inventions for the protection of our country, I turned my attention for a time to applying my inventions to commercial purposes and to prove the practicability of navigating on the bottom.

For this purpose I built, in 1894, the *Argonaut, Jr.*, which I mentioned in the preceding chapter, and will now describe more fully. This vessel was provided with three wheels, two on either side forward and one aft, the latter acting as a steering wheel. When on the bottom the wheels were rotated by hand by one or two men inside the boat. Her displacement was about seven tons, yet she could be propelled at a moderate walking gait when on the bottom. She was also fitted with an air-lock and diver's compartment, so arranged that by putting an air pressure on the diver's compartment equal to the water pressure outside a bottom door could be opened and no water could come into the vessel. Then by putting on a pair of rubber boots the operator could walk around on the sea bottom and push the boat along with him and pick up objects, such as clams, oysters, etc., from the sea bottom.

Experiments with this vessel on the bottom of Sandy Hook Bay convinced a sufficient number of people who were permitted to witness the experiments that submarine navigation in this manner was practicable, and I succeeded in raising sufficient capital to build a larger vessel to continue my experiments on a broader scale. Therefore, in 1895, I designed the *Argonaut*.

"ARGONAUT" AS ORIGINALLY BUILT. LAUNCHED IN AUGUST, 1897

Built to further demonstrate the possibility of navigation over the waterbed of seas or the ocean. She covered thousands of miles in her experimental work, testing out the practicability of the submarine for various kinds of commercial work.

At this time I was living in Baltimore, Md., so I made a contract with the Columbian Iron Works and Dry Dock Company, of that city, for her construction. This company was also building for the Holland Torpedo Boat Company the *Plunger*, which was being constructed for the government under the 1893 appropriation. Both vessels were completed about the same time. They were launched in August, 1897, and went into dry dock together.

The *Argonaut*, as originally built, was thirty-six feet long and nine feet in diameter. She was the first submarine to be operated successfully with an internal-combustion engine. She was propelled with a thirty-horsepower gasolene (petrol) engine driving a single-screw propeller. She was fitted with two toothed driving wheels forward, which were revolved by suitable gearing when navigating on the water-bed. They could be disconnected from this gearing and permitted to revolve freely, propulsion being secured by the screw propeller. A wheel in the rudder enabled her to be steered in any direction when on the bottom. She also had a divers' compartment to enable divers to leave or enter the vessel when submerged, so as to operate on wrecks or to permit inspection of the bottom or to recover

150

shellfish. She also had a lookout compartment in the extreme bow, with a powerful searchlight to light up a pathway in front of her as she moved along over the water-bed. This searchlight I later found of little value except for night work in clear water. In clear water the sunlight would permit of as good vision without the use of the light as with it; while, if the water was not clear, no amount of light would permit of vision through it for any considerable distance.

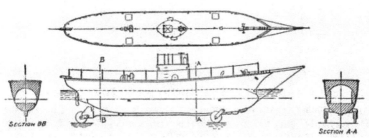

THE "ARGONAUT" AFTER LENGTHENING AND ADDITION OF BUOYANT, SHIP-SHAPED SUPERSTRUCTURE, INCREASING THE SURFACE BUOYANCY OVER 40 PER CENT

As the *Argonaut* was principally built in order to further test out the possibility of navigating on the water-bed in exploration and commercial work, she was propelled, both when on the surface and submerged, by her gasolene (petrol) engines. Storage batteries were carried only for lighting purposes. The air to run her engines was first drawn into the vessel through a hose extending to a buoy floating on the surface. Later she was fitted with pipe masts, which enabled her to navigate on the bottom in depths up to fifty feet. She functioned satisfactorily from the start. We found we could readily navigate over any kind of bottom, soft or hard, by regulating her buoyancy to suit, and she would, due to her buoyancy, readily climb over any obstruction that did not reach higher than her forefoot.

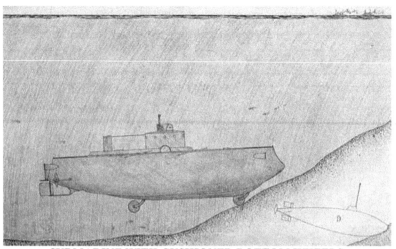

SUBMARINE WITH CUSHIONED BOTTOM WHEELS

Showing how such a vessel will surmount a steep declivity while a boat of the diving type (D) will likely "bury her nose" into it or strike with sufficient force to disarrange her machinery. If the submarine has sufficient statical stability she will maintain substantially a level keel even when riding over a steep declivity.

There were three things which caused us to delay her departure on a submarine exploration trip for a few weeks. The first was the escape of gasolene (petrol) fumes in the boat. When first built, fuel tanks were built in the hull itself and formed an integral part of the vessel. Special care was given to make these fuel tanks tight. They were tested under hydraulic pressure and found to be tight, but the fumes from gasolene (petrol) are very searching, and, after filling the fuel tanks and keeping them filled over night, gasolene fumes were found to exist in the boat the next morning to such an extent that I would not venture to make a start until a fuel tank had been built outside of the vessel, where any escape of fumes would not form an explosive mixture. I followed this practice in all our later gasolene-engined boats, which largely eliminated the danger from carrying gasolene as a fuel. A number of explosions have occurred in other types of gasolene-propelled boats, in some cases with fatal results, from gasolene fuel being carried in built-up tanks within the hull itself.

The next cause of delay was due to the escape of and collection of carbon monoxide within the vessel. This developed on our first submarine run. After we had been down about two hours some of us commenced to experience a dull pain at the base of the brain and a decided feeling of lassitude. On coming to the surface a couple of our men collapsed completely, and one was very sick all night. I could not understand the cause of this, as nothing of the kind had occurred in my previous hand-propelled vessel, so we made another submerged run the following day, and after about the same period of time the pain in the head and weariness came on again. I then discovered that the engine would occasionally backfire out into the boat and that gas was escaping past the piston rings into the base of the engine and from there into the boat. To overcome this difficulty I installed what I called an induction tank, which was piped up to the air intake of the engine and also the engine base. A check valve admitted air into this induction tank. When the engine was started the check valve was automatically lifted and induced a flow of air through the tank, in which a slight vacuum was maintained, which also served to draw the gases out from the engine base. In case of a backfire, the check valve automatically closed and the gases from the backfire were caught in the induction tank, from which they were drawn out on the next stroke of the engine. This solved the difficulty, and thereafter the air was always fresh and pure when running submerged even after a submergence of several hours' duration.

Like Mr. Holland, I also had difficulty on our first submergence in always knowing where we were going. Our compass was first installed in the boat itself, where it was surrounded by steel. The compass adjuster had searched for and found what he considered the most *neutral* place in the ship to install the compass, and had adjusted it by magnets in the usual manner, but it was too "loggy" for correct navigation and we were forced finally to install it in a bronze binnacle directly over the conning tower, where it could be viewed by mirrors from the steersman's station. This cut out most of the adjusting magnets, and the compass was nearly accurate on all courses. Submarine navigation thus became reliable.

On the completion of these changes the *Argonaut* was taken down the Chesapeake Bay to Hampton Roads, where several months were spent in examining the bottom conditions in the bay and out on the ocean, and in locating and picking up cables and in examining wrecks. The Spanish-American War was on at this time, and an effort was made to interest the government officials in charge of the mines at Fortress Monroe. I tried to get some of the officers to go down in the

Argonaut and see how easily observation mine cables could be located and cut if desired, as I was making almost daily submerged runs in their vicinity. Finally I received peremptory orders not to submerge within a mile of the mine fields, as I might accidentally sever one of the cables, and then, as the officer in charge said, "There would be the devil to pay in Washington."

It was about this time that Admiral Sampson's fleet was holding at great expense its long vigil outside of Santiago, waiting for Cervera's fleet to come out. Our fleet was kept outside the harbor for fear of the mines, while here in Hampton Roads all this time was a vessel capable of clearing away the mine fields, but which was not given serious consideration, as it was thought that the submarine was impracticable. Experiments were also made showing the possibility of establishing submarine telephone stations at known locations on the bottom of the ocean. In January, 1898, while the *Argonaut* was submerged, telephonic conversation was held from submerged stations with Baltimore, Washington, and New York. In 1898, also, the *Argonaut* made the trip from Norfolk to New York under her own power and unescorted. In her original form she was a cigar-shaped craft, with only a small percentage of reserve buoyancy in her surface cruising condition. We were caught out in the severe November northeast storm of 1898 in which over two hundred vessels were lost, and we did not succeed in reaching a harbor in the "horseshoe" back of Sandy Hook until three o'clock in the morning. The seas were so rough, and broke over her conning tower in such masses, that I was obliged to lash myself fast to prevent being swept overboard. It was freezing weather, and I was soaked and covered with ice on reaching harbor.

This experience caused me to apply to the *Argonaut* a further improvement, for which I had already applied for a patent. This was to build around the usual pressure-resisting body of a submarine a ship-shape form of light plating which would give greater seaworthiness, better lines for surface speed, and make the vessel more habitable for surface navigation. It would, in other words, make a "sea-going submarine," which the usual form of cigar-shaped vessel was not, as it did not have sufficient surface buoyancy to enable it to rise with the seas, and the seas would sweep over it as they would sweep over a partly submerged rock.

**THE "ARGONAUT," AFTER BEING LENGTHENED AND REBUILT, IN 1898,
SHOWING SHIP-SHAPED, WATERTIGHT, BUOYANT SUPERSTRUCTURE**

The *Argonaut* was therefore taken to Brooklyn, twenty feet added to her length, and a light, watertight, buoyant superstructure of ship-shape form added. This superstructure was opened to the sea when it was desired to submerge the vessel, and water was permitted to enter the space between the light plating of the ship-shape form and the heavy plating of the pressure-resisting hull. This equalized the pressure on the light plates and prevented their becoming deformed, due to pressure. The superstructure increased her reserve of buoyancy in the surface cruising condition from about ten per cent. to over forty per cent., and she would rise to the seas like any ordinary type of surface vessel, instead of being buried by them in rough weather.

This feature of construction has been adopted by the Germans, Italians, Russians, and in all the latest types of French boats. It is the principal feature which distinguishes them in their surface appearance from the earlier cigar-shaped boats of the diving type. This ship-shape form of hull is only suited to level-keel submergence, and must be controlled by hydroplanes.

I also departed from the cigar-shaped inner hull and was granted a patent on a form of pressure-resisting hull with rising axes. This improvement overcame the tendency to dive by the head common to the cigar-shaped form, increased the surface speed on an equivalent displacement, and gave a considerable increase in metacentric height over a vessel of equivalent length and beam.

Some incorrectly informed writers of books and magazines have, through their lack of complete information, given the credit of inventing and developing this seagoing type of submersible to the Krupps of Germany, to former Naval Constructor Lauboeuf, of France, or to former Naval Constructor Laurenti, of Italy. For the purpose of giving a correct history of this development, perhaps I may be pardoned and not considered overconceited if I mention a few facts in connection with the development of this type of boat in European countries.

On April 2, 1897, I applied for a patent on a combined surface and submarine vessel, the specifications of which began as follows:

"This invention relates to a combined surface and submarine vessel and may be employed either as a torpedo boat *or for freight and general cruising purposes*, or for submarine work of all kinds. It has for its object, first, to combine with a submarine vessel cylindrical in cross-section a superstructure built upon the submarine vessel and affording a large deck surface, buoyancy, and a high freeboard for surface navigation, the space between the submarine vessel and the superstructure adapted to being filled with water when the vessel is submerged, and thus rendered capable of resisting the pressure of the water, etc." A patent was granted in due course with fifty claims, and, according to the records of patent offices throughout the world, this is the pioneer patent covering this form of vessel.

When Krupps took up the matter of constructing submarines for the Russian and German governments, they decided upon this type of vessel, as they held that it offered a greater opportunity for development than the diving type. A contract was drawn with their directors for the construction of the "Lake" type of boat, which they accepted by wire. This contract covered the erection of a plant in Russia for the manufacture of "Lake" submarines on a division of profits and also the construction of ships in Germany on a royalty basis. It also covered my employment by them in an advisory capacity. I was living abroad at the time, and the papers were sent to my directors in America for their approval.

In the meantime I had submitted to them various plans of submarines, copies of my patents, and even my secret data, including copies of patents pending, all to enable them to go ahead, as I considered the agreement settled by their wire of acceptance. I had also advised them how to overcome certain difficulties in boats which they then had under construction for the Russian Government at their Kiel plant, the Germania Werft.

Before I succeeded in getting the power of attorney from my directors in America authorizing me to sign up the agreement, the great industrial revolution started in Russia, immediately after the Russo-Japanese war, and the Krupps informed me that, owing to that fact, they had reconsidered their idea of going into Russia and withdrew from the arrangement. Their attorney in Berlin informed me that on looking up the patent situation they had found that "I had not protected myself in Germany and that they were free to build 'Lake' type boats in Germany and expected to continue to do so." This was true, for, like most pioneer inventors, I had not succeeded in securing sufficient capital to finance and protect my fundamental inventions in all countries, which would have involved very large amounts in taking them out and paying the yearly tax.

So much for Germany.

In 1905, while residing in Berlin, Germany, I was called to Rome and sat three days with a commission appointed by Admiral Mirabello, at that time Italian Minister of Marine, regarding their construction of submarines. I then learned that the Italian Government had started on a plan of building submarines of substantially my type, that they had several under construction at their Venice Arsenal after the design of Major Laurenti, a naval constructor; that certain difficulties which they explained to me had arisen, and that they had not succeeded in getting any of their boats to function satisfactorily submerged. I came to the conclusion that their trouble was due to lack of longitudinal stability, and advised the Commission how to increase this. Shortly afterward I was advised that they had corrected their trouble and that the boats then worked satisfactorily.

Major Laurenti, at this time, resigned from the Italian Navy and became affiliated with the Fiat Company, and has designed quite a large number of successful submarine boats, all of which have buoyant superstructures and are designed to operate on a level keel by the use of hydroplanes. These boats are of the "Lake" type, so far as invention goes.

There is a difference, however, between invention and design. Invention introduces a new method, a new principle, or a new form of construction, to accomplish a certain purpose in a new way. Many modifications of design may be made which do not involve invention.

As an illustration, on August 14, 1907, Major Laurenti applied for a United States patent on a submarine or submersible boat in which the attempt was made to secure a patent on slight variations of design over the "Lake" type. The patent office records show that many amendments were made and hearings held in the endeavor to evade the foundation patent of Lake, No. 650,758, which was applied for April 2, 1897, over ten years before Laurenti applied for a patent. The patent office consistently and persistently held that the slight difference in design did not involve invention over "Lake." After arguments and hearings, extending over a period of over three years, Major Laurenti was finally obliged to accept a patent restricted to details of construction, most of which were in themselves not new to me, as they had already been used in various modifications of my inventions and consisted in such changes as would naturally be worked out by any good hull or engine draftsmen while developing the designs of a vessel.

Our patent laws are too free in allowing the granting of patents on modifications of design while fundamental patents are still in force. This works great hardship on original inventors, forcing them to take out a great many patents on features of design rather than on invention. I have taken out nearly one hundred United States patents with over one thousand one hundred claims covering a few fundamental inventions, some of which cover details of construction for which I should not have been forced to seek protection.

All original inventors complain of this system. I know of several instances where patents on modifications of design have been granted, which modifications have been in common use for several years by others, but were only considered as a design and not as an invention. Then some designer hits on the same arrangement and considers he has made an invention, and applies for and takes out a patent which has already been in common use but has been looked upon purely as a design by its originator rather than an invention. Then the original designer may be hauled up before the courts and put to great expense to prove that it was in prior use as a design.

While Captain Lauboeuf and the Krupps have taken out several patents on detail mechanisms for use on submarine boats, they have never—so far as I am aware or the patent records show—attempted to claim to be the original inventors of the type of submarine with buoyant ship-shaped form of hull consisting of a pressure-resisting body surmounted by a watertight, non-pressure-resisting body which gives suitable form for surface speed and seaworthiness, which is the principal characteristic of vessels built by them. I feel, therefore, that certain misinformed authors should, in the interests of the truth, correct their statements if they issue new editions of their work or write further on the development of the submarine.

During the years of practical experimental work with the *Argonaut*, Mr. Holland continued in his efforts to get the *Plunger*—building under the 1893 appropriation—in shape for submerged trials, but without success.

The large steam installation, sixteen hundred horsepower, was largely responsible for this. As I remember, there was only about eighteen inches between the main engines, with large steam supply and exhaust pipes overhead and under foot. These engines were designed to run at over four hundred revolutions per minute. The boiler was located nearly in the centre of the vessel and so nearly filled the ship that there was barely room between the top of the boiler and ship to creep from "forward to aft."

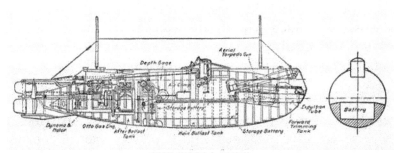

THE "HOLLAND"

This vessel, while holding to the same general principles of construction and method of control as used in the "Plunger," was much better proportioned and had a much better distribution of weights. It was her performance that led the House Naval Committee in 1900 to authorize the construction of additional submarines of the Holland type. Her armament consisted of one torpedo tube forward and an aerial torpedo gun for firing aerial torpedoes, designed to be used somewhat on the same principles as used on the gunboat "Vesuvius."

The heat was so intense that the trial crew found it impossible to live in the boat, so for their full power dock trials valve stems were run up through the deck to enable the engines to be started from there. Arrangements were made also to take the indicator cards from the deck. She was also fitted with a heavy armored conning tower, as per Mr. Holland's description previously quoted. This, combined with the high position of the boiler and engines, together with her cigar-shaped form, which gives a diminishing water plane, reduced her stability almost to zero. I was informed that when the attempt was first made to start up one of her engines her stability was so little that the turning effort on her propeller shaft nearly caused her to "turn turtle," and that she rolled over on her side to such an extent that the conning tower struck the dock stringer. The constructor at the Columbian Iron Works then put heavy chains on her so that she could not turn over. Every inducement was made to the Holland Company to enable it to make this vessel satisfactory, as Congress, in 1896, authorized the Secretary of the Navy to contract for two more "submarine torpedo boats of the Holland type, *provided* that the Holland boat now being built for the Department shall be accepted by the Department as fulfilling all the requirements of the Contract." She was finally abandoned in 1900 without ever making a submerged run or fulfilling any of her guarantees of performance under which the award was secured. Mr. Holland as early as 1897 must have concluded that the *Plunger* was destined to failure. In fact, no submarine, even up to the present day, has ever equalled the performance guaranteed under the *Plunger's* contract. He therefore built a much smaller boat, called the *Holland*. This vessel was fitted with internal-combustion engines instead of steam, and was finally accepted by the United States Government in lieu of the *Plunger*, and placed in commission in 1900. She was the first submarine torpedo boat to go into commission in the United States Navy. Her characteristics were: Length, fifty-three feet four inches; beam, ten feet three inches; displacement, sixty-four tons surface, seventy-five tons submerged; power, internal-combustion engines, fifty horsepower; surface speed, six to seven knots claimed; submerged speed, five knots claimed. The only official report I have seen gave her a surface speed of five and two-thirds knots. I believe she was purchased by the authority of the Act of June 7, 1900, which read as follows: "The Secretary of the Navy is hereby authorized and directed to contract for five submarine torpedo boats of the 'Holland' type of the most improved design, at a price not to exceed one hundred and seventy thousand dollars (£35,000) each: *Provided*, That such boats shall be similar in dimensions to the proposed new 'Holland,' plans and specifications of which were submitted to the Navy Department by the Holland Torpedo Boat Company, November twenty-third, eighteen hundred and ninety-nine."

THE "HOLLAND" RUNNING ON THE SURFACE
Courtesy of the Engineering Magazine

The United States was, therefore, at the beginning of the twentieth century, fairly launched on a policy of submarine boat construction, and other governments rapidly followed suit. France had, in the meantime, brought out two new boats, the *Morse*, 1898, and the *Narval*, after the designs of M. Lauboeuf, launched October 26, 1899. The *Gustave Zédé* had also been modified by adding hydroplanes so that she became controllable submerged.

The *Morse* was one hundred and eighteen feet long by eight feet three inches beam, with a displacement of one hundred and thirty-six tons, of about the same type as the *Gustave Zédé*. The *Narval* was one hundred and eleven feet six inches in length by twelve feet four inches beam; one hundred and six tons surface displacement and one hundred and sixty-eight tons submerged. She was, like the author's 1893 design, a double hull vessel controlled by hydroplanes. She was fitted with "Dzrewiecke" apparatus for carrying and discharging torpedoes, two of which were carried on either side. The *Narval* was a successful type and appears to have been the first French naval vessel to adopt a ship-shape outer hull of lighter plating. She was also, so far as my records show, the first French boat to be fitted with two motive powers—viz., steam for surface work and electricity for submerged work. To distinguish her in these particulars from the purely electric boats of cigar-shaped form, like the *Gustave Zédé* and *Morse*, Mr. Lauboeuf called her a submersible.

Very little was known about the French boats at this time (1900), as their method of construction and experiments were kept secret, but enough information leaked out as to their reported success to cause the British public much uneasiness, and they began to demand that their Admiralty should also take up the development of the submarine. No one had, so far, evolved a satisfactory type in England, so when the fact became known that the United States Congress had made an appropriation for five Holland boats, the British public became still more insistent that they should also have submarines.

About this time, so I was informed by Sir William White, who was then chief constructor of the British Navy, Lord Rothschild brought to him Mr. Isaac L. Rice, president of the Electric Boat Company, who controlled the Holland patents and who offered to build duplicates of the United States boats for England. Sir William thought this gave the Admiralty the opportunity to satisfy the public demands and to meet the French, their hereditary enemy—this was before the establishment of the "Entente Cordiale"—in their development of the submarine. Consequently an arrangement was made for the manufacture of this type of vessel for England by the Vickers Company. An agreement was drawn, so Sir William informed me, giving "Vickers" an exclusive monopoly of building submarines for the British Navy for a period of ten years, the consideration being that they should have available for the use of the British Admiralty all the details of the development work of the Electric Boat Company in America. This, plus their own experience and development work in England, which should be kept secret, should enable England to keep on an equal footing with France.

Sir William informed me that he thought this had been a mistake in policy, as it had deprived the government of the opportunity to secure improvements that had been developed by other inventors and builders who had made greater progress on independent lines.

England, therefore, started to build her first submarine, known as the "A" type. These were practically duplicates of the United States *Adder* and *Moccasin* type, now also designated as "A's" Nos. 1 to 7. England has been particularly unfortunate with this class of submarine, several of them having plunged to the bottom with the loss of their crews during peace-time manœuvres.

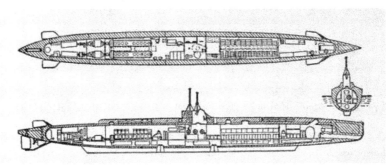

Modern French Submarine of Lauboeuf Design. Constructed by Schneider and Company

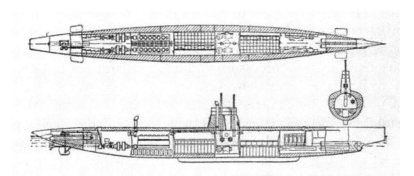

Modern Italian Submarine—Fiat Construction—Laurenti Design. Vessel of the Double Hull Buoyant Superstructure. Hydroplane Controlled Type

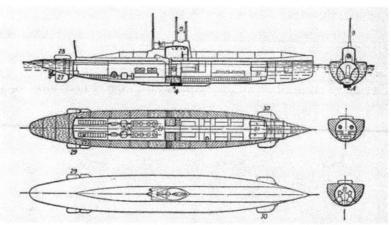

German "U" Boat—Krupp Design VARIOUS TYPES OF MODERN FOREIGN SUBMARINES

27 and 28, vertical rudders; 29 and 30, hydroplanes for controlling depth of submergence; 9, periscopes; 21, engines; 20, motors; 22, storage batteries; 4, drop keel; 31, torpedo tubes.

The majority of the British and American boats are developments from the original *Holland* of Mr. Holland's design. Increasing the stability, greater subdivision of ballast compartments, refinements in steering gear, and the addition of hydroplanes forward have enabled Mr. Holland and his successors to produce submarines that operate very well. These boats, however, with only one pair of forward planes, still require constant manipulation of the horizontal rudder to control them when submerged. This rudder, controlled by power gear, is very effective and will, by expert manipulation, hold the submarine to practically even depth. The only danger the writer can see is that the diving rudder gear might fail to function after it is set in the diving position, in which case the vessel might continue diving until she struck bottom or reached a depth great enough to cause her to collapse.

The modern submarines, therefore, as built and used in all the world's navies, owe their final success to principles of construction and control devices invented and introduced into the art by two American inventors.

CHAPTER V

USE OF THE SUBMARINE IN WAR

The submarine boat is the guerilla in warfare. Its tactics are the tactics of the Indian who fights under cover or lies in ambush for his enemy. These are necessarily the tactics of all weaker individuals and are an essential method of procedure in preventing the weaker party from being annihilated by the strong and more powerful. Some people have contended that the submarine is an unfair weapon, but the old statement that "all's fair in love and war" applies to the submarine as it does to every weapon which has been invented since the days when men struggled for supremacy with their bare hands. The first man who wielded the club might have been accused of being unfair; the same term might have been applied to the man who invented the sling-shot or the bow and arrow. When people fight for their existence, the existence of their families or of their country, they do not fight according to the "Marquis of Queensberry Rules." A revolver in the hands of a weak man or a defenceless woman is a proper weapon to enable them to protect their property, their honor, or their life; and, no matter what theorists may claim, the submarine will remain as a weapon to be reckoned with in all future wars, provided there are future wars upon the high seas. In making this assertion I do not intend to justify a great many of the acts performed by the submarines of one of the belligerents in the present war. I do claim, however, that the submarine is a perfectly legitimate naval weapon, and that it deserves a place in the armament of any nation whose military power is maintained for purposes of self-defence.

Above all, I believe the submarine most fitted to act as a weapon in coast-defence operations. Coast-defence submarines will probably be found to be the most important adjunct to the navies of every country whose policy is to defend their own coast lines, rather than to attempt aggressive warfare. Vessels for this purpose do not need to be of great tonnage nor of high speed. Speed is the one thing, more than anything else, which runs up the cost of the submarine vessel. While speed is desirable for the cruising submarine, it is not an essential for a defensive submarine. It is possible to get a speed of fourteen or fifteen knots in a submarine of about five hundred tons displacement, and at the same time have comfortable living quarters for the crew. A boat of this size may carry eight Whitehead torpedoes, each torpedo being capable of destroying a fifteen-million-dollar battleship, and as a five-hundred-ton displacement submarine can be built for about one-half million dollars, and is capable of carrying eight Whitehead torpedoes, potentially good for eight fifteen-million-dollar battleships, or a total of one hundred and twenty million dollars' worth of capital ships, it seems as if that would be sufficient to ask of one little submarine boat. Now to double that speed would require a much larger vessel, and would cost approximately two and one-half million dollars. A two and one-half-million-dollar boat for the defence of harbor entrances or seacoast cities would not carry as many torpedoes as five of the five-hundred-ton boats. A torpedo fired from a small boat is fully as potent as one fired from a two and one-half-million-dollar boat.

These small boats could be located at five different points covering a portion of our coast, and the chances are that at least two of these smaller boats could reach an objective point on the coast line under their protection in shorter time than one large high-speed boat would be able to do. At the same cost they could cover the same area of coast line to a much better advantage, as there would be five of them to protect that area instead of one.

We will assume, for purposes of illustration, that the Sandy Hook entrance to New York Harbor is to be defended. If we strike a fifteen-mile radius from Sandy Hook point, running from the Long Island to the New Jersey shore, and have four submarines take station on that radius line about five miles apart, no ship could pass that radius line without coming within the range of vision of the commander of the submarine, either from his periscope in daylight or at night within the range of hearing of his "submarine ears." The Fessenden oscillators, or microphones, now installed in all submarines, would readily detect the approach of a surface ship or ships. These instruments have been improved to such an extent that it is now possible to carry on wireless conversation under water between one submarine and another for a considerable distance. Communication by the Morse code, or other special codes, may be carried on between submarines up to a distance of several miles.

It would be possible for groups of submarines on station, or picket duty, so to speak, to be in constant communication with shore stations, either by submerged telephone stations or by wireless. In that way the submarines can be kept in constant touch with the country's scouting fleet of high-speed surface vessels or aeroplanes and immediately be notified of the approach of an enemy's fleet or ship. There is no way in which they can themselves be detected, so far as I am aware, as there is no need to run the machinery of the submarine while lying at rest on picket duty, and it would be impossible for a surface ship or flying machine to detect them, providing a constant watch was kept on the horizon or the heavens through the aeroscopes.

As the effective range of the modern Whitehead torpedo is about three miles, no ship could pass between the submarines without passing within torpedo range. However, a commander of a submarine would hardly take a chance of making a hit at such great distance, and on sighting the enemy he would leave his station and attempt to intercept her, so as to get a shot at shorter range. If the enemy succeeded in running the gauntlet of the outer circle it would have to pass the submarines distributed on, say, a ten-mile radius. Three submarines would be able to protect this radius line. A five-mile radius might also be established with two submarines, and one located at the entrance. To enter Sandy Hook, therefore, a ship would have to run the gauntlet of five or six submarines without it being necessary for them to leave their stations.

Submarines with high speed will become valuable as commerce destroyers and for carrying on an offensive warfare. Page 32 shows a high speed, sea-keeping, fleet submarine of the "Lake" type. Its principal characteristics are the same as those of the coast-defence type, except that the buoyant superstructure is increased in height sufficiently to form living quarters for the crew when cruising in surface condition.

One of the essentials of a high-speed sea-going vessel is high-powered machinery. A large portion of the interior of the pressure-resisting hull, therefore, must be devoted to machinery space. The quarters would necessarily be somewhat cramped without a buoyant superstructure, which gives plenty of room for the crew to take exercise and secure plenty of fresh air when off duty, even in rough water. As it is very important to keep the physical and mental condition of the crew in a satisfactory state, it is essential that the men be not kept in restricted quarters for a long period of time.

This vessel is designed to carry torpedoes firing in line with the axes of the ship both fore and aft, and carries, also, torpedo tubes in the superstructure which may be trained to fire to either broadside. Of course, such a vessel as this should be fitted with wireless and sound-transmitting and detecting devices, and, to be effective, should have a speed of at least twenty-five knots, in which case she would be able to pursue and overtake any battle fleet that could be assembled from existing ships in any navy in the world. Undoubtedly such high-speed submarines will come into being within the next few years.

Congress, in 1914, appropriated money to build "fleet submarines," in which they expressed the desire to secure twenty-five knots. A certain amount of discretion, however, was left with the Navy Department, which would permit them to accept boats of not less than twenty knots. There is no difficulty in the way of making such vessels function satisfactorily when submerged, but up to date no internal-combustion engine has been produced suitable for such high-speed submarines, and steam has many disadvantages in a military submarine, which should be able to emerge and get under way at full speed after a long period of submergence.

The tactics of the fleet submarine would be to search for and destroy the enemy's warships or commerce carriers wherever they could be found. A seagoing submarine of such character would also carry rapid-fire guns of sufficient calibre to destroy surface merchantmen. Having sufficient speed to overhaul them, they would be able to capture the merchantmen and perhaps take them as prizes into their own ports, something which it is impossible for the commander of the small-sized submarines now in commission to do, as they have neither the speed to overhaul swift merchantmen nor guns of sufficient range and power to destroy them if they refuse to follow the instructions of the submarine commander. The only alternative, therefore, has been to destroy the merchantmen, and, in many cases, the crews and passengers of the merchant ships have been destroyed as well. This latter policy, however, is much to be regretted.

From a study of the submarine problem as it stands to-day, the one thing lacking to make the submarine sufficiently powerful to stop commerce on the high seas between countries at war is speed. We have seen from the foregoing that sufficient speed to accomplish this purpose means great additional cost, and, as the engine situation exists to-day, it may be considered that it is impossible. My own personal opinion is that we shall not see satisfactory twenty-knot submarines, let alone twenty-five-knot submarines, for a matter of several years. In the meantime the people of this country, now engaged in the gigantic conflict which is taking place across the water, are becoming much exercised as to the possibility of some condition arising which may bring about an attack upon our own country.

There is a method of preparing this country with a type of submarine which may be navigated, so to speak, at much greater speed than that called for by the 1914 Congress; namely, twenty-five knots. The boats would have the further advantage in that they would be much less expensive even than the fourteen-knot submarines now called for in the latest specifications for the coast-defence type. This new method calls for the construction of a moderate-size submarine, which, for the want of a better term to distinguish it, I have called an "amphibious submarine"; that is, a submarine which may be carried on land as well as on or under the water.

"AMPHIBIOUS" SUBMARINE
Making up a train to ship a Lake submarine across Siberia during the period of the

170

Russian-Japanese war. Note the special trucks with sixteen wheels each, used to carry the load (about 130 tons). As the Trans-Siberian road had light rails, it was necessary to design these special trucks to distribute the weight so as to carry this heavy load. It is remarkable that several of these unheard-of weights should have been transported by vessel and rail a distance of over 10,000 miles each without accident or damage. Boats mounted on trucks especially designed to pass through tunnels could be transported from one port to another at railroad speed and be ready for immediate action in defending threatened sections of the country. The Germans have since made extensive use of this method of transporting submarines, giving them access to the Dardanelles and other points not easily accessible to their submarines by water.

These submarines would be much smaller than the present coast-defence type of submarine, and of a diameter that could pass through our tunnels and over our bridges. They could be of about two hundred and fifty tons submerged displacement. A railroad truck would be provided for each submarine, with a sufficient number of wheels to carry the load. The submarine itself would be constructed with proper scantlings to carry her entire load of machinery, batteries, fuel, and supplies without injury when mounted on her special trucks. Vessels of this type, which would have a surface speed of ten to twelve knots and a submerged speed of ten knots, would be readily constructed. They could carry as many as eight Whitehead torpedoes and have a radius of action on the surface of about two thousand miles at eight knots. Fitted with telescopic, or housing, conning towers and periscopes, nothing would need to be taken apart to ship these submarines from one section of the country to another at railroad speed. Fifty submarines of this type would probably be more efficient in time of need for protecting our thousands of miles of coast line than would many times the same number of fourteen-knot boats distributed over the same number of miles of coast line.

In the war game no one can tell where the enemy may decide to strike in force. An attack might be made in the vicinity of Boston, New York, Charleston, Pensacola, New Orleans, or Galveston on the eastern coast; it might be made at or in the vicinity of San Diego, Los Angeles, San Francisco, or Seattle on the western coast. There should be, of course, a certain number of the coast-defence type of submarines permanently stationed at these ports for their protection during war-time periods. But wars come suddenly, and the old saying that "the one who gets in the first blow has the advantage" is a true one. The history of recent wars shows that the declaration of war usually comes after the first blow has been struck. It is readily conceivable, therefore, that before we knew that we were going to become involved in war a fleet of battleships and transports stationed off our harbors, or off a suitable landing place on our extensive coast line, might be able to establish a shore base before we knew it or had time to get sufficient of our slow-going submarines at the danger point to prevent the landing of an invading force.

If we had one hundred submarines distributed over our Atlantic and Pacific coast lines, it would take weeks or months to mobilize many of them at the point of attack, for the reason that a submarine, when submerged, has such a small radius of action. The best in the service to-day have a radius of action of about one hundred miles at five knots, or eleven miles at ten and one-half knots, or twenty-four miles at eight knots. The enemy, with light, shallow-draft, high-speed picket boats, could probably make it very unsafe for a submarine to travel any considerable distance along the coast in the daytime, or even at night, in surface cruising condition. As it takes considerable time to charge the batteries to enable the boat to run in a submerged condition, should the enemy have control of the surface of the sea, the average submerged radius to-day of a submarine would probably be less than one hundred miles, unless it ran a grave risk of being captured while on the surface. The chances are, therefore, that if we had one hundred submarines distributed over our Atlantic and Pacific coast lines, not over ten or a dozen of them would be able to reach the point of attack in time to prevent the landing of an invading force with sufficient men, guns, and ammunition to do a great deal of harm in some of the thickly populated sections of the country.

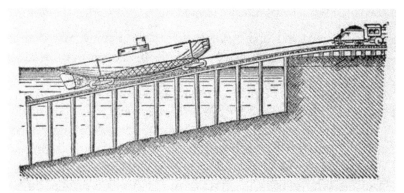

AN AMPHIBIOUS SUBMARINE BEING HAULED OUT OF THE WATER

If, however, the country were provided with fifty "amphibious

172

submarines" located at ten of our important Atlantic and Pacific ports, they could all be mobilized at an objective point within a week. If the government made arrangements with the railroads to run a track down under the water at each railroad coast terminal, or to run special tracks into the water at other suitable localities along the coast where there would be sufficient water to float a submarine, submarines could be rapidly mobilized to ward off a landing at any point.

To illustrate the point which I wish to make, assume that this country should become involved in war with nations lying both to the east and west of us. To get submarines from one coast to the other would require a long period of time. The "amphibious submarine," on the contrary, could in an hour's notice be run on to the tracks at New York and three days later be run into the water at San Francisco, with her crew, fuel, stores, and torpedoes all ready to go into action at once. A submarine could make a trip from Boston to New York in five hours, or from Boston to New Orleans in thirty-five hours. These boats could be built in quantities at a cost of about $300,000 (£61,500) each. Fifty of them could, therefore, be built at approximately the cost of one modern battleship.

There has been much talk recently about the so-called "baby" submarines—little one-or two-man boats. A large number of one-man submarines were built for the Russian Government previous to 1880 by Mons. Dzrewieckie, the well-known inventor of the Dzrewieckie type of torpedo launching apparatus. Mr. Holland, Goubet, and practically all inventors and builders of submarines commenced with "baby" submarines. One of the designs which I submitted to the United States Government in 1901 called for a one-man boat to be carried on the davits of a battleship or cruiser. A boat of that kind might have had a place a number of years ago when attacking vessels came near the shore. Such small craft must necessarily have a very limited range of action and very slow speed; they also would be unseaworthy. It would be impossible for a man to remain submerged in a vessel of this type for a considerable length of time, so that personally I can see very little use for them at present.

It has been well established that submarine boats should be divided into two classes: one a torpedo boat with as high surface and submerged speed as it is possible to attain with a large radius of action, capable, if possible, of exceeding battleship speed when on the surface, so that it may intercept a battle fleet on the high seas and submerge in its path of approach before being discovered; the second class should consist of smaller, slower-speed, mine-evading submarines, with torpedo and mining and countermining features. Such submarines are essentially defensive, but if they have sufficient radius of action to reach the enemy's harbors and to lie in wait off the entrance to such harbors, or to enter submerged the harbors themselves and there destroy the enemy craft, they have become potent offensive weapons of the raiding class. For a European power it is relatively easy to give such boats the radius necessary for them to invade an enemy's ports.

We have not pushed the consideration of the submarine of the second class, with its anti-mine features, because we have been kept busy trying profitably to meet the wishes of the various governments which demand constantly increasing speeds at a sacrifice of some characteristics which I personally regard very highly. Most government officials have been more attracted to vessels of the first class, as speed in all classes of vessels more than anything else seems to appeal to the imagination, but I think it may be the old story of the tortoise and the hare over again.

As regards the first class of submarines, the present submarine boats engaged in the continental war consist of vessels only a few of which have a surface speed exceeding twelve knots, or a submerged speed exceeding ten knots for one hour or eight knots for three hours. There may be a few in commission that exceed these speeds, but very few. Some are in course of construction that are expected to give a surface speed of seventeen and eighteen knots for forty hours and about eleven knots submerged for one hour, or a slower speed for a greater number of hours.

Governments are asking for bids for submarines of greater speed, and some have been designed which are expected to make twenty knots on the surface; but they are not in service as yet. One reason that higher surface speeds have not been reached is the difficulty of securing a perfectly satisfactory high-power, heavy-oil, internal-combustion engine, suitable for submarine boat work. As soon as a proven satisfactory heavy-oil engine is turned out by the engine builders, capable of delivering five thousand horsepower per shaft, submarine boats may be built capable of making up to twenty-five knots on the surface.

The submarine, even at its present development, has shown its superiority over the battleship in coast operations; to intercept a battleship at sea, however, even a high-speed submarine must lie in wait, perhaps for days or even weeks at a time, much like a gunner in a "blind" waiting for a flock of ducks to pass within gunshot. Because of its relatively slow speed it would have to wait for a long time, also, for a battleship or fleet to pass sufficiently near to be headed off, especially if the submarine were entirely submerged, because the moment the periscope appears above water the quarry will take to its heels, if it follows the latest ruling of the British Admiralty, to "steer away from the vicinity of submarines at full speed, even if it is necessary to abandon a torpedoed sister ship and its drowning crew to their own fate."

I believe that this apparently heartless order is justified by the loss of the *Aboukir*, *Cressy*, and *Hogue*, the only flock of ducks, figuratively speaking, that has come within the shot of the submarine torpedo gunner.

The conclusion must be reached, therefore, that on the high seas the only advantage the costly dreadnought has over the pigmy, cheap submarine, as at present constructed, lies in its ability to run away and to rule commerce far offshore on the high seas.

So little is known of the possibilities of submarine vessels of the second type that it seems necessary for me to devote some time to describing their possibilities and my experience in their construction. In 1905, while living in Berlin, Germany, I prepared plans for a mine-laying submarine for submission to the Russian Government, a general description of which was published in 1906. This submarine was designed to carry thirty-six of the regulation naval mines, which could readily be placed in a desired locality while the submarine was entirely submerged. A vessel of this type might be useful for either offensive or defensive purposes. Where used for offensive purposes the mine-laying submarine could readily, with comparatively little danger to herself, plant mines off entrances to the enemy's harbor. Equipped with the "mine-evading" guards, they might even work their way into an enemy's harbor and plant mines under a vessel at anchor, or destroy shipping lying tied up at the docks. For defensive purposes a mine-laying submarine would be of great value, as it could readily plant mines, even under the guns of a powerful fleet, to protect its own entrances and harbors.

The submarine *Protector*, built in 1901 and 1902 at Bridgeport, Connecticut, was fitted with a diving compartment which corresponds to the mine-laying compartment of the 1905 design above referred to. The importance of a mine-laying submarine for the defence of the country was first officially called to the attention of the American people by a board of officers appointed by ex-President Taft, then Secretary of War, as early as January, 1903. This board of officers consisted of General Arthur Murray, late chief of Coast Artillery Corps (then Major); Captain Charles J. Bailey, and Captain Charles F. Parker, of the Artillery Corps. The following is a copy of their recommendations for this type of vessel for the defence of our coast:

"First and second, the board believes that this type of submarine boat is a most valuable auxiliary to the fixed-mine defence, and in cases where channels cannot be mined, owing to the depth, rough water, swift tides, or width of channel, it will give the nearest approach to absolute protection now known to the board. The boat can lie for an indefinite time adjacent to the point to be defended in either cruising awash, or submerged condition, by its anchors, or on the bottom ready for instant use, and practically independent of the state of the water and in telephonic connection with the shore, or can patrol a mined or unmined channel invisible to the enemy and able to discharge its torpedoes at all times. It possesses the power of utilizing its engines in every condition except the totally submerged, and can always charge its storage batteries while so doing, necessitating its return to shore only when gasolene (petrol) must be replenished. In narrow channels the boat or boats would have a fixed position with a telephone cable buoyed or anchored at the bottom. In wide channels they would patrol or lie in mid-channel where they could readily meet approaching vessels. Third, as a picket or scout boat, outside of the mine field, or even at extreme range of gun fire, telephone communications can be sustained and information received, and instructions sent for attacking approaching vessels. Fourth, the test at Newport demonstrated the ease with which the boat can locate and pick up cables, and with minor alterations in the present model, junction boxes, etc., can be taken into the diving compartment and repaired at leisure while absolutely protected from hostile interference. The faculty possessed by the boat of manœuvring on the bottom and sending out divers leaves little or nothing to be desired in its facilities for doing this work.

THE "PROTECTOR" (LAKE TYPE, 1901-1902)

"The boat shows great superiority over any existing means for attacking mine-fields known to the board. First, it can be run by any field, as at present installed, with but little or no danger from the explosion of any particular mine or from gun fire during the few seconds it exposes the sighting hood for observations, and can attack at its pleasure the vessels in the harbor. Second and third, the board personally witnessed the ease with which cables can be grappled, raised, and cut, while the boat is manœuvring on the bottom; mine cables can be swept for, found and cut, or a diver can be sent out for that purpose. The crew of the boat is a skilled one, trained for its tests in every way likely to be requested by the Naval Board. It should be noted that, with one exception, no seamen are used, this exception being the man who steers and handles the boat. The crew is as follows: One navigator, who is also a diver; one chief engineer, one assistant engineer, one electrician, one machinist, one deck hand, and one cook.

"The board recommends consideration of the foregoing by the General Staff. The question of the use of the Whitehead torpedoes as a part of the fixed-mine defence, fired from tubes on shore, is now receiving consideration. Where channels are wide and water swift, this use of the Whitehead will be very limited. With boats of this type the Whitehead can, it is believed, be carried within certain effective range in all ordinary channels, and this alone will warrant the consideration asked for.

"The board recommends, in consequence of its conclusions, that five of these boats be purchased for use in submarine defence as follows:

"One for the School of Submarine Defence for experimental work, one for the eastern entrance of Long Island Sound, one for the entrance to Chesapeake Bay, one for San Francisco harbor, and one for Puget Sound.

"The necessity for this kind of defence in the four localities named needs no demonstration to those acquainted with them.

Arthur Murray,
"Major, Artillery Corps, President."

The recommendations of this board were submitted to Congress, and the Senate passed the bill for the purchase of the *Protector* to enable the authorities to test out the merits of this type of boat as an adjunct to our coast defence, but at this time it seemed as if certain politicians and financial groups were able to control the policy of the United States Government in its development of the submarine. The result indicated, at least, that these influences had been sufficiently strong to take out of the hands of the Navy Department and of the officers connected with the Coast Artillery, who had charge of the laying of our mines and the protection of our coast from hostile invasion, the right to specify the kind of appliances they should use. Instead of leaving the question of defence of our country in the hands of the expert officers who had been trained to study the problem, Congress in this instance specified the exclusive use of a type of boat which did not possess the characteristics called for by these expert students of defence.

Strange as it may seem, the opportunity of the United States to be a leader in the development of the type of boat which Germany has proven to be of such great value was lost by the dictation of a manufacturer of gloves from an inland county. It is a sad commentary on our laws that such a state of affairs could exist, but I accidentally happened to learn that this was the case in this instance, and I fear it has been the case in many other instances where financial and political influences have been permitted to overrule the recommendation of officers of the army and navy.

The *Protector* had been built by private capital at the suggestion of the Board of Construction of the United States Navy, at that time composed of Admirals Melville, O'Neil, Bradford, Bowles, and Captain Sigsbee. In 1901 I had been called to Washington by a telegram from the late Senator Hale, who was then chairman of the Committee on Naval Affairs in the Senate, and was asked to submit plans and specifications for a submarine torpedo boat. Accordingly, I submitted plans for the three types above referred to. The Board of Construction complimented me upon the plans, and stated that they believed the plans of the vessels I had proposed showed great superiority over any type of vessel that had been heretofore proposed, either in this country or abroad, but at the same they stated that all appropriations made by Congress had specified the particular type of boat that must be used, and the Navy Department did not have any authority to authorize the construction of a different type. They suggested further that if I or my friends had sufficient capital to construct such a vessel, they would see that it had a fair trial upon its merits, and if it proved of value to the service they would recommend its adoption, and they did not believe that Congress would then ignore their recommendations. Consequently the *Protector* was built. Her performances and capabilities for defence of the United States were strongly endorsed by the Board of Officers which had tested her, and many of her characteristics have been copied by all European builders of submarines.

After the Senate passed the bill authorizing her purchase, the matter was referred to a sub-committee in the House. As the boat had been built by private capital, and the lifetime savings of a number of friends, as well as all my own capital, were tied up in her, I was naturally desirous to learn if the House committee having the matter in charge was also going to recommend her purchase. One day I called at the committee room to inquire. There was no one present in the main committee room, so I took a seat at the table. After sitting there for a few moments, I heard a conversation in the chairman's room, adjoining the general committee room. Soon the voices took on an angry tone, and I heard one member of Congress accuse the chairman of the sub-committee which had the matter in charge of intention to report unfavorably the recommendations for the purchase of the

Protector. I recognized the voice of the gentleman who was making the accusation as that of an old retired general. He did not use polite language in accusing the chairman of the sub-committee of intending to defeat the purchase of the *Protector* in the interest of the company which had had sufficient influence to maintain a monopoly of submarine boat construction in the United States up to that time.

The chairman of this sub-committee did report unfavorably, and, as I have already stated, a manufacturer of gloves from an inland section of the country was able to defeat the recommendation for the adoption of a means of defence for this country which the best qualified officers in the United States service of both the army and the navy had recommended as of great value, and superior to other defensive means known to them at that time. It was this type of vessel which Germany later developed and which has so far been able to keep great fleets of almost the entire world from her shores. Recently the ex-member of Congress referred to in this connection was sentenced to imprisonment for attempt to defraud the government in other matters.

OFFICIAL DRAWING OF THE CAPTURED GERMAN MINE-PLANTING SUBMARINE, U. C-5

Copyright by Munn & Co., Inc.

Published exclusively in the *Scientific American* by permission of the British Admiralty and here reproduced by its courtesy.

I am a great believer in the value of this type of vessel for harbor and coast-defence work, and I believe that in one country vessels of this type are now engaged as mine layers in the present war. Our own government has to this day no submarine vessel equipped for the laying of mines, although the Commandant of the School of Submarine Defence repeatedly urged their adoption. I quote from the annual report of the Commandant of Submarine Defence, 1904-1905:

"As in the case of movable torpedoes, the question of the use of submarine boats as adjuncts to the fixed-mine defence of the country has been under consideration by the board for the revision of the Report of the Endicott Board during the past year, and the Torpedo Board has been called on for remarks on this subject.

"It is now again desired to invite special attention to the unquestionable value of submarine boats as an adjunct to fixed mine and movable torpedoes for the defence of the particular places named in the report of the second committee; and also to the need of a boat of the Lake type, or similar type, at the School of Submarine Defence for experimental work, as this is the only submarine boat, so far as known, that can be efficiently used in countermining electrically controlled mines. The advisability of procuring submarine boats for the defence of the places named, it is believed, will also be seen to be unquestionable when it is considered that the cost of such a boat is about one-fortieth of that of a modern battleship; that without such boats as an adjunct to the mine and gun defences of those places a more expensive boat of the navy will undoubtedly be called for as a home-guard for those waters in case of war; and that with submarine boats as an adjunct to the army's defences it will be impossible so to defend those waters as to enable the more expensive and seagoing boats proper of the navy to cut loose from those harbors with impunity and go wherever naval strategy may demand.

(Signed) "ARTHUR MURRAY,
"Lieutenant-Colonel, Artillery Corps."

The principal means used in my mine-planting, mine-and net-evading submarine are the bottom wheels and diving compartment which were incorporated in my 1893 design, which also carried my pioneer features of lateral hydroplanes to get even-keel submergence; high, water-tight superstructure, which is indispensable for high-speed, ocean-going submarines; anchors, and lifting and lowering sighting instruments. Excepting the bottom wheels and diving compartment, most navies have now incorporated these features into their submarines. Three navies have adopted the bottom wheels, etc. These mine-evading craft are able to enter the enemy's own territory with impunity and destroy their merchant ships and warships in their own harbors. The *Niger* was sunk at Deal by a German submarine which is reported to have passed through a mine field.

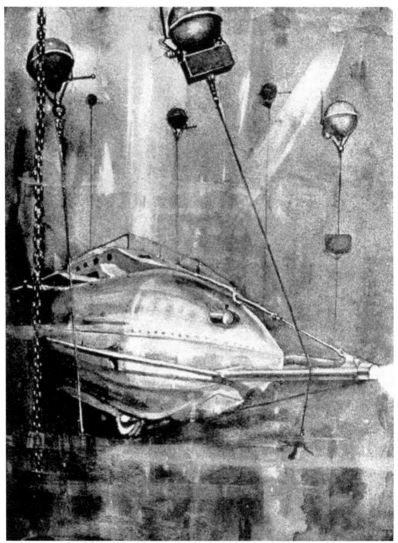

A BOTTOM-CREEPING SUBMARINE PASSING THROUGH A MINE FIELD
Courtesy of the Scientific American
Fitted with guards and gently pushing aside the cables which anchor the buoyant

mines, the bottom-creeping submarine can proceed slowly and cautiously over the bottom and pass through a mine field with impunity.

The necessity of such features as bottom wheels and diving compartment is now being brought out in the present war. I believe the mining and countermining features must be incorporated in one type before the submarine reaches its full development. The impotency of the great combined English and French fleets of battleships, cruisers, destroyers, and submarines must be galling to the people who have paid for them by the sweat of their brows. These fleets are impotent because the Germans will not come out from behind their mines and forts and wage an unequal battle against superior numbers, but prudently are sending out their submarines to destroy gradually the enemy which is trying to blockade the German ports.

A MINE AND NET EVADING SUBMARINE UNDER-RUNNING A NET

Courtesy of the Scientific American

A submarine fitted with a device of this kind can readily under-run any net; running slowly on the bottom the net may be seen through the aquascope or felt with its advanced feelers. Even if mines are attached, divers may cut them loose, or they may be exploded by counter mines to make a safe passage under the nets. Surface ships attempting to guard the nets may be sunk by torpedoes or heavy gun fire from disappearing guns on other submarines, giving the bottom-working submarines ample time to clear away nets and mines.

Winston Churchill, former First Lord of the British Admiralty, expressed the bitterness of this impotency when he said: "If they don't come out and fight, we will go in after them and dig them out like rats"; regrettably, the German mines and submarines stand in the way, and are themselves taking their toll of ships.

The mine-evading submarine can enter with comparative safety through a mine field, like a shuttle passing through the woof of cloth during the weaving process, and I take the opportunity to explain this method of entering harbors.

To comprehend thoroughly the safety with which this is accomplished, it is necessary to appreciate the almost insuperable difficulty of discovering an object like a submarine vessel when once sunk beneath the surface of the water. There are many sunken ships containing valuable treasures and cargoes that lie along our coast, and in most of the harbors of the world, that have been known to have sunk within a radius of less than a mile from some given point, but which have never been located. Some of these vessels have been searched for for years and never have been found. Dozens of vessels have been sunk in the waters of the North and East Rivers and never have been located. Some of the British and French submarines have been lost in localities well known, but it has been impossible to locate them.

During several years of experimental work with submarine investigating bottom conditions I have travelled many miles in the Chesapeake and Sandy Hook bays, along the Atlantic coast and Long Island Sound, and later in the Gulf of Finland and the Baltic Sea; and it is a fact that cannot be successfully disputed, technically, by any one, that a submarine of the type recommended by the United States Army Board may be taken into any harbor in the world entirely unseen, and remain there, if necessary, for a month at a time, destroying shipping, docks, and war craft deliberately and leisurely, and yet defy discovery.

My method of entering harbors or through mine fields consists principally in providing submarine vessels with bottom wheels and other component undisclosed details. When submerged, the vessel is given sufficient negative buoyancy so that she will not be drifted off her course by the currents when resting on the bottom. The vessel is what may be termed a submarine automobile, and it may be navigated over the bottom as readily as an automobile runs on the surface of the earth. The submarine automobile has one great advantage over the surface type in its ability to mount steep grades or go over obstructions, because the vessel is so nearly buoyant that she will mount any obstruction she can get her bow over.

My early experience proved to me that a submarine could not be satisfactorily navigated submerged in shallow, rough water by the same method of control as was found to be practical in deeper water, for the reason that the vessel would pump up and down with the rise and fall of the sea. Neither could the vessel lie at rest on the bottom, as the lift of the ground swell in bad weather was sufficient, even with a considerable negative buoyancy, to cause the vessel to pound so badly that the storage battery plates would be destroyed in a few minutes. I therefore suspended the wheels on swinging arms and applied a cushioning cylinder. The hull of the vessel was then free to move up and down, synchronizing with the lift of the ground swell, and at the same time the weight of the wheels kept the submarine close to the bottom and able to keep her position while at rest or to be navigated over the bottom at any speed desired.

Most of our Atlantic coast, Long Island, and Chesapeake Bay water-beds are comparatively uniform as to depths. In other countries I have navigated over rocky bottoms filled with giant boulders. A rough bottom limits the speed at which it is advisable to travel, but I have never seen a bottom so rough that it could not be readily navigated.

"Lake" boats, fitted with bottom wheels, have, in a competitive test abroad, entered landlocked and fortified harbors without discovery, where the entrance from the sea has been through a tortuous channel. All other vessels, except the one fitted with bottom wheels, were discovered long before reaching the outer fortifications, because it was necessary for them to show their periscopes to sight their way. They struck the sides of the dredged channel, which caused them to broach and be discovered, because they had to maintain a comparatively high speed to be kept under control. In tests carried out in Russia the boat fitted with bottom wheels simply wheeled along in the channel at slow speed and stopped and backed to change course at will. The revolutions of the bottom wheels gave the distance travelled, the manometer gave the depth, and the compass the proper direction; consequently, with a correct chart as to courses and depths, navigation on the bottom in entering harbors is very much easier than on the surface, unless the channels are well buoyed.

Most mines, as at present installed, are either of the observation or contact type; the observation mines are fired usually from shore stations when the enemy is seen to be over them, while the contact mine is anchored a few feet beneath the surface and is either exploded by contact with the surface of the vessel's bottom or by the agitation caused by the rush of water due to the swiftly passing vessel. The European belligerents have put out contact mines to protect their capital ships from the submarines. The dread of these mines is holding the submarines outside of the mined areas, and the mines are therefore effective. None of the British vessels are fitted with bottom wheels and diving compartments, and they must be navigated at such speed to keep submerged control that they would explode a contact mine if either the mine or its anchor rope were touched. This also applies to some of my later boats, as the bottom wheels have been omitted to meet the demand for greater speed on the surface and submerged.

I am inclined to the belief that this has been more or less of a mistake, because the bottom-wheeled submarine can go to and dig the enemy out of its base in addition to hunting the big surface craft of the enemy on the high seas.

With the bottom wheels, navigation can be conducted so carefully over the bottom that inspection of the course can be made, if desired, foot by foot, as progress is made, and all mines can be avoided.

MINES PLACED UNDER SHIPS AT ANCHOR

Permission Scientific American

A submarine of the mine-planting and mine-evading type may, by means of its periscope, range finders and direction indicators, ascertain the exact distance and bearing of vessels at their anchorage. On securing this exact knowledge the submarine may then be submerged to the bottom and creep up under the anchored craft and plant a mine under her which may be exploded by electricity after the submarine has backed a safe distance away, or a mine might be fitted with a powerful

186

magnet and allowed to ascend (by the diver) until it attaches itself to the bottom of the ship.

The diagrammatic sketches illustrate the "Lake" method of operation in cutting cables, evading mines, planting countermines, clearing away mines, or passing under chains, cables, and nets that may be stretched across the entrances of the harbors to effectively stop the progress of surface vessels and submarines not fitted with bottom wheels.

SUBMARINE SUPPLY STATION
(Drawing by Robt. G. Skerrett.)

Illustrating the use of the submarine supply station, which may be anchored on the bottom in positions known only to the commanders of submarines, who may visit such station and renew their supplies of fuel, foodstuffs and torpedoes. The submarine boat approaches alongside of the supply boat, then, by utilizing the air lock, divers may pass out of the submarine and enter into the supply boat through its air lock compartment. A hose may be led from the fuel tanks of the submarine to the fuel supply tanks in the submerged station, compressed air admitted to the tanks and fuel driven from the submarine station to the military submarine. The author's experimental cargo-carrying submarine as tested out in 1900, proved the practicability of transferring cargo from one submerged vessel to another submarine, all the operations being performed under water.

The diving compartment is another feature of submarine construction which has been neglected by the majority of the world's naval authorities. This device is of value not only to vessels of the type just described, but is of general usefulness to all submarines of whatever size or speed. A submarine crew is able by this means to go outside the vessel while submerged and make repairs on the propellers, periscopes, and other exterior parts without the necessity of rising to the surface or of returning to their base. Further, it is capable of use in such a way as to add immensely to the cruising radius of submarines. The method by which this may be accomplished I will briefly outline.

As matters stand now, the submarines are forced to return to their home ports to refill their fuel tanks, to take on fresh provisions for the men, and to replenish their exhausted ammunition and torpedoes. Thus, even though their personnel gets relief by the boat's halting upon the sea-bed, a cog is slipped in the matter of continued military efficiency. Without a fresh supply of fuel oil and more food and munitions of war the submarine is ineffective, and when her objective is a distant one she must draw heavily upon her stores to get her there and to carry her safely back to her revictualling base. Indeed, she may overreach herself through her commander's desire to strike his remote enemy and then find herself forced back to the surface and without the means to take her home again, floating impotently upon the sea, an easy target for attack, and certain to be sunk or captured.

These present handicaps need not be permanent ones, and there is no more reason why a submarine should not take on fresh stores in the open sea than a surface vessel. Indeed, a submarine should be able to replenish her fuel tanks and to ship provisions under some circumstances even more securely than its rivals that run upon the water.

In short, a submarine should be capable of sinking to the sea-bed and there, beyond the reach of its foes, of drawing new strength, so to speak, from a suitably designed submergible supply boat. This scheme is not at all visionary. In part it has already been done in the past by vessels planned by me for commercial work, and there is no inherent difficulty in modifying both the military submarine and its revictualling consort so that they can thus function in unison for the purpose of giving the fighting undersea boat a wider field of action.

While the torpedo-boat destroyer, the submarine's logical pursuer to-day, is battling with wind and wave, jarring well nigh her sides out, and hunting over the tumbling seas for elusive periscopes, the submarine can lie in ambush upon the ocean-bed if the water be not too deep, or at rest at any desired depth, held in suspension between the surface and the bottom by her anchors, thus conserving her energies so that when she does rise for a peep through her observing instrument she can strike more certainly with all of the sinister force of her chosen weapon of attack. She can lurk in wait for her quarry not only for one day but for weeks at a time, especially when sand banks a hundred feet below the surface offer the needful haven.

What I propose is to provide every seagoing submarine with one or more mobile submersible bases of supply in the form of boats without motive power of their own which can be towed by the military under-water boat and sunk upon the sea-bed at convenient points where they will best suit the purposes of the subaqueous torpedo vessel. Naturally you ask what would happen if submarine scouts should sight a submarine towing a convoy of this sort. Wouldn't the submarine have to desert her supply vessels and sink alone beneath the surface? My answer is no.

Of course, this assumes that the submarine at the time is traversing waters that are not too deep for her to go to the bottom. She would take her tender or tenders down with her under such circumstances, for the supply boats would be built to stand safely the test submergence of the military submarine; that is, a depth of two hundred feet. The question may arise as to how I can control the sinking of the crewless consorts, holding as they would only supplies, and having none of the operative mechanisms that constitute a necessary functional part of the fighting undersea boat.

This is illustrated by the method with which I controlled the submergence of a tender with which I salvaged the coal from a sunken barge in Long Island Sound years ago. That cargo boat had tanks into which water could be admitted from the sea, and certain of the inlet passages were closed by means of check valves which were automatic, seating themselves by the tension of springs. In order to submerge the boat it was only necessary to admit water purposely and to open a valve on the deck for the escape of the air as the water entered.

To refloat the tender after it had reached the bottom and was loaded, a diver went from the submerged *Argonaut* by way of the diving compartment and attached a hose to the deck vent. This hose was then connected to the compressed-air flasks in the submarine. The air was blown down through the pipe into the ballast tanks and the water forced outboard, past the check valves that yielded in that direction, but reseated and closed themselves as soon as the air pressure stopped. In this fashion buoyancy was reacquired and the tender rose to the surface.

Of course, the initial sinking operation required the presence of someone in a small boat alongside the tender which I have just described. This would not be feasible in the case of the military supply boats I have in mind. These must be made to sink by suitable controlling devices manipulated from within the military craft, but in principle the cycle would not differ from that which I have outlined.

The deck valve allowing the air to escape from the tanks and the inlets admitting sea-water could be operated by suitable electrical mechanisms, and, once opened, the sea-water would enter and destroy the reserve buoyancy, thus causing the tenders to sink. Again, compressed air supplied from the submarine or compressed air carried by the supply craft themselves could be turned on by electrical control, and the boats brought to the surface at the will of the military commander.

The supply boats, like the fighting submarine, would have diving compartments, but these would be arranged so that the bottom door could be opened from the outside by divers, who, by manipulating suitable valves, would fill the chambers with compressed air and thus permit the door to be opened and allow entrance into the tender. An air-lock would then facilitate a passage into the inside of the craft, where stores would be stowed. This air-lock would have to be operated each time materials were brought into the diving chamber for transfer to the submarine.

The provisions and other portable supplies would be packed in metal cylinders capable of keeping out the water at any depth in which a diver could work safely. I should count upon carrying on this transfer of provisions, etc., on depths of one hundred feet and less, but deep enough to constitute a sufficient cover against detection by aeroplanes. To facilitate disguise in clear water the tenders could be painted mottled colors which would make them blend into the background of the sea-bed, much after the fashion of a flounder.

These provision tanks, when loaded, would have a negative buoyancy of only a few pounds, just enough to make them sink, and a diver would have no trouble in either carrying or dragging one of them from the tender to the open diving compartment of the submarine. Only food, drinking water, the ammunition for guns, and the disjointed sections of torpedoes need to be transported in this way. Fuel oil for the engines, and even lubricating oil, could be sent from the tender to the submarine in a very simple manner. The outboard connection of the oil tanks of the supply craft would have hose joined to them leading to the fuel tanks of the submarine, and the contents could be transferred simply by pumping them across.

The supply boats should have fenders in the shape of long metal rods reaching out from the bow and the stern and both sides. These would give the tenders the appearance of gigantic water-bugs, but they serve to form smooth surfaces over which the loop of a mine sweeper would glide freely without encountering any projections to which it could cling. Thus, while the mine sweeper could certainly pick up a floating mine, it would pass without warning over a submerged supply base capable of holding stuff sufficient to keep a submarine going for weeks without return to her home port.

With such a system of revictualling, submarines should be able to operate secretly for long periods and virtually hold to the sea during the entire time, doing in that interval what would be absolutely impossible for any type of surface fighting craft of kindred displacement and military power. The submarine commander would be the only one having knowledge of the position of his submerged supply bases, and he could place them under cover of night just where they would contribute best to the carrying out of the operations planned for him.

SUBMARINE "SEAL"—LAKE TYPE U. S.

This vessel is unique in that she was the first vessel built that was provided with deck torpedo tubes that could be trained and fired to either broadside when the vessel is submerged, in addition to the vessel's hull tubes. In her acceptance trials her crew took her down to a depth of 256 ft. She broke the record for speed in the U. S. Navy.

On almost every coast there are areas where submarines could sink safely to the bottom in moderate depths of water, and there are also quiet coves but little frequented where ideal resting places could be found for the submerged supply boats. With these failing, however, the tenders could be sunk to the water-bed in the open sea, and with their bottom wheels to rest on, working upon pneumatic buffers, they need not feel any vertical motion of the sea even in the stormiest weather. I have found that such motion actually exists forty feet and more below the surface when the ground swell is deep.

BRITISH SUBMARINE B-1 (HOLLAND TYPE)

A sister ship to B-11, that sank the Turkish battleship "Messudieh" in the Dardanelles.

Of course, the submarine must rise to the surface from time to time in order to draw in fresh air to fill her pressure tanks and also to recharge her storage batteries. The electrical accumulators are charged by means of the oil motors, and these engines are so greedy for air that they must have the free atmosphere to draw upon when working. Therefore the submarine would rise to the surface to perform these services during the night time, and boats seeking submarines after dark have a task cut out for them pretty much like that of hunting for the proverbial needle in a haystack. If the commander of a submarine recognizes that the first principle of successful submarine raiding is never to betray his position by exposing his periscope while under way when within sight of the enemy, his vessel becomes invulnerable, because it is an invisible object. The submarine vessel is then invincible, because all the science of naval architecture has not been able thus far to devise a protection against the mine and torpedo.

CHAPTER VI

THE POSSIBILITY OF DEFEATING THE SUBMARINE

In the present European war, for the first time in the world's history, the submarine, as is also the case with the airplane, has taken an important active part, and has become a weapon of unlimited value. We have seen that even as early as the war of the American Revolution the submarine was utilized, but up to modern days the submarine had never been a really significant or consequential factor in naval warfare; its use had been previously but sporadic and experimental. In the wars of the past it had no bearing upon the destinies of nations or the outcome of naval battles. To-day the situation is very different: the submarine has been called into action as a weapon of primary value and is producing tremendous results.

In the conflict in which we are now engaged the destructive capabilities of the submarine have been made use of, for the most part, in the work of commerce destruction and in the task of hampering communication by sea. It has not taken a great deal of active part in actual naval battles, although on some occasions its presence has been severely felt by the fleets of its enemies. But the submarine has been an important factor in naval warfare by reason of the fact that its very presence and the possibility of its use have checked the actions of belligerent fleets of battleships in no inconsiderable way. In writing of this I am reminded of the fact that a short time ago I was introduced to a pleasant-faced, motherly old lady who, when she learned that I was an inventor of submarine boats, exclaimed, "Why! I should not think you could sleep nights from thinking of all those poor people who have been drowned by the U-boats!"

I asked the old lady if she had ever considered the submarine from another angle of view—viz., as a life and property saver in the present war—and she said, "No; how could that be possible?" I then explained to her that had it not been for the existence of the submarines many more lives would have been sacrificed than have been lost by the use of submarines. I asked her to consider what would have been the loss of life if the battleships, cruisers, gunboats, destroyers, etc., had met on the high seas and fought as they were intended to fight. A submarine carries a crew of but a few men, while a battleship may carry a thousand, consequently thousands of men would have been killed in the old-time methods of fighting, compared with the few that have been killed in the submarine warfare. Then again, had it not been for the submarines lying off Russia's, Germany's, England's, France's, Italy's, Austria's, and even Turkey's shores, many seacoast cities, towns, and hamlets would undoubtedly have been bombarded and destroyed, and countless thousands of lives and enormous property valuations lost forever to the world; for one must remember that a life, or a property once erected by hands that are gone, if lost, can never be economically replaced. The only reason such bombardments have not occurred is the fleet commander's fear of that waiting, watching invisible sentinel, the submarine, which lies off the respective combatants' shores; and thus because of its existence thousands of lives and great property valuations have been saved. Thus, while the submarine has not been much of a fighter in naval battles, it has, in my opinion, been of great power as a preventer of fighting, and that, after all, is rather more in its favor than against it.

It is, however, the submarine in the role of commerce destroyer which is attracting attention at the present time. The democratic nations of the world are face to face with the problem of transporting men, food, ammunition, and supplies to Europe. The submarine threatens to cut off communication between Europe and the other continents. It is very necessary that means be taken to offset the activities of the submarine. It is this problem which leads me to write upon this topic.

BRITISH SUBMARINE C-2 ARRIVING AT PORTSMOUTH IN A GALE
Note hydroplanes at centre of conning tower; in later types these were placed under the water, as they were found ineffective in this position

The devices which have been proposed for capturing and destroying the U-boats in order that navigation upon the Atlantic Ocean may be made safe have run into the thousands. I have had hundreds of impractical schemes sent to me, and the Navy Department and the Naval Consulting Board have been almost swamped by the various suggestions that have been pouring in from all over the country in response to editorials in the newspapers to "Save us from the U-boat!"; "American inventors, rise in your might and strike down this peril which works unseen, like an assassin in the dark!" etc. The devices proposed run all the way from blowing up the whole restricted area or war zone of the ocean to fishing for submarines from aeroplanes, which latter method offers a good chance for sport, at least; and if the submarine designers and commanders were asleep the fishermen might have a good chance of making a catch. Many of my engineering friends with whom I have discussed the U-boat problem have urged upon me that I ought, in order to save the time, energy, and money of many earnest and patriotic—but misinformed—citizens, to publish some material showing the fallacies in many of these schemes which apparently are so promising, and at the same time to point out wherein some have value, and along what lines I believe success to be attainable.

At the beginning of the war I myself sent to the Navy Department a number of devices for detecting the presence of and destroying submarines in shoal waters, some of which may have already been known to the Navy Department, and several of which I have since seen published as being the ideas of others; this goes to show that where many minds are working toward the solution of any particular problem several are likely to arrive at the same point. In the interest of public policy I do not think that any device hitherto unknown which offers a chance of success if used against an enemy U-boat should be described, and therefore I should not describe any such device if such were known, but shall limit my remarks to a discussion of some of the devices that have been proposed and described publicly. Trying to serve the country by developing a certain idea, when that idea is itself old or impractical, is evidently a waste of mental energy and money. Further, to show how some of these methods of attack may be offset by the submarine commanders will also serve to prevent the country from relying on false defences; the submarine is a real menace, and should not be lightly regarded. I hope to impress upon people that this is a very serious proposition. It is a problem which should and does attract the leading minds of the mechanical world; and it is not to be coped with by any fanciful notions. While the devices proposed thus far are individually very numerous, they may be classified into a few distinct categories. I would designate them as follows:

Offensive Devices:

    I. Airplanes and dirigibles for the location and destruction of submarines.
        (*a*) By bomb attacks.
        (*b*) By directing surface boats to the attack of sub-vessels.
    II. Offensive appliances for use of surface vessels:
        Sound detectors.
        Submerged mines operated from shore stations.
        Deck guns.
        Under-water guns.
        Aerial torpedoes.
        Searchlights.
        Echo devices.
        Magnetic devices for locating and destroying submarines.

III. Channel and open-sea nets.
IV. Submarine vs. submarine.

Defensive Devices:

   I. To be installed on surface vessels to baffle and elude
   submarines:
      Sound detectors (spoken of above).
      Blinding searchlights.
      Blinding apparatus.
   II. To offset torpedo attack:
      Nets.
      Plates.
      Magnets.
      Bombs.
      Discs.
   III. Unsinkable ships.
   IV. Tactics to elude the submarine:
      Convoying a merchant fleet.
      Zigzag course.
      Smoke screen.
      Cargo submarine.
      High speed.

   In considering the practicability or value of these devices, we must
first consider the capabilities of the submarine and the proper tactics
for her commander to pursue. In a paper read before the Institution of
Naval Architects in London, in 1905, I described, illustrated by
diagrams, the proper method to be pursued in attacking a surface ship,
in which I contended that the commander of a submarine, on sighting
an enemy, should always keep the hull of his own boat below the
horizon in its relation to the enemy vessel, and try to intercept the
approaching vessel by taking frequent observations of her course and
speed. When the two vessels approach sufficiently near to make it
possible for the larger surface vessel to observe the smaller
submarine (the comparative range of visibility being proportionate to
the exposed surfaces of the two vessels above the horizon), the
submarine should then entirely submerge, with her telescopic
periscope withdrawn below the surface of the water to avoid the
making of a "wake"—which looks like a white streak on the water.

When the commander wishes to make an observation he should first bring his submarine to rest and then extend the periscope above the surface for a brief instant only, and thus avoid the chance of being seen. Earlier in the war it was common to detect the submarine by her wake, but now, since the fitting of merchantmen with guns, the above tactics are usually pursued, and the first intimation the crew has of the presence of the submarine is the shock of the explosion caused by the torpedo "striking home."

GERMANY'S U-9 AND SOME OF HER SISTER SUBMARINES

AEROPLANE AND SUBMARINE
(Drawing by T. E. Lake.)

For defense of coast lines aeroplanes and submarines may work in conjunction. Aeroplanes, with their enormous range and high speed can locate surface ships many miles away, beyond the range of a submarine's periscope or sound-detecting devices. It could then direct the submarine by wireless or direct communication. Aeroplanes, however, are of great danger to enemy submarines. Flying at certain altitudes they

200

can see submarines a short distance below the water and swoop down on them, dropping depth bombs or trailing torpedoes.

Aeroplanes and Dirigibles.—These are undoubtedly valuable near land in shallow water, *providing* the water is clear and has a bottom in striking contrast to the hull of the submarine. I should consider the dirigible likely to prove of more value than the aeroplane, owing to its ability to hover directly over and regulate its speed to that of the submarine and thus enable itself to drop depth bombs more accurately. Experience has shown that it is almost impossible to calculate where a bomb will strike when dropped from a swiftly moving aeroplane. The chance of its striking the submarine would be very slight. The use of aeroplanes has, however, forced the submarines away from shoal clear water and probably has been instrumental, also, in causing them to become equipped with high-angle rapid-firing guns. In a battle between swiftly moving aeroplanes and submarines with high-powered guns firing shrapnel, the chances are nearly all in favor of the submarine, as they can carry the most powerful guns and are firing from a much more stable platform; in fact, the best analogy I can think of is that of a gunner in a "blind" firing at a flock of ducks passing overhead. Aeroplanes have been used, however, as scouts, merely to detect a submarine and direct surface ships to the attack; also, aeroplanes have directed trawlers to a submarine lying submerged at a shallow depth. This method of attack has undoubtedly been successful in some instances, but where success might have been met with in this manner with the earlier submarine boats, which were not provided with guns, it is now a problem easily met by submarine architects. Submarine boats may be built which have no fear of this combination. One of my earliest designs provided for a revolving armored turret to carry heavy-calibre guns; this revolvable armored turret would extend only above the surface and would carry guns of sufficient calibre to sink any trawler, destroyer, or other craft except an armored ship. It has recently been reported that the Germans are bringing out ships fitted with turrets of this type, and as they are familiar with my designs from the Patent Office specifications, and also have my working drawings of a large cruiser submarine mounted with guns, in 1905, I have no doubt that the report is true, as they have consistently been the first to adopt such new devices as may be needed to offset any attack against their submarines, or to increase their means of offence against surface craft without relying upon torpedoes alone. As far back as 1902 the *Protector* was fitted with a small gun on top of her conning tower, with the breech extended into the sighting hood and a tampon controlled from within the turret for closing the muzzle, so that no water would enter the barrel when the vessel was submerged, thus permitting a new cartridge and shell to be inserted into the breech when submerged; then, by momentarily bringing the conning tower above the surface, we could fire, then submerge and reload, rest and fire again, etc., thus providing a disappearing gun on a very stable platform.

In deep water the submarine may readily escape detection by aeroplanes by sinking below the depth to which vision can penetrate. This depends upon the amount of foreign substance held in suspension in the water. Along the Atlantic coast it is possible to see only a few feet; as you go off shore vision becomes clearer, and it would probably vary during the dry seasons from four to five feet near shore to forty or fifty feet well off shore. The greatest distance I was ever able to see in my experiments in the Chesapeake Bay with a powerful searchlight was forty feet. In Long Island Sound one can seldom see over fifteen feet, and after storms, when sediment is carried into the Sound, sometimes it is difficult to see over three or four feet. I have been down on muddy bottom at a depth of one hundred feet and could not see my hand held close to my face. At a depth of one hundred and twenty-five feet in the Baltic on sandy bottom I was able to see twenty-five feet. This was about eight miles off shore, opposite Libau, Russia. In the English Channel the frequent storms stir up so much sediment that it is seldom possible to see over fifteen feet, while in the Mediterranean and our Southern waters near the Florida coast, near Nassau, and in the Caribbean Sea, it is possible at times to see seventy-five or even one hundred feet. Now there are means available to the submarine to enable it to lie at rest submerged at depths exceeding one hundred feet, and yet have a full view of surface ships and also to scan the heavens, therefore I would say that aeroplanes and dirigibles will prove ineffective against submarines fitted with revolvable turrets, high-angle firing guns, or where they may be operating in clear water exceeding one hundred feet in depth or in shallow water where the sediment held in suspension is in sufficient quantity to prevent discovery. Aviators with whom I have discussed this problem tell me they can seldom detect objects lying on the bottom, even in comparatively shallow water.

RUSSIAN CRUISER-LAKE TYPE SUBMARINE IN SHED BUILT BY PETER THE GREAT—1905

This was the first large submarine of the cruiser type, built substantially after the design submitted by the author to the U. S. Navy in 1901.

Sound Detectors.—We have heard many claims put forth concerning the great results which were to be attained in fighting the U-boat by the use of various sound-receiving devices in the nature of microphones, in detecting the presence of submarines by hearing the hum of the motors and the noise of their machinery. These devices are proposed both for offensive and defensive purposes. A vessel equipped with such mechanism is believed to be able to escape upon hearing a U-boat, or to seek out the submarine and destroy it. Those who have been expecting so much from this source are probably not aware of the fact that submarine inventors themselves were the first to utilize this method of sound detection under water to enable them to apprehend the presence of other vessels in their vicinity before coming to the surface; they have made use of such devices for years.

I well remember my first long submergence of ten hours' duration down at Hampton Roads, near the mouth of the Chesapeake Bay, July 28, 1898. During this period of submergence the machinery was shut down for a time, and one of the first sensations we experienced was the strange sounds which came to us of the propellers and paddle-

203

wheels of surface vessels passing in our vicinity. The first vessel that we heard was a tugboat; we could tell that by the sound of her puffing exhaust and the characteristic sound of her machinery. We thought at first she was coming right over where we were submerged, and feared she might carry away our masts, which extended above the surface, but she passed on, and then we heard coming at a distance the uneven and characteristic sound of a paddle-wheel steamer as her paddles slapped the surface of the water. Then we heard the slow, heavy pound of an ocean liner coming in, and knew that she had a loose crank-pin or cross-head bearing by the pound every time the crank-pin passed over the dead centre of its shaft. The click, click of the little high-speed launch was also easily detected—all this without any sound receiver on the vessel. Any of us simply sitting or standing anywhere in the submarine could hear outside sounds. By putting the head of an iron bolt against the skin of the ship and sticking the end of the bolt in my ear the sound was much intensified, as the whole steel fabric of the ship became a great sound collector. This led me to make experiments toward determining the direction of the sounds under water, and I applied for a patent on a device which could be swung in different directions, on the theory that the sound waves would be stronger when coming straight from their source, but shortly after this the experiments of Professor Gray and Messrs. Munday and Millett were published and I dropped my application and did nothing further in the matter, as they seemed to have solved the question in a satisfactory manner. Afterward Professor Fessenden brought out his oscillator and improved sound detector, with which it is possible for submarines to carry on wireless conversations under water when at a distance of several hundred feet apart, and to pick up the characteristic sounds of different types of surface ships at considerable distances. Sound detectors are of greater benefit to submarines lying in wait for their enemies than they are to surface vessels, as they enable the submarine to lie at rest, submerged and invisible, herself giving no betraying sound, while no surface ship can come within the zone of her receiving apparatus without betraying its presence.

Submerged Sound Detectors.—It has been stated that sound detectors connected to shore stations have been able to detect submarines when passing in their vicinity, and, by the triangulation method as applied to the intensity of sounds, observers have been able to tell approximately the location of the U-boat from the sound of the U-boat's machinery. The obvious thing for submarine designers and commanders to do to offset this danger to the submarine is to use noiseless machinery in the U-boats, or to send other U-boats with a wire-cutting grapnel to cut the shore connections of the sound transmitter. It is apparent that this method of attack is applicable only to points close to shore or in places like the English Channel.

A GROUP OF GERMAN U-BOATS
Note their broad decks, due to buoyant superstructure.

RUSSIAN-LAKE TYPE CRUISING SUBMARINE "KAIMAN" MAKING A SURFACE RUN IN ROUGH WEATHER IN THE GULF OF FINLAND

Deck Guns.—The mounting of deck guns on merchantmen for defence against the submarine has proved of slight value. When it was first proposed to mount guns on American merchant ships I wrote the Navy Department on March 11, 1917, in part as follows: "I have tried, in the interest of this country, to impress this fact upon the people (that the submarine, because it is invisible, is invincible), but I find in talking with many intelligent people, that they do not and cannot comprehend the possibilities of the submarine when it is taken seriously and the effort is made to get all there is out of it, without reference to political, financial, or prejudiced interests. The *destructiveness* of the submarine is growing; devices which were effective in detecting and trapping submarines early in the war are now becoming useless. The theory that putting a gun on a merchant ship is going to protect that ship, her crew and passengers, will, I fear, be equal to the signing of the death-warrant of all that are on that ship if we are at war, as the slogan in to-day's headlines (as per copy clipping enclosed)—'Sink any ship you see'—will be met, I fear, by a German slogan of 'Sink every ship you meet, but don't let them *see you* do it.'"

Since that time many ships fully equipped with arms have been sunk by torpedoes and have never seen the submarines which destroyed them. There is no way to attack submarines by gun fire unless they are seen, and commanders of submarines are becoming expert in concealing their presence.

Submarine Guns, Aerial Torpedoes, Searchlights.—For an under-water gun to be effective, there must first be discovered some way to locate the target; this, of course, is almost impossible. Aerial torpedoes or depth bombs might be effective if the submarine were seen, but it is the business of the submarine commander to keep out of sight. Powerful searchlights have very little chance of picking up the periscope or conning tower of a submarine. I remember lying all one night in the *Argonaut*, during a storm, at the outer edge of the mine fields off Fortress Monroe, at the time the whole country was in dread of an invasion by Cervera's fleet during the Spanish-American War. We were in forbidden territory, having been delayed by the storm in getting into harbor before "Curfew" rang, so to speak. The powerful searchlights of Fortress Monroe were playing all night, but they did not detect our presence, as only our sighting hood was above water, and presented such a small object, and being painted white, it was not distinguished from the "white caps" on top of the sea caused by the storm.

Searchlights under water are useless because of the particles of foreign matter held in suspension which reflect back the glare of the light. The *Argonaut* was fitted with powerful searchlights and reflectors located in her extreme bow, with a pilot-house or lookout just above the three searchlight windows. The greatest distance we were ever able to see was during some night experiments in the Chesapeake Bay during a long dry spell, when the sediment had had an opportunity to settle, and that was only forty feet. The light would penetrate through the water several hundred feet and make a glow on the surface, but vision could not penetrate the water. For instance, it is said that after a storm a glass of Mississippi River water will show fully an inch of sediment. To see through three or four inches of that kind of water, therefore, one must see through an inch of mud. It is well known that no light has yet been found that will enable vision to penetrate through a heavy fog, due to the reflection of light upon the minute crystals of water held in suspension in the air. It appears hopeless, therefore, to expect vision to locate submarines by seeing through the opaque substance held in suspension in all water.

Echo and Magnetic Devices.—Locating submarines by echo has been proposed, but apparently without thought as to what would happen to the vessel giving out the sound in the effort to get an echo back from a submerged submarine, lying in wait with her "ears" waiting to hear some suspicious sound. Also, magnetic devices for the purpose of detecting submarines, if ever found practical, will probably be kept so busy leading their operators to and investigating large steel ships that have already been sunk by submarines that they will probably miss the little submarine, which can easily sink them while they are investigating these other sunken ships.

Channel and Open-sea Nets.—These have been and are being used with some success, but that success has been attained only because at the beginning of the war the submarines had no means for determining the presence of the nets before becoming entangled in their meshes, and when they once became entangled they had no means to cut themselves loose. Devices are now available which enable the commander of a submarine to locate a net before reaching it, and to destroy that net and all its attached mines with but little danger to his own vessel. To what extent these devices are being used is unknown. However, when the submarine is not especially fitted for the detection and destruction of nets and attached mines, they are probably the most efficient type of trap yet provided for capturing and destroying these "submarine devil fish." The *Scientific American* published an article by me in 1915 describing a submarine fitted with mine-evading devices and meant to under-run nets, which has been reproduced in the previous chapter.

THE U-65

Photograph copyright by Underwood & Underwood

One of the large German U-boats fitted with deck guns hailing a Spanish merchantman which they have held up.

RUSSIAN-LAKE TYPE

These vessels are powerfully armed, fitted with four torpedo tubes firing fore and aft, also Dzrewiecke apparatus for firing torpedoes to either broadside.

The above articles having been published previous to our country entering the war, and being thus of public knowledge, it is permissible to republish them as a method which might be used to advantage in preventing the German submarines from coming out from their bases. It is admitted that the allied fleets are overwhelmingly superior to the

208

German fleet, yet they are impotent to attack the German battle fleet or to make reprisals on Germany for the constant depletion of their merchant fleet, because Germany's fleet of battleships, cruisers, and merchantmen will not come out in the open, but lies safe behind nets and mine fields as their inner defence, using her submarines on her outer line of defence. As mentioned, Winston Churchill said we must "dig them out like rats out of a hole." That was over three years ago, but not one has been dug out as yet, and, although it would be a very expensive process to do so, it might be possible, by the coöperation of submarines, surface ships, trawlers, and aeroplanes, to move forward gradually and expansively a double or treble line of nets and to defend such a line of nets just outside of the range of the most powerful shore-defence guns. The battleships should be protected by operating between the line of nets to prevent attack upon them by submarines in the rear. Bottom-working submarines would be needed to clear away the mines and nets of the enemy as the mines and nets were moved forward. Constant patrol and repair of the nets would be maintained under the guns of the net-protected fleet, and allied submarines must be on constant attendance in advance of the first line of nets to meet the concerted attack of a portion of the German fleet in "rushing" the line—which must be expected in the attempt to break the same—in order to let out a fleet of their submarines into the open sea to continue their attacks on the allied and neutral commerce of the world. This seems to me the only practical way of stopping up the hole or holes through which the German submarines come out, and to make it effective it would require a double line of nets and patrol fleets extending from Norway to Scotland, and across the English Channel, and across the entrance to the Dardanelles from Brindisi, Italy, to the Albanian coast. Also, battleships which should be unsinkable and provided with longer-range guns than those of the enemy would be required. Perhaps the combined navies of the world as arrayed against the Central Powers could accomplish it, but unless their guns were more powerful and far-reaching than the shore guns, even then they could not land an invading army.

Submarines vs. Submarines.—Submarines to search for and sink other submarines have been proposed in all sorts of forms and advocated in the press under various titles, such as the "Bloodhounds of the Sea" and other fantastic and sensational captions. Submarines cannot fight submarines, because they cannot see each other, and if they are fitted with noiseless machinery they cannot hear each other. Therefore one might put thousands of submarines in the great ocean, and so long as they kept submerged the chance of their ever finding or colliding with one another would probably be not once in a year.

Derelicts have been known to keep afloat on the ocean for years, although constantly searched for as a menace to navigation. Here the searchers have had sight to aid them, and the object of their search has floated on one plane, the surface of the water, while submarines may navigate or remain at rest at various planes up to a depth of about two hundred feet, which is equivalent to multiplying the area of the ocean to be searched several times, and that in darkness, without the aid of sight to assist. It is ridiculous to think that anything can be accomplished except by the merest chance by one submarine searching for another.

Our attention will now turn to consideration of devices of the second class; namely, those which have been offered as a means of defence against the submarine.

Blinding Searchlight; Blinding Apparatus.—*Blinding devices* have been proposed which aim to direct powerful searchlights against the periscope so as to blind the commander. These are schemes based on very false notions. Submarine commanders frequently have to con their ship against the sun's rays, and have colored glasses to enable them to withstand the intensity of the sun's rays, so that it would be impossible to blind them this way. Further, I cannot imagine a more desirable target for a commander to direct his torpedoes against than a bright spot, either on the surface or submerged, as he knows the searchlight is probably on what he wants to hit; it becomes an illuminated bull's-eye for his target. Again, it has been proposed to blind the periscope by putting a film of oil on the surface to obscure the object glass of the periscope when it emerges through this oil, and a member of one of the British commissions told me he knew of shiploads of oil being pumped overboard, possibly for this purpose, or to show the course of a periscope through its "slick." Some periscopes have been built with means for squirting alcohol, gasoline, or other substances to clear the object glass if ice or salt forms on it. A device of this kind would clear off the oil.

Nets; Plates.—There have been many devices proposed for

warding off the torpedoes, the usual weapon of the submarine. The most common of these schemes designate the use of nets or plates suspended from booms carried out from the sides of the ship and extending down into the water. Any device of this kind seriously handicaps the ship's speed, and, if she is once sighted by a submarine, is almost sure to be come up with and attacked. Plates, to be effective against a broadside attack, would need to be the full length and extend to the full depth of the ship. Now, skin friction of a ship's plating is the principal resistance to be overcome in forcing a ship through the water up to speeds of about ten knots, the average speed of the cargo-carrying ship. If you increase the speed beyond ten knots, other resistances come more prominently into effect, such as wave-making resistance, etc. Now a ship afloat has two sides, while a plate suspended in the water equal to the length and depth of the ship also must have two sides, and thus presents nearly the same square feet of plate surface to the friction of the passing waters as the two sides of the ship, and two plates, one on each side, present nearly twice the area and thus very materially reduce the speed. This resistance is further augmented by the roll and pitch of the vessel, and in a severe storm the plates would be unmanageable and of great danger to the ship itself. The resistance of nets with its vertical members is much greater than that of plates. To get some idea of what the resistance of a vertical rod extending down into the water is, take a broom handle and attempt to hold it vertical when it is extended down into the water from a launch running at about ten knots; it is almost impossible to hold it. A net with a mesh fine enough to catch a torpedo would consist of thousands of vertical members as well as horizontal members extending down into the water.

I have been informed by one naval architect of standing who investigated this phase of the problem that nets of sufficient strength to protect the sides of a ten-knot ship from a torpedo attack cut the speed of the ship from ten knots down to two and one-half knots per hour. It would therefore take a ship protected in this way four times as long to make her voyage; her chance of discovery would therefore be four times as great and her chance of destruction, if once discovered, be almost certain, as a submarine could readily overtake her and plant mines in her course or even tow a mine underneath her bottom and explode it there, which would destroy the ship much more completely and quickly than a Whitehead torpedo exploded against her side.

Devices have also been developed which enable a torpedo to dive under a net and explode under a ship's bottom by a slightly delayed detonator.

Torpedoes have also been built with net-cutting devices, and they have been known to penetrate a ship's plating and sink the vessel without exploding. It is not an easy matter to stop a projectile weighing nearly a ton speeding at thirty-five or forty miles an hour. I can see no hope in stopping the submarine menace by any device in this class.

Magnets.—Some proposals have been made to divert the torpedo by powerful magnets extended out beyond the sides of the ship or at the ends—on the theory, I suppose, of fishing for little fish in a pan of water—the Whitehead torpedo being built of steel in this country and England. It is not generally known that the Schwartzkopf torpedo built by the Germans is built of bronze, or at least it was when I went through their works in Berlin several years ago. Even were it of steel, I doubt if a magnet could be built powerful enough to attract or divert a Whitehead steel torpedo from its course unless it passed very close to the magnet, as any artificially erected magnetic force diminishes in strength very rapidly as the distance from the object is increased. Recall, for instance, the powerful magnets used in handling scrap and pig iron; while they will lift pigs or billets of iron weighing tons when in direct contact, they will not exert sufficient magnetic force to lift any iron at a distance of only a few inches.

Bombs.—The throwing of bombs in the water to intercept the oncoming torpedo might possibly divert its course if the torpedo were seen, but of all the ships that have been lost how few have seen the torpedo which did the damage! The white wake due to the air exhausted from the engines of the torpedo is frequently seen, but the air wake does not show on the surface from a torpedo running at any considerable depth until after the torpedo itself has passed on, as it takes quite some time for the air bubbles to reach the surface, and in a choppy sea the wake is very difficult to see in any case.

Discs.—Whirling discs spinning through the water to catch the nose of the torpedo and whirl it out of its course is one of the fanciful schemes which has attracted some press notice. The horsepower required to whirl the discs during one voyage would probably tax the full capacity of the ship to provide fuel and power enough to keep them whirling.

C-1, ONE OF THE LATER TYPE FRENCH SUBMARINES
French-Official   Courtesy of Sea Power & Pictorial Press

Unsinkable Ships.—Unsinkable ships are possibly practical to a limited extent. Numerous proposals of ship construction along this line have been made, mostly of ships built up on the cellular system. Some proposals have also been made for carrying the cargo in hermetically sealed tanks that would assist in floating the ship if she were torpedoed. The objections to the construction of vessels of this class are its enormously increased cost over the ordinary cargo ship, the reduced carrying capacity per ton of displacement of such vessels, and the impossibility of preventing injury to ships of this sort to such an extent as to make them unmanageable. Any surface ship, to meet fully the submarine menace, must be not only *unsinkable, but it must also be indestructible.* When a ship once becomes unmanageable and incapable of getting away, a powerful mine or mines may be placed at considerable depth under her bottom and the whole fabric blown up into the air.

CARGO-CARRYING SUBMARINES OF THE AUTHOR'S DESIGN
They will carry 7500 tons of cargo on a surface displacement of 11,500 tons; their submerged displacement is about 13,500 tons.

Convoys.—Convoying a merchant fleet offers perhaps some safety to the individuals on the ships in case some of them are lost, but I cannot see that it offers much protection to the fleet as a whole, as the speed of the fleet is limited to that of the slowest ship, and the smoke or appearance of the leading ships are more apt to give a waiting slow-speed submarine time to catch up with the tail end of the fleet. If it came to a gun fight the fleet might have the advantage, but in experimental work I have frequently run in amidst a fleet of ships, and their first knowledge of my presence was when the periscope was extended above the surface. As it is only necessary to extend this for a period of a few seconds' duration to get the range and bearing of one of the ships to aim the torpedo, the chance of a gunner getting the range and hitting the periscope is very slight, and, even if the periscope were destroyed, it is easy to replace it with a spare one.

Smoke Screens.—To hide vessels in clouds of smoke so as to avoid being seen by submarines has been proposed as a method for eluding the U-boats. This procedure would really assist submarine commanders in their search for prey, for the smoke would notify them of the presence of vessels far below the horizon, whose location and course they would otherwise not be aware of. They have a term in the British navy called "firing into the Brown," which means firing at a group of vessels, expecting that a certain percentage of hits will be made, depending on how close a formation of ships is being kept; firing into the "smoke" would be apt to get some. Smoke screens can be used effectively only when the wind happens to be proportionate to the speed of the ships and blowing in the right direction. With a head wind or a strong side wind some of the vessels forming the convoy are sure to be exposed to attack.

Zigzag.—Steering zigzag courses adds to the time of crossing from one port to another, and affords only a slight measure of additional safety, as a ship running a zigzag course takes much longer to make a crossing, and is therefore longer exposed to danger; besides, this process adds very materially to the cost of the voyage. It probably does add somewhat to her chances of escape, as a submarine lying in wait anticipating that she will pass within torpedo range might be fooled by her zigzagging out of the way. On the other hand, a submarine might be lying in wait too far to one side of her course to be able to intercept her, and the ship might just as likely as not, not knowing she was there, zigzag right toward her and get caught.

In facing the submarine problem, the nations at war with Germany are thus forced to adopt tactics of three kinds: First, to destroy the enemy submarines—I have been informed from reliable sources that England has over five thousand vessels searching for U-boats; second, to make cargo vessels invulnerable to torpedo attacks; and, thirdly, to elude and escape the U-boats. No great measure of success, no great results, have come out of attempts of the first two orders; the U-boats have in general gone unscathed, and they have inflicted damage of such an appalling nature as to terrify those cognizant of the shipping needs of Europe. In my judgment, however, efforts to combat the submarine should be concentrated on devising ways and means to elude it; this is the only solution which promises results. I shall therefore devote the remainder of this chapter to a discussion of the problem of eluding submarines and how it may best be accomplished.

Cargo Submarines.—In my judgment, the only way that any nation will be able ultimately to continue its commerce with any degree of safety or certainty when blockaded by submarines will be by the construction of large merchant submarines which will be able to evade the enemy U-boats successfully.

I have pointed out above that "submarines cannot fight submarines," because they cannot see or locate each other. It is this very thing which will enable the cargo-carrying submarine to evade the military submarine. They are also able to evade all surface craft, either friend or foe. Captain Paul Koenig, of the *Deutschland*, told me that most of his journey in the *Deutschland* was upon the surface. He stated that her low visibility enabled him to see all approaching ships before they could see her, and that it was only necessary for him to submerge and rest until the surface ship had passed on her way. The tactics of the larger cargo-carrying submarines would be the same. They need not have much radius of action when submerged; all they need to do is to hide until the danger has passed. If desired, however, their radius of submerged action may be increased to equal or largely exceed that of a military submarine, but this would unnecessarily increase their cost of construction; otherwise the cost of building such vessels should not exceed twenty-five per cent. more than the cost of constructing a first-class surface ship.

Now I have prepared a few diagrams showing the advantage of various types of vessels in evading the submarine, and of these I shall treat immediately, as they illustrate the points of my contention perfectly. There was a time when everybody thought the earth was flat, but now I believe it is generally conceded that it is round. Every one knows that when the sun or moon sinks beneath the horizon it cannot be seen, neither can anything else which is below the horizon, so if the horizon intervenes between two distant observers they cannot see each other. Now by referring to our text-books we find that if an observer is stationed at a height of fifteen feet above the surface of the sea the horizon is five and one-eighths miles distant, so that if there were another observer stationed on the other side of the horizon at the same distance and height from the surface of the sea they could not see each other, as the surface of the earth or sea, being round, would stand up like a hill between them.

THE "DEUTSCHLAND"

By Courtesy of Motorship

The "Deutschland" was the first submarine cargo-carrier to cross the Atlantic Ocean. She was under the command of Captain Paul Koenig and proved the practicability of running the English blockade four times before war between Germany and the United States caused her owners to discontinue her sailings. Had war not come between the two countries, her German owners would undoubtedly have had submarine cargo-carrying vessels making weekly sailings between the United States and Germany.

The diagram shown herewith shows the distance of horizon in miles from 0 to two hundred feet elevation above the surface of the water.

I have drawn a sketch—in which the scale of distance is exaggerated in order to better illustrate my meaning—of the earth's surface to show the comparative visibility of vessels when seen from a military submarine, lying in wait, with periscope extended fifteen feet above water. Now take such ships as the *Lusitania*, shown in

217

position No. 5 on the diagram, with her smoke-stacks extending over one hundred feet above the surface of the sea; their tops would appear above the horizon and become visible to a distant observer with a powerful glass, stationed at, say, fifteen feet above the surface, at a distance of about eighteen and three-eighths miles. Her smoke-stack would also become visible through a telescopic periscope, the object glass of which was extended fifteen feet above the surface, while men seated in a rowboat could not see each other because of the intervening "hill," so to speak, at a distance of four miles apart. If they were under water in a submarine they could not see each other at all unless they had the periscopes elevated above the surface. In that case it would not be possible for one periscope to see another at any considerable distance, because the periscope is such a small object, and vision through it does not compare with natural vision, owing to the fact that there is considerable loss of light in passing the image of external objects through lenses and prisms. Hence it has been found necessary to reduce the field of vision to about one-half that of natural vision to give the effect of true distance, and as soon as twilight falls it is practically useless. I have taken fifteen feet above the surface without the submarine's conning tower showing, for if her conning tower is shown above the surface she is in danger of being herself discovered.

From the above data we are able to determine the probability of being discovered. We take the case of the largest and fastest ocean liners, such as the *Lusitania* as one illustration. We will assume that the *Lusitania* is making her maximum speed of about twenty-five knots, which is about the maximum of speed yet attained in a large surface freight-and passenger-carrying ship, and from our scale of vision as applied to upper diagram No. 5 we see that her top works will become visible above the horizon at a distance of eighteen and three-eighths miles from the periscope of the submarine. The commander in the submarine, by using his range and direction finder with which all military submarines are fitted, finds the ship to be pursuing a course and speed that will cause her to pass probably within ten miles of the submarine station in about thirty-five minutes, which is too far off to attack by torpedo. Now, while submarines have a submerged speed of only about ten knots, the commander is quickly able to ascertain that he can intercept the twenty-five-knot boat by laying his own course at right angles to the approaching ship, and that, if the ship keeps her course and speed, in thirty-five minutes he can be within torpedo range, as will be seen by reference to this sketch (see diagram, position No. 5).

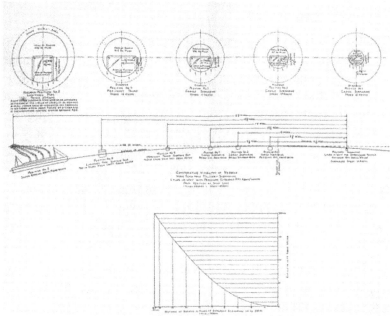

DIAGRAM TO ILLUSTRATE THE COMPARATIVE VISIBILITY AND CONSEQUENTLY THE COMPARATIVE SAFETY OF SURFACE SHIPS AND CARGO-CARRYING SUBMARINES

Now take for another comparison a slow-speed merchantman of the tramp type making ten knots, which is about the economical speed for this class of ship. Her smoke might be the first thing to betray her approach, but for purposes of comparison take her smoke-stack also, which is the first solid portion of the ship to appear. The smoke-stacks of this class of vessel would probably not be over forty feet in height above water level, therefore, if she were making the same course as the high-speed ship, it will be observed by referring to diagram, position No. 4, and the distance and speeds mentioned thereon, that the submarine at a speed of ten knots has more time to get nearer the course of the approaching ship and can have more time to calculate the enemy's speed of approach and direct course, and thus launch his torpedo with more certainty of making a hit. But assume that this approaching slow-speed ship had no solid opaque portion extending over fifteen feet above the surface of the water, as is the case in a cargo submarine as shown in position No. 3 on the diagram of the earth's surface. One now sees that she would pass the waiting submarine below the horizon, and the intervening round of the sea's surface would prevent the submarine from seeing her; thus she would pass by unseen and in safety.

The above series of diagrams will show the percentage of safety of ships of different characteristics when coming within the range of visibility of a submarine lying on the ocean highway waiting for passing ships; the submarine is assumed to have a submerged speed of ten knots in each instance. From an analysis of these diagrams it cannot be denied that practically one hundred per cent. safety could be secured could these cargo-carrying submarines cross the ocean from one friendly port to another and remain invisible during the entire journey, but at the present time this is impossible, because there is no known means of supplying sufficient power for long under-water voyages without drawing on the upper air in large quantities to assist combustion in either prime or secondary power-generating machinery.

The diagram plainly shows that a cargo-carrying submarine running awash, with her periscope and air intakes only above the water line, may approach within about five and three-quarters miles of any waiting military submarine without danger of being seen, as her "wake" would be below the horizon. Such cargo-carrying submarines can be built and can cross the Atlantic Ocean in this condition at a speed of about ten knots, and by maintaining a sharp lookout would have as much chance of seeing a military submarine as the military submarine would have of seeing them; and by the application of certain tried devices which I do not feel it proper to disclose at this time, but which are within the knowledge of our government authorities, the range of visibility can, I believe, be reduced to less than one mile. This type of vessel can almost instantly become entirely invisible by submerging at the least intimation of danger.

Such a type of vessel travelling with a freeboard of five feet would become visible to a submarine lying in ambush when she approached within eight miles. This increases the area of danger from one hundred and three square miles, as shown in diagram, position No. 1, in the first instance to two hundred and one square miles, as per diagram corresponding to position No. 2, but in comparison with the usual type of surface cargo-carrying ship of the so-called tramp type she is comparatively safe, as she has the ability to submerge in less than two minutes; and it is hardly likely that she would be attacked without warning, for fear she might be a friendly military submarine. Any communication in the way of wireless, sound, or other signals would, if she were a merchant ship, give her warning, and she would at once submerge, as her only business would be to deliver her cargo and not communicate with or expose herself to *either friend or foe*. When far from land she might take a chance and navigate entirely on the surface with a freeboard of fifteen feet, in which condition she can make a speed of eleven knots, as her position No. 3, on the surface of the ocean. This increases the danger area to about three hundred and thirty square miles, as on diagram, position No. 3, about three times the danger area shown on position No. 1, but as the area to be covered by the military submarine on the high seas, far from land, is also much greater, the real danger would be proportionately less than that with the lower visibility in a more thickly infested zone.

TORPEDO BEING FIRED FROM THE DECK TUBES OF THE SUBMARINE "SEAL"

This vessel was fitted with two double-barrel torpedo guns, housed in a superimposed superstructure. These four torpedoes could be fired to either broadside. The above photograph shows a torpedo in the act of leaving one of these tubes above water. They may be discharged either above or below the surface.

High Speed.—Speed is better than no defence, but no one would consider building twenty-five-knot freighters. The cost would be far out of proportion to the service. So long as U-boats do not betray their presence, a fast vessel is almost as liable as a slower one of less freeboard or lower top hamper. One can never tell where the submarine may be lurking, and her capacity to harm is determined by her ability to locate her prey. There are three means available to her to locate her target: first, her own sight; second, her sound-detecting devices; third, by wireless directions given to her by others who may advise her of the vessel's position. Her own sight is the best and usual means for locating her target. The above diagrams show that the largest and fastest ships can be located at much greater distances than the low visibility ships, and that the area of visibility becomes the area of danger, which is practically ten times greater in an expensive, large, high-speed liner over that of the comparatively low-cost cargo-carrying submarine.

BRITISH SUBMARINE NO. 3 PASSING NELSON'S OLD FLAGSHIP "VICTORY"

This submarine is of the Holland type, similar to the U. S. "Adder" and "Moccasin." This illustration shows the radical change made in naval warfare in one hundred years.

One should not imagine that the Germans are carrying on this campaign at random. It is well organized and systematic. Each vessel that comes in sight of a submarine is a marked vessel, and even if she is the fastest vessel afloat, she may speed unwittingly into a trap set for her by wireless. So long as she cannot disappear she has no real ability to elude. On the other hand, the cargo-carrying submarine of low speed has both these advantages: she has low visibility and the capability of disappearance. She may become invulnerable when danger threatens. She has all of the qualities possessed by her enemies. She may beat them at their own game. Vessels of the ordinary type will suffice in no way to meet the great problem presented by the U-boats. The cargo submarine, however, readily meets all the needs of the situation. This is the sole method of which I am cognizant by means of which a submarine blockade and the destruction of cargo-carrying vessels can be overcome with safety and with certainty. I have expected the Germans would blockade our own ports, as it is easily possible for them to do so; I believe the reason they have not done so thus far is because of political reasons, as it would undoubtedly be to their advantage to have our trade after the war, which they might not have if they arouse our hatred any more than they already have.

CHAPTER VII

THE SUBMARINE IN TIMES OF PEACE

So engrossed have been governments, inventors, capitalists, and the public in general, in the development of the submarine vessel for military purposes, and in the perfection and augmentation of its capabilities as a destructive agent, that they have never considered or realized that submarines and submarine appliances possess a wide range of utility as productive instruments in commercial and industrial operations.

This concentration of energy upon the construction of military submarines I believe to have been a very desirable thing, and the success which has been attained therein, I am convinced, augurs propitiously for the future well-being of the world. It is time now, however, to take up the development of the submarine for industrial purposes. The world stands in need, to-day, of services which the submarine is uniquely able to render.

While great publicity has been given to the art of submarine navigation as applied to warfare, little or nothing has been published, outside of scientific journals, as to the productive capacity of submarine devices. It seems desirable, therefore, to devote a few pages to consideration of the submarine in this other field of action. I myself have devoted the greater part of my own efforts to the construction of military submarines. But, in the early years of my work as a constructor of under-water vessels I was greatly attracted to this branch of submarine work, and from that time to the present I have spent a great deal of time and money in developing submarine appliances to be turned to peaceful uses. It is my aim to go into this work quite extensively when peace is restored to the world. At present, however, problems of national defence are occupying the attention of every naval architect.

I shall present in this chapter a few suggestions as to the uses to which submarine appliances may be turned as productive agents, and I shall speak briefly and simply as to the mode of operation of such devices. Many of the things of which I will write have actually been accomplished in vessels constructed by me. Others of which I write are now under process of construction. Still others are as yet visionary, but not at all impossible. Nothing of which I write do I believe to be impractical or improbable. The submarine can do many things in a new, more economical, and more productive way.

One important use to which the commercial submarine may be turned is that of navigating under ice fields, between ports which are bound with ice fields during great parts of the year, and also for purposes of exploration and of scientific study.

All navigators know the difficulty of attempting to break their way through the ice fields, since it requires a vessel of tremendous power and great weight to break down or through solid ice. A vessel of this type was first proposed by me in 1899 for exploration purposes in ice-covered seas. In 1903 experiments were made with the *Protector* in order to demonstrate the practicability of navigating in ice-covered waters.

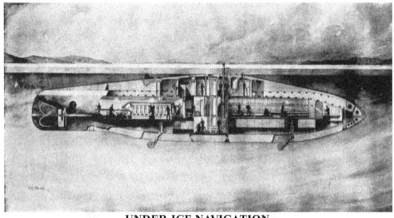

UNDER-ICE NAVIGATION

Under-ice boat designed by the author for navigating between ice-bound ports. A boat of this character could keep up communication between ports that are now closed by ice for several months of the year. Passengers, mail and freight can readily be transported in this manner with perfect safety. (See text.)

Professor Nansen, in his North Polar explorations, has stated in his book that his average rate of progress during eighteen months, in attempting to reach the North Pole, was only three-quarters of a mile per day, and that the thickest ice he found during these months of endeavor was fourteen feet. His progress was delayed by open waters, slush ice, and in the winter by the intense cold which compelled him to "hibernate" for a considerable period of time.

An under-ice submarine as illustrated, with large storage battery capacity, could navigate underneath the ice in perfect comfort and safety. The temperature surrounding the vessel, even in the most severe winter weather, would not exceed the temperature of the water surrounding the vessel. The vessel illustrated is designed to make a continuous submerged voyage of one hundred and fifty miles on one charge of the storage battery. After such a run, it would be necessary to stop and recharge the batteries. If open water should be encountered, this recharging process would be done by bringing the vessel to the surface. If the ice was not too thick, then by blowing out the water ballast the ice would be broken, since it is very much easier to lift the ice and break it than it is to force it apart or downward, as surface vessels are compelled to do. Provision is made for boring a hole up through the ice so as to permit the drawing in of sufficient air to run the engines and to recharge the batteries. Provision has also been made for putting out small mines underneath the ice to blow an opening to permit the submarine to come to the surface. A telescopic conning tower arranged to cut its way up through ice twelve or fourteen feet thick is also provided to enable the boat to remain under the ice and still permit the crew to reach the surface.

In navigating in an ice pack, the method of procedure would be to reduce the buoyancy of the vessel to, perhaps, a couple of tons, and then steam ahead, and it will be observed that the forward portion of the boat extends downward a considerable distance under the water, so that when the forward portion of the boat contacts with heavy ice the reserve buoyancy will not be sufficient to lift or push the ice out of the way, and the vessel will then be automatically pushed under the ice and run along in contact with the under surface of the ice. A toothed recording wheel would give the exact distance travelled, and, of course, the compass will give the direction. Progress could be made in perfect comfort and safety under the ice at a rate exceeding one hundred miles per day.

The *Protector* was fitted out in 1903 for experimental navigation under the ice with an inverted toboggan built up over the conning tower. This arrangement enabled her readily to navigate under ice fields, and she successfully navigated under an ice field in Narragansett Bay eight inches thick.

Ice two feet in thickness is sufficient to close navigation to the most powerful of ordinary surface ships, and great power is required to crush or break a lane through it by the specially equipped ice-breakers now used in northern latitudes.

While ice is a deterrent to surface navigation, it is actually an aid to under-water navigation, providing the submarine boat is specially equipped with guide wheels or "runners" on top of the hull to enable her to slide or wheel along under the ice.

A design of the under-ice submarine illustrated was prepared by me a number of years ago to meet the desires of an associate of Captain Nansen, the Arctic explorer, for a vessel that could be navigated either on the surface or under the ice. I explained the principal features and possibilities of a vessel of this type for under-ice navigation before the faculty of Johns Hopkins University, in Baltimore, in 1898, and at one time I thought one of the prominent New York newspapers was going to finance the building of such a vessel for North Polar exploration work, but the submarine was then looked upon as too much of an experiment and nothing ever came of the negotiations.

Some years afterward, in Christiania, Norway, I met and discussed the project with Captain Scott Hanson, R.N., who was associated with Nansen in his historical search for the North Pole, and he became quite enthusiastic over the possibilities of a submarine of this type for North Polar exploration.

An under-ice submarine of the type illustrated, fitted with large storage-battery capacity, would be able to average one hundred miles per day under the ice and about two hundred and fifty miles per day in open water. Starting from Spitzbergen, therefore, and going over Nansen's route, if the same conditions were met as he describes, the round trip to the Pole should be made in about ten days' time and in perfect comfort, as, no matter how cold the weather is above the surface, the temperature of the water is always above the freezing-point below the ice.

Later I was asked to submit to the chief engineer of one of the Canadian railways plans for an under-ice cargo-carrying submarine to enable them to transport passengers, mail, and freight from their mainland terminal at Vancouver to an open harbor on the island of

Victoria.

Cargo-carrying submarines fitted to under-run ice fields will shorten trade routes by opening up to navigation the Northwest Passage, and will also open up new ports in northern Europe and Asia, and provide an outlet for Siberian-grown wheat and other northern products which are not now utilized because of lack of transportation facilities.

Investigation of the geological formation of sea-bottoms, the flora and fauna of the sea, will be greatly assisted by bottom-creeping submarines. Fitted with powerful searchlights and moving-picture cameras, actual sea-bottom conditions may be reproduced up to depths of one thousand feet or more. The author, in 1898, succeeded in taking photographs through the windows of the *Argonaut* by means of an ordinary kodak, and last year the Williamson brothers showed in moving-picture houses throughout the country some wonderful submarine moving pictures they had secured by the use of their collapsible submarine tube.

One of the greatest pleasures in life so far denied to most men is to witness the constantly changing scenery of under-sea life in tropical waters. It has been one of the great desires of my life to explore the bottom of the southern seas. All of my submarine work has been in the more northern waters, covering the Chesapeake Bay, Long Island Sound, on the Atlantic coast north of Virginia Beach, and in the Baltic Sea and Gulf of Finland. The range of vision in any of these waters did not exceed forty feet, but that has been sufficient to create a zest for more. The beauties of under-sea life can be described only by a poet. It is impossible for me to convey to the imagination the wonderful beauty of some of the under-sea gardens when seen through the windows of a submarine automobile. Imagine, if you can, these under-sea gardens with masses of vegetation, swaying to the current and waves of the sea, of a great variety of form and color and with myriads of many beautiful and variously colored fishes swimming among them, with perhaps a background of a wonderful coral reef of fantastic shapes, with the octopus, or devil-fish, lurking at the mouths of dark caverns, and the long, gray man-eating shark, like a ghost now and then flitting within one's range of vision. Instead of the sky above you, you see a scintillating mirror which reflects the sun's rays as they penetrate the clear blue waters and strike the white sands and are reflected back to this under surface of the water and are then re-reflected back in multitudinous rainbows of color.

Such sights await the tourist of the future who visits some of the southern seas, with the further privilege of seeing some of the old wrecks, many of which have been lost since the days of the Spanish galleons by striking on some of these same coral reefs, and whose skeletons now lie at their base. I have built for my own use a combination house-boat and exploring submarine automobile, and hope in the near future to explore some of the southern waters along the Florida coast and in the Caribbean Sea; also, later to build larger submarine automobiles to enable "sight-seeing" parties to see some of the beauties of "Davy Jones' locker."

The Williamson brothers—Ernest and George Williamson—have, by the use of the Williamson extensible and flexible collapsible tube, invented by their father, Capt. Charles Williamson, and fitted with an observation chamber, succeeded in taking some wonderful moving pictures of under-sea life, which have been shown throughout the world and have thus given pleasure to millions of people in this country and abroad. I am indebted to the Williamson brothers for the loan of some of their wonderful under-sea pictures taken in the vicinity of Nassau, in the West Indies, where the waters are particularly clear, and the under-sea floral gardens, noted for their beauty, have been visited by tourists for many years, who view them through the glass-bottom boats. This method discloses some of their beauty, but does not begin to do them full justice, as compared with a view from under the water in their natural perspective. When viewed from above it is much like judging of the beauties of architecture of a city from a balloon, as one can only get a plan view.

The Williamson brothers commenced their experiments in submarine photography during the summer of 1913. Their first experiments proving satisfactory, the following year, 1914, they fitted out an expedition and visited the West Indies and there took several thousand feet of films of submarine motion pictures, showing some of the submarine gardens, divers fighting with sharks, an old wreck, etc. These were the first moving pictures of under-sea life that had ever been produced. "Still" under-water photography had been done by Dr. Francis Ward in a pond on his estate in England and by several others, but none of these experimenters had ever succeeded in getting the wonderful results such as those secured by the Williamsons in their 1914 expedition.

A SUBMARINE GARDEN AT THE BOTTOM OF THE SEA

Submarine Photo by Williamson Bros.

This photograph, taken in the vicinity of Nassau, shows a great variety of tropical submarine growth and fishes.

Since 1914 the Williamsons have produced many remarkable submarine scenes in the film productions known as "Twenty Thousand Leagues Under the Sea," "The Submarine Eye," and other photoplays.

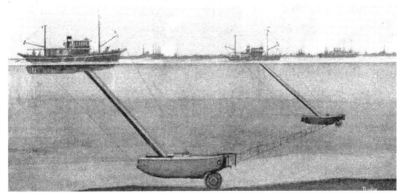

SUBMARINES FOR HYDROGRAPHIC WORK AND WRECK FINDING

Permission of Scientific American

A sweep line extending between the two submarines running parallel courses locates any intervening obstructions. (See text.)

As it is of historical value to record some of their experiences, I quote from Mr. Ernest Williamson's notes:

"During the first experiments in Hampton Roads, I found the condition of the water to be such that objects could be seen clearly for a distance of about six feet, and the photographic results showed that the fish and other objects photographed clearly at about four feet through the water. My theory, judging from the experiments, was that it would be possible to photograph through the water at almost the distance you could see clearly with the eye, and if it were possible to see through the water a distance of one hundred feet or more, as we were informed could be done in the West Indies, I reasoned that we could possibly get good photographic results at a distance of seventy-five feet.

"The latter proved to be correct, although in the middle of the experimental work I was a little bit concerned about a published record at that time of the experiments made by a Dr. Francis Ward in England. This Doctor Ward had built a cement well in the edge of a pond in his estate, and through a plate-glass window in the side of this well, under water, he had photographed fish and water-fowl. The *Illustrated London News* devoted four or five pages to his photographs and technical description of his work, and he made a point, in drawing his conclusions, that he believed that under the most favorable conditions it would be possible to photograph through water at a distance not exceeding three feet. None of his photographs showed any more than this, and he seemed to have technical reasons for believing that three feet was the limit.

"During the extensive work we have carried on in the West Indies, making scenes for our various productions, I have been down in the operating chamber at the base of the Williamson tube, when the water was so clear at times I have seen objects at a distance of two hundred feet—possibly more. At such times we have made motion pictures showing objects clearly at a distance of one hundred and fifty feet. These results were obtained at a depth of thirty feet. I have been down sixty feet in the chamber, and, of course, the greater the depth the less the sunlight under water and naturally the photographic results are not so good, but with the banks of Cooper-Hewitt lamps, which I successfully encased in watertight containers for the purpose of illuminating the under-sea, we obtained excellent results within a radius of the greater volume of this artificial light.

"For exploration and scientific work the artificial lights are a valuable adjunct, as they make it possible to photograph at any depth and at any time; but, there being so many other details to be taken care of in the taking of a scene under water, we try to do them all in the daytime. With as many as five divers operating in a scene, the divers wearing self-contained suits with no connection with the surface, having the tide and wind and the photographic apparatus and other things to be all worked at the same time, it is better to be working in the daylight, when you can keep your eye on the sharks and take care of the divers."

The reproduction of under-sea photographs shown in this book will give the reader some intimation of the "wonders of the deep," but unfortunately the wonderful colors and the play of light and movement cannot be reproduced.

Similarly, for scientific purposes as well as those of safeguarding navigation, submarines equipped for hydrographic work will prove of immense value. My work with submarine boats, both in the United States and foreign countries, has taught me that most charts are very unreliable, so far as their recorded depths are concerned. While they may be fairly accurate as to the average depths, they do not record many of the peaks or depressions that exist, especially where the water-bed is formed over a rock foundation. Silt and sand may fill in the depressions between peaks so that the average depth is fairly constant, yet here and there are outcropping peaks or humps that have, in many instances, proved fatal to shipping.

The method of charting our coast lines and the estuaries of the sea has been by the use of the sounding lead, taken at points a greater or less distance apart. The depths recorded at these points are plotted by the triangulation method of location from tripods or known structures, or objects on shore, and shown on the chart. These points would need to be taken every few feet to give an accurate topography of the bottom, the cost of which, in time and money, would be prohibitive. Assuming that our coast waters were sounded and depths recorded, at points only fifty feet apart in all directions, even such close soundings would not guarantee that some peak might not project above the bottom and prove disastrous to some ship.

I remember some few years ago the battleship *Missouri* struck such a peak in New York Harbor, seriously injuring her bottom. Thousands of ships of equal draft had passed this vicinity, but none of them had happened to strike this particular spot and no one suspected that such a rock existed in this much-frequented highway. In 1900 the steamer *Rio de Janeiro* struck an unknown rock in entering the harbor of San Francisco, with a loss of one hundred and thirty-one lives and over two million dollars in property.

In Long Island Sound we found, during a deep submergence trial with one of our submarines, a depth of two hundred and fifty-six feet, whereas the chart indicated a depth of only twenty-seven fathoms (one hundred and sixty-two feet).

In one instance in Russia we were conducting submerged trials on the official trial course of the Russian Government in the Gulf of Finland, this being the course on which they tried their surface torpedo boats, and we were assured that there was not less than sixty feet of water on the course, yet we struck rock peaks twice on this course in less than thirty feet depth. The record of ships that have been lost, due to striking uncharted rocks and shoals, is a large one, and a more correct topography of the water-beds of our coast and inland waterways should be worked out. In 1899 and 1901 considerable time was spent in experimental work with the submarine boat *Argonaut* in locating sunken ships and recovering their cargoes. To find a sunken ship it was necessary to search the bottom thoroughly, and many experiments were made and success attained to such an extent that we could search thoroughly an under-water area of from ten to twenty square miles per day. It is the result of this experimental work that has led to the design of the herein-described apparatus, which will give very accurate contour records of the bottom within such depths as would prove of interest to navigators of either surface vessels or submarines. The advent of the submarine has made it more important to know where obstructions exist, as they require at least seventy feet depth to navigate at speed entirely submerged and to enable them to keep below the bottom of surface ships. This method of water-bed surveying consists of using two or more submarine boats of my bottom-navigating type, with access tubes extending to surface vessels. Instead of using two bottom wheels arranged in tandem, as is used on my military submarine, I use a single pair of toothed driving wheels capable of being swivelled and driven to propel the submarine in any desired direction over the bottom. The submarine vessel contains also a diver's compartment, so that examinations of the bottom may be made and a record kept of the materials and conditions found, which are recorded as frequently as may be desired directly on the contour sheet, on which the soundings are being automatically recorded.

Navigators of surface vessels are interested principally in knowing the amount of water they have beneath their keel and the nature of the bottom, so that they may judge of their location by soundings, especially in time of fog. It is not essential, therefore, to know every foot of the bottom, but it is essential to know that no obstructions exist extending nearer to the surface than their keel. It is also essential for submarine commanders to know that there are no obstructions nearer the surface than their depth of submergence, if they are running submerged at speed. It is possible that collisions with submerged obstructions may have been responsible for some of the mysterious submarine fatalities.

This method of bottom investigation permits of very accurate contour lines being run as close together as may be desired for harbor work. On the coast, in depths exceeding fifty to seventy-five feet, if contours were run one-half mile apart, it would probably be satisfactory if a guaranty could be given that there were no obstructions over five or six feet in height which lay between such contours. Two vessels as herein described are capable of automatically recording parallel contours at the rate of two or three miles per hour and to guarantee that there are no dangerous obstructions lying between them.

Referring to page 267, a surface vessel is shown with a well which extends from under the pilot-house and out under her stem. An access tube extends from this well forward to a small submarine vessel. The upper end of this access tube is pivoted to strong bearings secured in the sides of the well, and is further secured by tension rods extending from part way down the tube to bearings secured to the outer skin of the ship in line with the bearings in the well. Large bearings with stuffing boxes in the submarine boat end of the access tube permit of access through a door to an air-lock compartment, and a second door leads from the air-lock into the diving compartment, a sliding door in the bottom of the diving compartment permitting the door to be opened for inspection of the bottom. By donning a diving suit members of the crew may also leave or enter the vessel when on the bottom. The water is kept from entering the diving compartment by air compressed to the same pressure as the surrounding water pressure, corresponding to the depth of submergence, the same as is done in my military submarine boats. A motor, drawing its power from a dynamo on the surface vessel, drives through suitable gearing the tractor wheel arranged near the bow of the submarine. This tractor wheel may be turned by its vertical steering post so as to propel the vessel in any desired direction.

The weight of the submarine upon the bottom is regulated by water ballast. A depth-recording device operates in connection with a distance-recording apparatus, so that an exact contour of the bottom is reproduced on a roll of paper, the record being made by the revolution of the tractor wheels. Corrections of errors are made by taking observations from the surface vessels from known points on shore by the usual triangulation method.

A drum is mounted on the submarine on which is wound a double wire. The upper wire is an insulated wire and is used to telephone between the two submarine vessels. The lower wire is a bare wire and is used to locate obstructions. The two wires are secured together as shown. Suitable recording devices in the interior of each vessel give the amount of wire unwound from its drum. A tension regulator holds a certain desired strain or pull upon the sweep lines, and another indicator gives the direction of lead of the wires during the "sweeping" operations. The surface vessel has a propeller in her skeg operating athwartship in addition to the usual stem propeller.

The method of operation is as follows: Two vessels are required, which proceed to the location to be charted. In surface navigation the submarine, carried at the forward end of the access tube, is emptied of her water ballast and floats on the surface in front of the surface vessel, being pushed ahead of the latter vessel by the access tube, the pivoted bearings at each end of the tube giving sufficient flexibility to prevent any damage to the tube because of strains set up by the waves.

One of the vessels takes her station at the point of beginning the day's survey and anchors; the other vessel then comes sufficiently near to secure the end of the sweep line from the anchored ship and then moves over to her starting point, which might be only a few yards away or as much as a mile. I have found, in wreck-sweeping operations, that it is practical to go as much as a mile apart, depending upon how close together the contours are desired. These sweep lines of the two vessels are then joined together and the submarines sink to the bottom, on which they are allowed to rest with sufficient weight to prevent their being drifted out of their course.

We will assume that their starting points are one-half mile apart, and that they are to run contour lines due west from their respective starting points. The boats should therefore lie due north and south from each other, and the sweep lines should lead at right angles from each toward its companion boat. The dynamo is now started in the surface vessel to supply the motors in the submarines with power. The two submarines now start ahead.

The surface vessels, by means of their athwartship propellers, are always kept headed due west, therefore the course must also be due west. Each operator in the submarine keeps watch on his indicator, which records the amount of line paid out, and also enables him to be kept advised, by frequent inquiry through the telephone, of the amount of line his companion vessel has out. The operators also keep each other advised of the distance their respective vessels have travelled and the direction of lead of sweep line. Thus they can always keep each other on lines due north and south. If now an obstruction is struck, such as a rock, a sunken ship, etc., the strain on the sweep line becomes greater than normal, and the line commences to run off its drum. After running a short distance the sweep line will begin to lead aft instead of at right angles to the course. The two operators then stop and advise each other of the lead of the line. The one whose line leads the greater number of degrees off from right angles to the course is nearest the obstruction. He now turns his tractor wheel in the direction of the lead and wheels over to the obstruction, taking in his sweep lines as fast as he goes. The characteristics of the obstruction are noted, and its position accurately located by the triangulation method and recorded on the chart. In practice this sweep line extends a few feet above the bottom so as not to pick up small boulders, stones, etc., and would be caught only on the larger submerged objects. In taking off the readings from the contour sheets, when plotting the depths on the charts, the assurance can be had that no obstructions exist between the surface and the depth of the sweep line, as the depth and contour recording gauge is located at the height of the sweep line. The actual contour depth would be the distance between the sweep line and the water-bed, which could be added if desired.

As the submarine may be used for purposes of making navigation more safe, so also may it be used for the recovery of ships' cargoes and for salvaging ships which have had the misfortune to be sunk.

In searching for sunken vessels two boats are used, of the same general type as the "hydrographic submarine." When a wreck is located divers go out and examine it. If it is concluded that she has cargo on board worth salving, her location is plotted on the chart and then the recovery boats are sent out to remove the cargo. I have done much experimental work in locating sunken wrecks and recovering their cargoes. In 1898, 1899, and 1900 the *Argonaut* and special wreck-finding apparatus were used in this experimental work. Numerous wrecks were found and a number of cargoes were profitably recovered, notwithstanding the fact that the apparatus used was crude and experimental. In 1901 I was called from this line of work to take up the construction of submarine torpedo boats, and have been too busy ever since, building for the United States and foreign governments, to find the time and opportunity to push on this very interesting phase of submarine work.

THE "ARGONAUT" SUBMERGED

Drawn by C. McKnight Smith for *Harper's Weekly*, April 1, 1899. (By permission. Copyright 1899 by Harper & Brothers.) This shows the remodelled "Argonaut" with her buoyant ship-shaped superstructure, on a submerged wrecking expedition, as was actually accomplished in the years 1900-1901.

Searching for sunken vessels is, perhaps, the most interesting of all submarine work. It is like fishing. One is always on the *qui vive* for a "bite." There is hardly a location along our coast or in Long Island Sound that does not have a tradition about lost treasure ships, and every time one gets a "bite"—that is, our lines get fast to some sunken object—excitement runs high in the expectation of some valuable find. In my experimental work in the vicinity of Bridgeport, Connecticut, we located sixteen sunken vessels, the great majority of them containing coal, which we recovered at a cost of about fifty cents per ton. Most of these vessels had been sunk a long time. Only a few of them were known by name, and some had evidently been sunk many years. One that we searched for during several months had a cargo of copper ore and copper matté which was quite valuable. We finally found her several miles away from where people testified they saw her disappear.

Somewhere off Bridgeport lies the wreck of the old Sound steamer *Lexington*. Legend has it that she has a fortune in her safe. Many a ship has been sunken in the waters about Hell Gate; search was carried on there for years for the old British frigate *Hussar*, which struck on Pot Rock and sank during the Revolutionary War. Tradition has it that she had four million dollars (£820,000) in gold on board to pay off the British troops, and that she carried this treasure to the bottom with her. There is a cargo of block tin somewhere in a sunken barge off the Battery, and many a ship with valuable cargoes lies along the coast from Newfoundland to Key West. The yearly loss in ships and cargoes throughout the world has always run into many millions of dollars, and since the war this has been multiplied a hundred-fold, and amounts to billions. The time will come when many of these ships will be found, and such of their cargo as is still valuable will be salvaged. Salving a sunken cargo is not a difficult engineering feat, providing the proper apparatus is at hand. It is the novelty of the enterprise and the mystery surrounding submarine work that make it so difficult to the layman. Diving, as heretofore conducted, has been difficult and dangerous work, and only the strong could stand the hardships connected with it. The advent of submarine salvage vessels fitted with proper machinery and in the application of scientific methods, however, will clear away many of the hardships and dangers connected with salving a sunken cargo, and more experience and proper apparatus will prove that certain cargoes may be removed from sunken ships in moderate depth with almost as much rapidity as they can be lifted from the hold of a vessel alongside of a dock. Take anthracite coal, for instance. With a six-inch pump, on the old *Argonaut*, I have transferred fifteen tons of nut coal from a sunken barge to a sunken freight-carrying submarine in nine minutes. A turn of the air valve then sent the sunken freight boat to the surface. The coal was transferred while all the boats were submerged in seven fathoms of water. It was this kind of experimental work which has enabled me to devise apparatus which will undoubtedly operate successfully on a much larger scale, as explained in the illustrations.

EXPERIMENTAL CARGO-RECOVERING SUBMARINE

This vessel was built in 1899 and experimented with in 1900, to demonstrate the practicability of transferring cargoes from sunken vessels to submarine freight carriers. (See text.)

The crucial feature of diving operations lies in the time required in decompression, which, if held within the limits given by Fleet Surgeon Mourilyan, would practically limit diving operations to half the present depth of submergence and greatly increase the cost and the time demanded for such undertakings. Strange as it may seem, the human body will stand an immense amount of compression, but the greatest care must be taken to make the recovery to normal a very slow and deliberate process. Doctors Leonard Hill and Greenwood, of the London Hospital Medicine College, have conducted a series of scientific investigations regarding the physical limits of a normal man to compression without risk of strain or ultimate injury. Remarkable as it seems, they have shown that it is possible to submit to a pressure of seven atmospheres—the equivalent of a submergence to a depth of two hundred and ten feet, a depth considerably in excess of the best diving records up to the time of their experiments. These gentlemen proved conclusively that immunity from serious consequences could be assured, provided the period of decompression was sufficiently long. The experiments were not made under water, but were made in an experimental air-chamber especially fitted up for them by one of the big English submarine engineering companies.

SKETCH DRAWING ILLUSTRATING A METHOD OF TRANSFERRING CARGOES FROM SUNKEN VESSELS TO SUBMERGED FREIGHT CARGO-CARRYING SUBMARINES

Demonstrated as practical in 1900 by the combined use of the "Argonaut" and the demonstrating freight-carrying submarine shown above.

Under the conditions usually prevailing in the fields wherein divers are employed, it is not possible, with the systems of working generally adopted, to provide this period of decompression nor to work with this studied deliberation when descending from or when ascending to the ordinary surface vessel. The suit of a diver weighs over two hundred pounds, and when inflated the bulk is considerable. A diver being lowered from a vessel is swung to and fro like a pendulum, and if there is any sea on—the open sea is never entirely still—the surge naturally affects the diver so that it is beyond human possibility to limit his descent to a nicety or to take the time either in going down or coming up that science has proved necessary to his physical well-being in the most generous sense. The greater the depth the greater the difficulties, and to reach a submergence of one hundred and fifty feet is now practically prohibitive except under ideal conditions. The semi-submergible boat has, however, met the problem squarely and has overcome many of the difficulties heretofore deemed insuperable. The simplicity and the practicability of the working principle involved are graphically shown by the accompanying drawings.

This combination consists of a tube which may be built of any desired length or so constructed that this may be increased by the insertion of additional sections. This tube is provided with an operating compartment or working chamber at the free end, and water-ballast tanks are distributed throughout the length of the tube so that the structure can be placed in equilibrium with the water when ready for submergence. In the working chamber there are also water-ballast tanks by which that end of the tube can be sunk and caused to rest upon the bottom with any desired pressure or dead weight. This operating chamber has a hatch and door located in its bottom. This bottom door can be opened when needed—the whole compartment becoming then a virtual diving bell, so that divers can be sent out if so wished, or operations through this open passage to the water-bed can be pursued by means of tools and appliances controlled from within the compartment. There is also an air-lock or equalizing chamber. Its purpose is to enable the operators to become gradually accustomed to change of pressure when entering or when leaving the working chamber when the latter is being used with the bottom door open; the air pressure within the compartment would be maintained in constant accord with the water pressure corresponding to the particular depth at which this tube would be in use. The tube itself may have its upper end attached to the side of a surface craft, but preferably it floats in the well of a craft especially designed to work in combination with it, as shown.

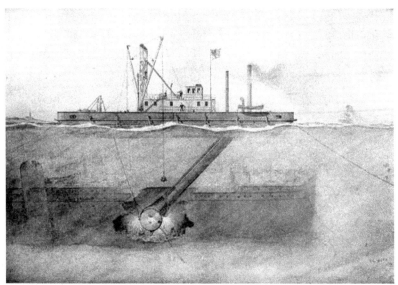

SEMI-SUBMERGIBLE WRECKING APPARATUS

The submergible tube has the diver's operating compartment shut off from the rest of the apparatus by means of an air lock which permits passage from the surface vessel and normal air pressure to the diver's compartment, where the air is under pressure equal to the compartment's depth of submergence, when the diver's exit door is open. The above illustration shows divers "breaking" the cargo out of the hold of a sunken ship and sending it to the surface.

The general method of operating upon a submerged wreck is as follows: The vessel carrying the tube is brought to the place of operation; it may be carried there either by towing or by its own power. The carrying vessel is moored over the wreck by quartering lines; anchor lines connect with anchors run out abeam on each side of the vessel. These lines are controlled from within the operating chamber, when once the anchors are planted, so that the lower end of the tube, when submerged, may be swung through the arc of a circle within the pivotal point at the buoyant end attached to the surface vessel.

The operating chamber and tube are lighted electrically, and electricity also supplies power control within the chamber. Compressed air is led into this compartment to supply the chamber when operating under pressure and also to supply any divers sent out therefrom at such times.

The surface vessel being properly moored, the ballast compartments are flooded and the working end of the apparatus

244

allowed to settle near enough to the wreck to permit of inspection through the "aquascope," or the bottom door may be opened and divers sent out for more intimate inspection, and instructions may then be telephoned to the surface vessel so to change her position that the working compartment may be located in the place most convenient to act as a base for carrying on the operations of recovering cargo, making repairs, etc., as the occasion may demand.

The position of the operating chamber may be over the hatchway of a ship, or, in the case of an old and worthless hulk, the decks may be blown off and the working end of the apparatus lowered right down through and on to the cargo itself. Sufficient additional water ballast may now be introduced to hold the working chamber securely to the bottom, or it may be held fast to the hulk itself, if that course be preferable. It will thus be seen that communication is now established between the surface and the submerged vessel at the point where it is desired to carry on the operations, and it will be realized that this can be accomplished without the use of divers and in absolute safety throughout the range or reach of the apparatus. The operators are protected by a strong steel tube, which now forms a sheltered passageway to and from the surface under normal atmospheric pressure, and no more skill is required to go down within working reach of the sunken ship than that required to go up or down a flight of stairs. It will also be seen, by referring to the sketch, that the operators are where they are protected from the currents, and even quite a severe storm on the surface would not interfere with work below, so long as the surface vessel could be held to her moorings.

The illustration shows a wrecking plant of the "Lake" design as it appears when operating on a sunken steamship. The case taken for illustration is that of a vessel that had been sunk for some time and where it had been considered advisable to blow away the decks in order to enable the operating compartment of the tube to be lowered right down into the cargo hold. The ship's hold is lighted up electrically, and the work of removing the material follows. A light down-haul line leads from the lower block of each set of derrick falls, and is led through a block secured conveniently to the diver's station. This line is handled by an electric winch in the operating compartment. Its purpose is to return the hoisting line with its sling to the divers after each load has been discharged upon the surface craft.

As the divers operate only a few feet from the working chamber, they are protected from the surge of the surface boat, with its attendant pull on air-hose and life-line, and also from possible aggravation by currents; and, as the handling of all lines is done by mechanical power, work of recovery may be carried on in a very expeditious manner with a minimum of stress upon the operator.

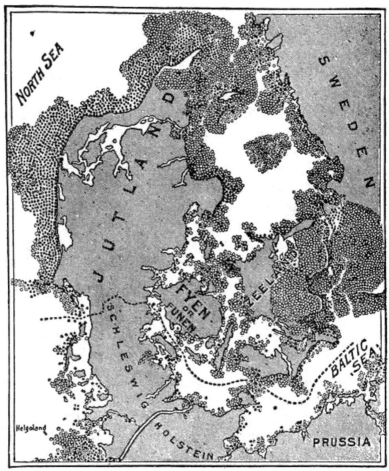

THE "CAVIAR MAP" OF SHIPPING'S GREATEST GRAVE-YARD
(The little circles represent wrecks.)
Reproduction of a chart published by the German Hydrographic Office, giving a list of wrecks which have occurred in the locality pictured during a period of only fifteen years. This great loss of shipping was one of the principal causes leading up to the construction of the Kiel canal.

In many waters the divers would be engaged in plain view of their tenders in the operating compartment, who would handle the down-pull lines and transmit signals by bell or telephone to the control station on the boat above. Work is thus carried on continuously by relays of divers who are thoroughly conversant with the progress of the undertaking and the circumstances affecting performance. Through the medium of the equalizing room the divers, who leave their helmets, shoes, and weights in the operating chamber, are able to undergo slowly and comfortably either decompression or compression after or before each shift. They can remain in the equalizing room as long as necessary to effect this in the way most conducive to their physical well-being. This compartment is well lighted, is fitted with seats, and provides every reasonable convenience for the diver during this intermediate stage.

Statistics have been published to show that practically the entire commerce of the world sinks in every twenty-five years. In the present war the rate of sinking has been, of course, enormously accelerated, and millions of tons of ships have been sunk, with billions of dollars' worth of cargo. Many of these vessels were sunk in the North Sea or the English Channel, where the water is comparatively shallow, and where many of the cargoes can undoubtedly be recovered with the proper apparatus. The loss of ships in peace times is such a common occurrence that little attention is paid to them except when their loss is accompanied by great loss of life, as was the case with the *Titanic*, the *Monroe*, the *Empress of Ireland*, or the *Lusitania*. There are therefore great opportunities for devices of this nature to operate profitably.

Another use to which the submarine may be put is the recovery of shellfish from the sea bottom. For such work as this adaptations of the submarine vessel are well fitted.

A submarine vessel of the "Lake" bottom-working type has been designed and is now being built for the location of and the recovery of shellfish on a large scale. Shellfish abound on both the Atlantic and Pacific coasts in great quantities. They are about the most delicious and nutritious food known to man. The most common shellfish are the oyster, the round or hard-shell clam, the long-neck or soft-shell clam, the scallop, and, on the Pacific coast, the abalone, which is valuable both for its mother-of-pearl shell and its meat, which is a great delicacy, the most of which is sent to Japan, either dried or canned.

My own sea-bottom investigations, combined with the sea-bottom investigations of the United States Fish Commission, have led me to the conclusion that edible shellfish abound along our coast in such great quantities that they can become an important rival to our meat-growing and packing industries, provided the proper apparatus is used for their recovery. I have, when "wheeling" along the bottom, found beds of the round or hard-shell clam in such great quantities that there must have been thousands of bushels to the acre. This was in waters too deep to be recovered by the usual clammers' apparatus. It is impossible to dredge for the soft-shell clam, as the shell is too delicate, and to pull them out of their bed would crush them. The abalone attach themselves to rocks, and it requires considerable force to break their hold, so there is no known means to recover them with surface ships.

The oyster industry is the only one that has thus far been developed by planting and cultivating methods, so that it is now a great industry, employing thousands of steam, internal-combustion, and sail boats in their cultivation and collection for the market. The method employed by the largest growers is by the use of power boats which drag dredges. These are rakes with a meshed bag dragging on the bottom back of the tooth bar of the dredge to collect the oysters after they are raked or torn up from their beds. This is not a scientific method, for the reason that many of the oysters are killed by the heavy dredge being dragged over them. It is largely a hit-or-miss or grab-in-the-dark method, as it is impossible to clean up the ground in this manner. Some oyster grounds will produce from three to four thousand bushels of oysters to the acre. When dredging is started it is only necessary to drag the dredge a few feet before it is filled; then, as the oysters become thinner, the drag becomes longer. They drag in all directions across the grounds, but, as they cannot see the bottom, there are places they never hit, because the wind and currents prevent a systematic covering of the ground.

SUBMARINE OYSTER-GATHERING VESSEL

By admitting water ballast into ballast tanks the vessel is allowed to sink to the bottom with sufficient weight to afford traction to the toothed driving wheels in the central operating compartment. This compartment is open at the bottom; water is prevented from entering it by the use of compressed air. As this apartment is well lighted the oysters may readily be seen lying on the bottom the full width and length of the compartment. When the boat is given headway the oysters are automatically transferred into the cargo holds by means of a system of pipes and suction pumps to induce a flow of water which carries the oysters from the dredges.

The design of a submarine oyster-dredging vessel is such that the vessel goes down to the bottom direct and the water is forced out of the centre raking compartment so that the oysters may be seen by the operator in the control department. With only a few inches of water over them, headway is then given to the submarine and the oysters are then automatically raked up, washed, and delivered through pipes into the cargo-carrying chambers, as shown. Centrifugal pumps are constantly delivering water from the cargo compartments, which induces a flow of water through the pipes leading from the "rake pans" with sufficient velocity to carry up the oysters and deposit them into the cargo holds. In this manner the bottom may be seen, and by "tracking" back and forth over the bottom the ground may be cleaned up at one operation.

The author's design of vessel illustrated has a capacity of gathering oysters from good ground at the rate of five thousand bushels per hour. The use of the submarine will make the recovery of oysters more nearly like the method of reaping a field of grain, where one "swath" systematically joins on to another, and the whole field is cleaned up at one operation.

In many other fields of industrial and commercial enterprise the submarine is qualified to render valuable services. In general submarine engineering work; in the construction of breakwaters, lighthouses, driving piles and building abutments, and in the deepening and improvement of waterways and harbors, the submarine will be utilized. In prospecting for, and the recovery and separation of, gold from river-beds and sea-coast bottoms submarine devices have been found to be very efficient and economical. A new method of laying tunnels under water has been proposed in which adaptations of the submarine boat will play a great part. However, these latter developments of the submarine are so highly specialized and a description of them would be so very technical that mere mention of these possibilities will be sufficient for the purposes of this book.

Thus it is evident that the submarine has a utility entirely apart from that of a military weapon. Its unique qualities fit it for the labors of peace as well as for those of war. Of course, in both cases, either as a naval weapon or as an industrial mechanism, it is the unique capacity of submergence possessed by the submarine which makes it of value, and in either case it is the question of accessibility which is all-important. In the war use the chief function of the submarine is to make itself inaccessible to the foe. It is immune from attack because it cannot be seen. It is able to strike at its foe with success because its presence is not detected by him. It is thus able to make use of its destructive energy in perfect safety. On the other hand, the chief value of the industrial submarine lies in the fact that it constitutes a means of access to places otherwise inaccessible to men. It is very desirable and very profitable for men to go down into the depths of the sea. There are things well worth doing on the bed of the ocean. Travel may be made safe, goods of great value may be brought up, foodstuffs of the first order may be obtained there; with submarines men may prosecute their labors beneath the sea with very little danger and at a minimum of cost. The diver's profession will become, through the use of this mechanism, an important factor in the economic affairs of the world.

CHAPTER VIII

THE DESTINY OF THE SUBMARINE

Studies of the submarine which deal with the subject solely from the engineering or military standpoint, or which treat of the development of this weapon simply in the light of its strategic value, fail to recognize the human aspects of the problem.

I have stated in the Foreword that at the present time the submarine is a tremendous factor in the political and industrial economy of the world, and I believe that a treatment of the submarine which gives no consideration to it in this broader relationship to the life and welfare of humanity is altogether incomplete. In my opinion, just as the submarine is to-day a power to be reckoned with in the world—an agency the prodigious capacity for destruction of which we realize but too well—so is it to be in the future an instrument the influence of which upon the progress and safety of the nations of the earth will be well-nigh incalculable. Temporarily, it presents itself as a power for evil, as the weapon, the bludgeon, as it were, of either a misguided people or of an overbearing and power-thirsty aristocracy; permanently, I believe, it will prove to be destined to work for the highest good of humanity, and will serve the noblest and most intimate interests of men; for, as I have asserted above, the submarine has by no means been brought to its fullest measure of development. The limit of its capabilities has not been approached by modern ship constructors, even remotely. It will have a future; it has a destiny; it will serve mankind.

There have been many criticisms and attacks directed at the submarine and against the designers of submarines within the past few years. These may be classified in general into two main categories: first, those which discredit the submarine on the basis of its mechanical limitations, and, secondly, those which assail the submarine on moral and humanitarian grounds and condemn the use of the weapon as piratical and murderous. For people who criticise the submarine on the grounds first stated I have little sympathy; they are those "who have eyes and see not, and having ears, hear not." They disavow the very testimony of the senses. I can, however, fully sympathize with those who attack the submarine on the latter basis; the events of the past three years may have borne this conviction upon them. Yet they also fail to realize that the submarine, in the end, will render great benefits and service to the world. They judge too much from the present and look too rarely into the future. By way of answering these criticisms I will be able to present the facts concerning the future of the submarine as they appear to me after years of thought and experimentation in this field.

THE "ARGOSY AND ARGONAUT III"

A house boat with submarine and access tube attached, built by the author in 1917, for pleasure and experimental purposes in making underwater explorations and investigation of sea coast waterbed formation, in locating beds of shellfish, wrecks, etc., and to demonstrate the practicability of their recovery. The house boat is 100 ft. overall, 20 ft. beam. The submarine can operate up to depths of 150 ft. by adding additional lengths of access tube.

There are many who believe that the submarine is limited in its power because of the inherent nature of its operation. These are the people who erroneously conceive that the submarine designers in some peculiar and miraculous way manage to get around the laws of the universe. They think that the activity of the submarine is in defiance of the law of gravitation; that it performs unnatural feats. People with such views, of course, are inclined to believe that the submarine by now must have reached the height of its development, and that in any case it is an unreliable mechanism. Criticism from such sources is worthy of notice solely because of its positive stupidity. Inventors never perform miracles and they never defy nature. Man can never master nature nor override her dictates. The inventor, rather, is one who comes to know the laws of nature with

254

intimacy, and devises ways to turn them to his use. He works in harmony with nature, perhaps a little more closely than ordinary men; the secret of inventors' successes lies in the fact that they are those who best know how to coöperate with nature. Just so the submarine, as we have seen, acts in response to the laws of gravity, hydraulics, pneumatics, and other natural sciences, and is in complete accordance with nature's dictates; it has no limitations set by nature upon its operation. Objectors on these grounds are in the same class with those who asserted some years ago that an iron ship could not float.

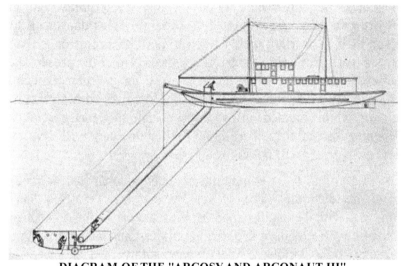

DIAGRAM OF THE "ARGOSY AND ARGONAUT III"

Sketch showing the submarine "Argonaut III" on the bottom and operator in diving compartment inspecting the waterbed through the open diver's door.

There is also a very numerous class of persons who hold that the submarine is a very risky and dangerous mechanism; they feel that the principles of its operation have not yet been brought to a point of safety or certainty. The facts upon which they base this judgment are found by them in the accounts of the many accidents which have occurred to submarines in recent years. As a matter of fact, these accidents have been due, as a rule, to either of two causes; namely, faulty construction or carelessness. There is not a case on record of a properly constructed, well-handled submarine coming to grief through any cause related to the principle of her operation. The principles of successfully navigating under the water were discovered twenty years ago, and have been applied with perfect safety ever since. Many designers since that time have failed to recognize the correct

255

principles, and their incorrectly built boats have given trouble; hence accidents have occurred. To-day, however, the true principles of construction are universally recognized. The modern submarine has passed the stage of experimentation.

Another source for notions of this same sort, as to the unreliability of submarine navigation, is the constant repetition in the daily press that our submarines are not operating satisfactorily. These complaints also lead people to conclude that the mechanical demands of under-water navigation are not completely fulfilled. Now, submarine vessels may be constructed to-day which are a great deal more trustworthy in their operation and considerably less dangerous to go about in than are certain well-known United States railroads. Nearly every submarine in use in the navies of the world at the present day is capable of functioning in perfect safety, so far as submergence and emergence are concerned. They may be operated with almost exact precision while located many feet beneath the surface. If given sufficient static stability, there is no danger that they will dive to the bottom or that they will not come up again.

The cause of all these complaints about our submarines is traceable to a single difficulty. The reader by this time realizes that the difficulty is with the engines, and not with the principles of submarine construction. The modern submarine builder cannot find an engine of sufficiently light weight to install with safety in a submarine hull which will give all the speed which the government demands that his boat should produce. On attempting to attain speed much engine trouble has developed, due to experimentation and trial, and from this source have sprung all the criticisms of the operation of our vessels. There is no such natural limitation to the possible utility of the submarine as many people believe; the only limitation is that of speed. Our boats are safe, they are seaworthy, they are capable of a tremendous radius of action. Sooner or later a reliable engine will be developed which will meet the needs of military submarines and which will deliver power sufficient to give the submarine battleship speed. This is at present the only limitation upon submarine development, and it is not an insuperable obstacle.

Those critics of the submarine who base their opinions upon moral and humanitarian notions are as self-deceived as those who disparage the mechanical success of the under-water vessel. People in this latter class, however, are not afflicted with a distorted vision of the truth, as are those of the other group, but rather, we may say, they suffer from nearsightedness. They do not look far enough ahead to judge as to the permanent utility of the submarine. They base their inferences entirely upon the use which one of the belligerent powers has made of its submarines. It is true, indeed, that the activities of a great many submarine commanders, and the policy of frightfulness which has been so consistently maintained throughout the course of the war by a certain group of autocrats, have temporarily put a moral stigma upon the submarine as a justifiable naval weapon. They have made it appear that the submarine cannot play a humane and legitimate part in warfare. While I have firmly maintained, and still believe, that a submarine blockade is a legitimate use of this weapon in warfare, I do regret that many acts committed by the submarines of one of the belligerents in the present war have been little short of outright piracy.

Strange to say, from the time when I first went into submarine work a fear has always possessed me that the submarine might be turned to piratical uses. I have often thought that some unscrupulous and adventurous group of men might terrorize the commerce of the world in times of peace by taking advantage of the invisible qualities of submarine vessels. Such a group of men with the use of such a weapon might make submarine attacks on peaceful merchant vessels and escape detection and capture for years. I did not, however, nor did any other submarine inventor, anticipate that any of the world's recognized governments would sanction piratical and barbarous actions on the part of their naval officers. In fact, it has been the aim of submarine inventors, from Fulton's time to the present, to devise a weapon that would ultimately bring war between maritime nations to an end. They have not had in mind the murderous designs which have been accredited to them from the very outset. It is my firm conviction that it is the destiny of the submarine to put an end forever to the possibility of warfare upon the high seas, and to eliminate warfare between nations which have no other access to each other except by sea. This is the wonderful opportunity of the submarine, and the submarine inventor has been and will be a laborer in the cause of peace, and not the cause of war and bloodshed.

Robert Fulton pointed out this possibility when he was working upon his own devices. In a letter upon the subject he stated:

"All my reflections have led me to believe that this application of it (the use of the mines placed by submarines) will in a few years put a stop to maritime wars, give that liberty on the seas which has been long and anxiously desired by every good man, and secure to Americans that liberty which will enable citizens to apply their mental and corporeal faculties to useful and humane pursuits, to the improvement of our country, and the happiness of the whole people."

Later on it was Josiah L. Tuck who recognized the same fact, and entitled the vessel of his construction *The Peacemaker*.

The reason which underlies this conviction held by submarine inventors was succinctly expressed by the late Mr. John P. Holland. He pointed out the fact that "submarines cannot fight submarines," the submarine inventors have long since grasped the significance of this fact, realizing as they have that the submarine eventually was to drive the battleship from the sea.

When the day comes that submarines are equipped with engines of battleship speed, and thus take away from the battleships the only means of defence which they now have—namely, the ability to run away from the submarine—the submarine will dominate the surface of the high seas. Submarines may be built of almost any conceivable size, and carry large-calibre disappearing guns and ten, fifty, or one hundred torpedoes. The battleship will be powerless before the submarine of the future; the advantage will always be with the submarines, as they are invisible.

When every country with a sea-coast is equipped with a sufficient number of defensive submarines, even of very low speed, attacks by invasion of their sea-coasts will become impossible. In case two maritime nations go to war, the submarines belonging to each will effectively blockade the ports of the other. Commerce will come to an end, but there will be no invasions and no naval battles. The submarines, not being able to see each other, will not be able to fight. The worst that can happen is a deadlock, and a commercial deadlock of this sort will soon be ended by mutual agreement. The smallest of countries may fear no country, however large, whose sole access to her is by way of water. With a few defensive submarines she may adequately protect herself from invasion. Her shipping may be bottled up, but she needs to stand in no fear of invading hosts and of rapine by armies from across the ocean. She stands prepared, with a fleet of a few tiny submarines, to stand for her rights and for her liberty.

Offensively the submarine will be of little value when brought to its highest point of development, for when every nation is fully equipped with submarines the menace of these vessels will keep enemy surface ships from venturing on the sea. There will be nothing for the submarines to attack except ships of their own kind, and that, of course, will be impossible. Thus wars between maritime nations will come to be nothing more than a mutual check; no surface ships or transports will dare to move in any direction. Offensive warfare will thus end, and each nation will be playing a waiting game, relying upon her submarines for defence.

This is the destiny of the submarine. This has been the aim and the prophecy of the pioneers in submarine development. There is nothing which will stand in the way of the accomplishment of this happy result. The success of the submarine in the present war has at last forced those in power—and among them many who bitterly opposed its development—to recognize the value of this weapon. Submarine designers and submarine inventors will from now on receive the encouragement and the attention of naval authorities throughout the world. Hence we may expect to see the submarine developed and improved until it has many times the efficiency, speed, and destructive power which is possessed by it to-day. We may also expect to see the industrial possibilities of the submarine developed to a high degree within a few years. Travel will be made safer, rich cargoes will be recovered, and the ocean will be forced to give up its wealth and its products to the uses of man in greater quantity than ever before. Thus, instead of following a career of murder and of piracy, the submarine is destined to protect the weak, to strengthen the strong, and to serve humanity in general as an agent for prosperity and for peace.

CPSIA information can be obtained
at www.ICGtesting.com
Printed in the USA
BVHW050945180623
666095BV00010B/803